Biorobotics

Biorobotics

Methods and Applications

Edited by

Barbara Webb and Thomas R. Consi

AAAI Press / The MIT Press

Menlo Park, California   Cambridge, Massachusetts   London, England

Copublished and distributed by The MIT Press, Massachusetts Institute of Technology, Cambridge, Massachusetts, and London, England.

An earlier version of "Construction of a Hexapod Robot with Cockroach Kinematics Benefits Both Robotics and Biology" by Robert Quinn and Roy Ritzmann firrt appeared in 1998 in *Connection Science,* volume 10(3–4): 239–254, and is reprinted here with permission.

Library of Congress Cataloging-in-Publication Data

Biorobotics : methods and applications / edited by Barbara Webb and Thomas R. Consi.
    p. cm.
    Includes bibliographical references (p.).
    ISBN 0-262-73141-X (pbk. : alk. paper)
        1. Animal behavior—Simulation methods. 2. Senses and senation—
    Simulation methods. 3. Robotics. I. Webb, Barbara (Barbara H.)
    II. Consi, Thomas R., 1956–

    QL751.65.S55 B56 2001
    591.5′01′13–dc21   2001041243

Printed on acid-free paper in Canada.

10 9 8 7 6 5 4 3 2 1

Contents

Introduction

Thomas R. Consi and Barbara Webb

Animals have long served as inspiration to roboticists. Their adaptability, flexibility of motion and great variety of behaviors has made them the (often unspoken) benchmarks for robot performance. Beyond inspiration, however, animals have not always yielded much in the way of concrete mechanisms that could be used to build robots, and robots have been almost comical representations of animals. The problem was that engineered components did not have the performance or form factor of their biological counterparts. Recently things have begun to change and robots are now capable, to a limited degree, of accurately mimicking the behavior of animals. Advances that have made this possible include microprocessors of ever increasing computational power and ever decreasing size, tiny solid-state sensors, low-power electronics, and miniaturized mechanical components. Robots can now be built that have some of the sensing capability of, for example, a desert ant or the motor skills approaching that of a cockroach. Animal-like robots (termed biorobots in this book but also known as biomimetic or biomorphic robots) are serving an increasingly important role as a link between the worlds of biology and engineering.

Biorobotics is a new multidisciplinary field that encompasses the dual uses of biorobots as tools for biologists studying animal behavior and as testbeds for the study and evaluation of biological algorithms for potential applications to engineering. There have been several recent reviews of biorobotics as a way to apply biological algorithms and mechanisms to engineered systems (e.g. Beer et al. 1993, Dario et al. 1993, Hirose 1993, Srinivasan and Venkatesh 1997, Bekey 1996, Beer et al 1997, Sharkey and Ziemke 1998, Chang and Gaudiano 2000) This book particularly concerns the role of robots as tools for biologists, a more recent phenomenon. Understanding how animals work is essentially a problem of "reverse engineering" i.e. rather than building something with a certain functional capability, we have something with a certain functional capability and want to work out how it works. Thus the application of engineering methodologies for modeling animals seems an appropriate and promising approach. However such a task is far from easy.

An animal can be described as mobile vehicle with a multimodal, high-bandwidth interface to its environment. One merely has to look at a cricket with a hand lens to see the thousands of sensory hairs studding its exoskeleton. Each hair is invested with many sensory cells and different types of cells "see" the environment in different ways (e.g. some respond to mechanical stimulation and others to chemical signals). Animals are therefore, deeply embedded in their environments and they are profoundly affected by the subtle and complex signals within those environments (e.g. turbulence, polarization patterns, acoustic noise, thermal micro-climates, etc). It is the complexity of the environment and the high degree to which animals can sense and respond to that complexity that makes it difficult to obtain a detailed understanding of the world as seen by an animal through its senses and interpreted through its behaviors. The situation is made even more complicated because the animal invariably disturbs its environment and creates a new set of stimuli that may also be important to the creature's behavior.

Biorobots are now enabling biologists to understand these complex animal-environment relationships. They can be thought of as micro-environment exploration robots that can detect and map sensory signals at the level of the animal and can measure how the presence and motion of the animal affects those signals. This data, coupled with observations of the animal itself, can lead to very sophisticated hypotheses as to what is causing a behavior and what is shaping the behavior as it plays out. These hypotheses can then be tested in laboratory or field-based experiments with the biorobot robot as well as with the real animals. The robot offers two distinct advantages over the real animal in such studies. First, the behavior under test in the robot is not affected by competing, uncontrolled, behaviors. Second, orders of magnitude more data can be obtained from a robot, compared to an animal, on its actions, its sensory input, and its internal states. Despite these advantages it must not be forgotten that the biorobot, however sophisticated, is only mimicking part of the animal. Biorobotics is a tool-based discipline, much like the microscopy, and one should never lose sight that biorobots are tools for use in studies of animals, not replacements for such studies.

Computer simulation has long been another tool used by biologists to model biological phenomena at all levels of organization, from populations of animals to individual creatures, to "subassemblies" such as the ear, down to individual components, neurons, sensory receptor cells and muscle fibers. The question naturally comes to mind as to why bother building robots at all when computer/numerical models have been so useful? The answer to this question comes from the complexity of the sensory world discussed above. A hypothesis implemented on a robot operating in a real environment can be tested more rigorously than in simulation because the hypothesis will be challenged with real, complex and often unmodelable stimuli. For example, hydrodynamic simulations of underwater turbulence are very complex yet still do not adequately represent real turbulent flow. This type of flow is what shapes the olfactory signal sensed by lobsters, fish and many other underwater creatures. It is far easier and cheaper to generate a real odor plume to test a plume following algorithm than to use a plume simulation that will produce an inferior stimulus compared to the real thing. Biorobots can be usefully thought of as physical models of animals that enable a level of investigation beyond that possible with simulation. Note that biorobots do not replace simulation, just as they do not replace real animals in experiments. Simulation is very useful both as a hypothesis testing methodology and as a design tool for developing biorobots. It often happens that there is a cyclic iteration of animal observations, simulations, and biorobotic experiments during the course of an investigation that, in the best case, leads to an increasingly more accurate picture of the animal's behavior and its physiological underpinnings.

A Brief History of Biorobotics

The attempt to make machines behave in a lifelike manner is as old as science (De Solla Price 1964). Ingenious mechanical devices have been built to mimic animal behaviors, sometimes with impressive detail e.g. Vaucanson's duck (de Vaucanson 1738, Chapuis and Droz 1958). However their clockwork mechanisms did not noticeably resemble the inner workings of biological systems. A more or less direct scientific lineage to biorobotics can be traced starting at the end of the nineteenth century with the advent of the then new discipline of electrical engineering. Nikola Tesla conceived "the idea of constructing [an] automaton that would ... respond, as I do myself, but of course, in a much more primitive manner, to external influences. Such an automaton evidently had to have motive power, organs for locomotion, directive organs, and one or more sensitive organs so adapted to be excited by external stimuli...." He built and demonstrated a radio controlled boat in the 1890s and discussed plans for an automaton that "will be able, independent of an operator, left entirely to itself, to perform, in response to external influences affecting its sensitive organs, a great variety of acts and operations as if it had intelligences [sic]" (cited in Rosheim 1994). The pioneering physiologist Jacques Loeb compared the behaviors of "lower" animals to that of an artificial heliotropic machine, a light following device made of motors, photocells and relays (Loeb 1918). Breder (1926) developed two model boats, one propelled by a flapping fin and the other by an undulating fin, to study fish propulsion. Fifty years ago the advent of cybernetics saw the building of a series of electromechanical devices intended to explore aspects of animal behavior, such as the "homeostat" machine (Ashby 1952) and the reactive "turtle" (Walter 1961). A number of similar devices built around this time are described in Young (1969).

Although the advent of modern transistor technology and computers might have been expected to support rapid further progress in building animal-like robots, in fact the main research emphasis diverged in somewhat different directions. One might be termed investigation of the "disembodied" brain: an emphasis on building machines with human reasoning powers (artificial intelligence) rather than human (or animal) physical powers. Although some of these mechanisms were "biologically-inspired," such as the neural network approach, the tasks investigated were still largely cognitive. Even within biology, where "analog" (i.e. electrical circuit models) of hypothesized animal control systems continued to be used as simulation tools (e.g. Harmon 1961, Collewijn 1972; Collett 1980) till replaced by today's software simulations, the systems rarely "closed the loop" with real actuators and sensors. On the other hand, investigation of the *physical* problems of sensing and control for artificial systems were somewhat subsumed by mechanization, with much robot research deriving from industrial concerns (with the main exception some notable research on humanoid robots in Japanese research groups such as that of Ichiro Kato). Cybernetic theory for operating these systems developed sophisticated mathematical formalisms, but was in the main not closely related to biology. One reason may have been the limited understanding of how biological systems actually worked.

Thus a parallel development in biology that was critical to the emergence of biorobotics was the application of control system theory and other engineering techniques to the study of animal behavior, most notably by the "European School" of neuroethology. This work was primarily focused on the sensory-motor behavior of arthropods and began with the work of von Holst and Mittelstaedt (reviewed in Schone 1984). Ground breaking studies on many arthropod systems were carried out in the mid to latter twentieth century. A few examples of the many systems studied include: fly vision (reviewed in Buchner 1984), ant navigation (Wehner 1989), walking in the stick insect (Cruse 1990) and crab oculomotor behavior (Horridge and Sandeman 1964). This work, and other similar studies, provided a rich baseline of quantitative data on the performance of animals that was ready to be incorporated into the biorobots that began to emerge in the last decades of the twentieth century.

Two notable event in the development of current biorobotics were the publication of the slender volume *Vehicles, Experiments in Synthetic Psychology* (Braitenberg 1984) and the emergence of behavior-based robots (Brooks 1986a). Braitenberg in "Vehicles" showed how animal-like behaviors might be produced in simple "thought" robots and how these vehicles may be used to interpret behavioral data. Brooks and colleagues expanded the field of artificial intelligence to consider the problems faced by relatively simple insect-like robots that must navigate within the real world. Other influential work done in this period includes the highly impressive running robots developed at the Massachusetts Institute of Technology's Lego Lab (Raibert 1986), and the application of Arbib's (1972) biologically based "schema theory" to autonomous robots by Arkin (1987). The fields of artificial life (Langton 1989) and adaptive behavior or "animats" (Meyer and Guillot 1990) also emerged around this time, with their emphasis on artificial replication of precognitive behaviors, though still largely in simulation. What these interdisciplinary movements helped generate was a meeting point between robot technology on one hand and mainstream biological models on the other.

This has resulted in recent years in a rapid increase in the number of models of specific animal competencies being implemented in robot devices, driven both by advances in technology, as mentioned above, and in our expanding knowledge of the sensory, motor, and nervous systems of animals. In table 1 we list papers from the last decade that fall within this description (not including the large amounts of work in biologically-based sensory processing except where it is used in behavioral control, i.e. on a robot), demonstrating both the quantity and breadth of current work in this field.

Overview of the Book

This book is an edited collection of papers that were presented at the "Robots and Biology: Developing Connections" American Association for Artificial Intelligence Symposium held on October 23-25, 1998 in Orlando Florida. The purpose of the symposium was to bring together scientists from a diverse array of disciplines all of whom are using biorobots as probes of animal behavior and brain function. The chapters are ordered with those primarily involved with sensory biology presented first, followed by chapters that focus on motor systems, and ending with chapters concerned with higher-level or cognitive processes. This ordering is, of course, artificial because it is difficult if not impossible to cleanly separate functional subsystems within animals. A prime example of this is the use of visual motion for object detection and navigation (Viollet and Franceschini, chapter 4) in which the motor and visual systems are closely coupled to perform this function. Nevertheless, the ordering does serve as a convenient organizational framework for the book and to direct readers with specific interests to specific chapters.

A chapter on neural mechanisms in cricket phonotaxis by Barbara Webb begins the Sensory Systems section. A robot model of a cricket is used to test a neuronal model for sound localization by these noisy insects. Next we dip underwater where Frank Grasso examines the world of olfactory-based guidance in lobsters. The robot presented in Grasso's chapter is one of the first examples of a marine biorobot. Polarized light navigation in insects has long been of interest to biologists and the next chapter by Ralf Möeller and colleagues presents a robot with a visual system modeled after that of the desert ant *Cataglyphis*. "Sahabot" is being used to test hypothesis on how *Cataglyphis* uses the pattern of skylight polarization to find its way back to its desert burrow. This is followed by an invited chapter by Nicolas Franceschini, a pioneer in biorobotics. In this chapter Franceschini and coauthor Stéphane Violett present a novel and robust visual tracking system that utilizes of low amplitude scanning of a photodetector. Such a system may have an analog in the compound the fly in which a tiny muscle oscillates the photoreceptor array.

Two chapters are presented in the Motor System section. In the first, Roger Quinn and Roy Ritzman review their work in developing hexapod robots with cockroach kinematics and control. This work is an excellent example of how the close collaboration of an engineer and a biologist can lead to advances in both fields. The chapter by Holk Cruse presents the intriguing argument that an understanding of how the brain controls complex, multiple degrees of freedom motor systems, such as the six legs of the stick insect, may give us important insight into how the so-called higher cognitive functions are implemented.

The issues addressed in Cruse's chapter lead us into the final pair of chapters on the use of robots to explore higher brain function. Olaf Sporns and Nikolaus Almássy explore the development of perceptual invariance in a neural model patterned after the mammalian inferior temporal cortex. This model was incorporated into a mobile robot with a visual system and was shown to develop pattern-selective "neurons" over time as the robot was permitted to move about within the real world. In the final chapter of this book Brian Scassellati discusses the application of humanoid robots to the study of human social development. The book ends with a discussion of the outstanding issues in biorobotics, given the current state of the art, that were derived from the lively discussions that occurred during the AAAI symposium.

It is our hope that the reader will find these chapters informative and insightful and perhaps inspirational. We do hope, however, that the reader also views these chapters with a critical eye. Biorobotics is an emerging field that will become scientifically strong only through vigorous debate and the application of rigorous standards of scientific utility. It must not be forgotten that a biorobot is a model of a living animal and, like all models, has its appropriate uses and its limits. To aid our readers in the evaluation of work in this field, and to help them develop their own research, we provide the following list of dimensions (Webb 2001) on which biorobotic modeling decisions need to be made:

- *Realism:* whether the model tests and generates hypotheses applicable to biology.
- *Level:* the elemental units of the model in the hierarchy from atoms to societies.
- *Generality:* the range of biological systems the model can represent.
- *Abstraction:* the complexity, relative to the target, or amount of detail included in the model.

Subject area	Examples	References
Simple sensorimotor control		
Chemical	Moth pheromone tracking	Kuwana, Shimoyama, and Miura 1995; Ishida, Kobayashi, Nakamoto, and Moriisumi 1999; Kanzaki 1996; Willis 2000
	Ant trail following	Sharpe and Webb 1998; Russell 1998
	Lobster plume following	Grasso, Consi, Mountain, and Atema 1996; Grasso, Consi, Mountain, and Atema 2000; Ayers et al. 1998
	C. elegans gradient climb	Morse, Ferree, and Lockery 1998
Auditory	Cricket phonotaxis	Webb 1995; Lund, Webb, and Hallam 1998; Webb and Scutt 2000
	Owl sound localisation	Rucci, Edelman, and Wray 1999
	Human localisation	Horiuchi 1997; Huang, Ohnishi, and Sugie 1995
	Bat sonar	Kuc 1997; Peremans, Walker, and Hallam 1998
Visual	Locust looming detection	Blanchard, Verschure, and Rind 1999; Indiveri 1998
	Frog snapping	Arbib and Liaw 1995
	Fly motion detection to control movement	Franceschini, Pichon, and Blanes 1992; Weber, Venkatesh, and Srinivasan 1998; Hoshino, Mura, Morii, Suematsu, and Shimoyama 1998; Huber and Bülthoff 1998; Srinivasan and Venkatesh 1997; Harrison and Koch 1999
	Praying mantis peering	Lewis and Nelson 1998
	Human oculomotor reflex	Horiuchi and Koch 1999; Takanishi, Hirano, and Sato 1998; Shibata and Schaal 1999
	Tracking/Saccade control	Clark 1998; Wagner, Galiana, and Hunter 1994; Schall and Hanes 1998
Other	Ant polarized light compass	Lambrinos et al. 1997, Lambrinos, Möller, Labhart, Pfeifer, and Wehner 2000
	Lobster anemotaxis	Ayers et al. 1998
	Cricket wind escape	Chapman and Webb 1999
	Trace fossils	Prescott and Ibbotson 1997
Complex motor control		
Walking	Stick insect	Cruse et al. 1998, Kindermann et al. 1998, Ferrell 1995; Pfeiffer et al. 1995
	Cockroach	Espenschied et al. 1996,Delcomyn and Nelson 2000, Nelson and Quinn 1998, Binnard 1995
	Four-legged mammal	Ilg et al. 1998, Berkemeier and Desai 1996
Swimming	Tail propulsion	Triantafyllou and Triantafyllou 1995, Kumph 1998
	Pectoral fin	Kato and Inaba 1998
	Undulation	Patel et al. 1998
	Flagellar motion	Mojarrad and Shahinpoor 1997
Flying	Insect wings Bat	Miki and Shimoyami 1998, Fearing 1999, Fearing et al. 2000, Dickinson et al. 1999, Pornsin-Sirirak and Tai 1999
Arms/hands	Spinal circuits	Hannaford et al. 1995;,Williamson 1998
	Cerebellar control	Fagg et al 97, van der Smagt 1998, Hoff and Bekey 1997
	Grasping	Leoni et al. 1998, Hauck et al. 1998
	Haptic exploration	Erkman et al. 1999
Humanoid		Special issue *Advanced Robotics* 116: 1997; Brooks and Stein 1993 Hirai et al. 1998; Yamaguchi and Takanishi 1997
Other	Running and Hopping	Raibert 1986, Pratt and Pratt 1998
	Brachiation	Saito and Fukuda 1996
	Mastication	Takanobu et al. 1998
	Snakes	Hirose 1993, Review in Worst, Miller forthcoming
	Paper wasp nest construct	Honma 1996
Navigation		
Landmarks	Ant/bee landmark homing	Möller 2000; Möller et al. 1998
Maps	Rat hippocampus	Burgess et al. 1997, Gaussier et al. 1997; Recce and Harris 1996
Search	*review*	Gelenbe et al. 1997
Collective behaviours		Beckers et al. 1996; Holland and Melhuish 1999; Melhuish et al. 1998; Kube and Bonabeau 2000
Learning		Edelman et al. 1992; Hallam et al. 1994; Sporns forthcoming, Scutt and Damper 1997, Saksida et al. 1997, Voegtlin and Verschure 1999, Chang and Gaudiano 1998

Table 1: Examples of biorobot research. This is intended to be a representative sampling not a fully comprehensive listing.

- *Accuracy:* how well the model represents the actual mechanisms of behavior.
- *Medium:* the physical basis by which the model is implemented.
- *Performance match:* to what extent the model behavior matches the target behavior.
- *Utility:* the biological understanding, technical insight or communication of ideas that the model provides.

Acknowledgements

The editors thank the American Association for Artificial Intelligence for sponsoring the AAAI Fall 1998 Symposium Series and our symposium organizing committee colleagues, Randall Beer and Holk Cruse. We thank our contributing authors and our other colleagues who participated in the symposium. Thanks also goes to our editor, Kenneth Ford, and our publisher the AAAI Press. Finally, we thank the following publishers for their generous permission to reprint some of the articles in this book: *Connection Science*, SPIE.

Note

1. Willis, M. 2000. Modeling Approaches to Understand Odor-Guided Locomotion. This paper is available at http://flightpath.neurobio.arizona.edu/Model/index.html.

Sensory Systems

1

A Spiking Neuron Controller for Robot Phonotaxis

Barbara Webb

In their 1988 paper about the auditory behavior of the cricket, Weber and Thorson suggest as a "first model" of phonotaxis:

> "… the simple rule 'turn toward the ear more strongly stimulated.' We use the word simple because a two-eared robot programmed to obey this rule (if suitable noise were incorporated) could be made to track a sound source in a manner like that of the female."

This chapter reports the latest in a series of studies (Webb 1994, 1995; Webb and Hallam 1996; Lund, Webb, and Hallam 1997, 1998) of what is required to make a two-eared robot track sound sources in a manner like the female cricket. In the process many questions have been raised, both about the "simple rules" of phonotaxis, the more general problems of understanding neural control of behavior, and what can be learned from robot models. The ultimate aim in these investigations has been to gain an understanding of how the sensory and neural systems of animals, embedded in appropriate environments, successfully control behavior. A general strategy has been to look for alternatives to the standard "information processing" conception of perception by focusing on how sensors can act as matched filters, how temporal dynamics of neurons can interact, and how environmental conditions control behavior. Consequently the models have the following features:

- As far as possible the models are built as real systems with actual sensors and motors, behaving in the real world. They are also built as whole systems, solving a complete problem of sensorimotor control rather than partial problems of sensing or moving.

- The architectures represent neural processes at appropriate levels of detail rather than using standard artificial neural net abstractions. Individual neuron properties and identified connectivity are included, rather than training methods being applied to generic architectures.

- The systems built are treated as models: the resulting behavior is compared in some detail with biological data, with the aim of assessing how the well the model really explains the observations.

The particular system studied—cricket phonotaxis—is a useful "model" to explore these themes. The behavior is stereotyped, yet nontrivial. The neuroethological understanding of this system is relatively well advanced. Thus an explanation of behavior in terms of neurons should be forth-coming. However, when the rigorous test of trying to build a replica of the system is applied it is quickly evident how far short of a full explanation current research falls. Moreover building the models suggest some alternative plausible explanations.

Cricket Phonotaxis

The female cricket can find a conspecific male by walking or flying towards the calling song the male produces. This sensory cue is sufficient (though not necessary) for finding a mate. Using only auditory cues, the female is able to cover a large distance—ten to twenty meters—negotiating uneven vegetation-covered terrain, and reliably locate a single male, despite other males and other sounds in the vicinity. In the lab the female will track sound for long periods on a treadmill and thus many details of the tracking ability are available (e.g. Thorson, Weber, and Huber 1982; Schmitz, Scharstein, and Wendler 1982; Huber and Thorson 1985; Huber, Moore, and Loher 1989). It is a tractable system for the neuroethological approach, involving a well-defined stimulus and response, an accessible nervous system and a relatively small number of critical neural connections (e.g. Wohlers and Huber 1982; Schildberger 1988; Horseman and Huber 1994; Stumpner , Atkins, and Stout 1995).

Thorson, Weber, and Huber (1982) suggested a basic hypothesis that still underlies most of the research on this system:

"Once a song is recognized as correct, the female apparently walks towards it by sensing whether the sound source is to the right or left and making suitable corrective turns."

This assumes that recognition of correct songs is an independent, prior event to localization of sound. However, whether a song is recognized is generally assessed by whether the female walks towards it, thus it is possible that failure to approach a song simply indicates failure to make the suitable corrective turns. It has been argued (Weber and Thorson 1988) that the fact that the cricket moves in typical "phonotactic" fashion i.e. stop-start movement with corrective turns, even when sound is played from above and hence contains no useful directional information, is evidence for explicit "recognition," but as will be discussed below this does not necessarily follow.

It is beyond the scope of the current chapter to review the extensive evidence on cricket phonotaxis (see e.g. Huber, Moore, and Loher 1989; Pollack 1998). The main finding that will be addressed is that the female cricket only turns towards and approaches the calling song of conspecific males. To be more exact, the carrier frequency of the song and the temporal repetition structure affect the likelihood and accuracy of taxis in the female: in general the best taxis is seen to the conspecific song.

Cricket song generally consists of short bursts (ten to thirty millisecond "syllables") of fairly pure tone (around 4-5 kHz) grouped in various distinctive patterns ("chirps"). A number of studies have shown frequency preference in the approach to temporally identical songs. For example, Popov and Shuvalov (1977), Stout and McGhee (1988) and Oldfield (1980) all report a higher threshold and decreased accuracy for taxis as the frequency is changed from the typical carrier, and no taxis below 2 kHz or above 12 kHz. The most important temporal pattern cue for recognition is given by the syllable repetition interval (SRI) in the song (Popov and Shuvalov 1977; Thorson, Weber, and Huber 1982; Stout and McGhee 1988). Thorson and colleagues argue for a "thirty Hz" hypothesis for *Gryllus campestris*: that a repetition rate of around this speed is necessary and sufficient for taxis in the female, whatever the length of syllables or higher order grouping of syllables. Doherty (1985) and Wendler (1990) suggest that chirp structure alone may also be necessary or sufficient for taxis in *Acheta domestica* and *Gryllus bimaculatus* respectively, but there is general agreement that syllable rate is a primary cue.

In previous work (Webb 1994, Webb 1995) it was hypothesized that the frequency selectivity of the cricket could be a simple consequence of the physical means by which it detects the direction of sound sources, and the temporal selectivity a consequence of using the relative timing of firing to control behavior rather than firing rates. The work discussed here will show that both these hypotheses are borne out by the robot model.

Robot Modeling

A good way to evaluate the completeness and usefulness of a hypothesis is to implement it in a model system. This will always quickly reveal gaps in information or inconsistencies in evidence, as well as potentially producing predictions for further testing.

In the case of hypotheses about sensorimotor function, there are a number of reasons why using a physical model rather than a simulation can be advanced. Although there has been much pseudo-philosophical debate over the merits of using real-world systems I believe that the pragmatic advantages are the ones to stress:

- It is easier to model physical constraints physically than symbolically. By using real-world physics there is little risk that the model violates the possible. Noise is natural rather than an arbitrary added randomness. Good simulations of real world constraints require substantial calculations, it is easier to let the "physics do the walking" (Flynn and Brooks 1989). Finally the testing of mechanisms is more straightforward and more robust—ideally one can use the same experimental paradigms on the robot as are used on the animal being modeled.

• Implementing a robot forces you to look for simple mechanisms that might make it work, rather than immediately implementing a given hypothesis. Thus each assumption about the system is questioned for its necessity and plausibility. The constraints imposed are appropriate because they are sensorimotor ones such as signal processing time, noise, and effects of self motion.

Implementation

The robot model of the cricket has undergone a number of incarnations. The main features of the current model (discussed in detail below) are (1) an electronic sound processing circuit that mimics the auditory processing of the cricket ear in real time, with programmable control of parameters; and (2) a neural-network model that operates at the level of dynamic changes in membrane potential

The robot base is a Khepera (K-Team 1994) miniature mobile robot. This measures roughly six centimeters in diameter and four centimeters high: the ears circuit described below adds six centimeters to the height. It has two drive wheels and two castors. It has a 68332 processor programmed in C. This platform was chosen because it is closer than most robots to the scale of a cricket, has precise motor control, and is relatively straightforward to interface. The processor speed turned out to be a limitation, requiring the invention of a pared-down version of the model of neural spiking previously used (Scutt and Webb 1997) to enable it to run in real time on the robot.

The Robot's Ears

The cricket has evolved a unique solution to the problem of determining the direction of the sound source it wishes to approach (Michelsen, Popov, and Lewis 1994). There is little direct amplitude difference in sound at the two ears either from distance attenuation or sound shadowing, and the cricket lacks the specialized neural processes found in other animals for detecting microsecond phase differences. Instead the phase difference is physically converted into an easily detected amplitude difference as follows. The ear-drums on the legs are connected by an air-filled tracheal tube to each other and to two additional openings on the cricket body. Sound thus reaches the tympani both directly and indirectly, via the tube, so that its vibration reflects the summation of these different waves.

The phase relationships of these waves depend on the distances traveled (and internal delays in the tube), which depend on the direction of the sound source. Thus a sound source on the left side produces a larger vibration in the left tympanum than the right tympanum, and consequently quicker firing of auditory neurons on that side.

This mechanism was modeled electronically (Lund, Webb, and Hallam 1997), using two microphones with a small separation. The output of each microphone was combined with the inverted, delayed output of the other microphone. The delay represents the time for sound to travel through the tracheal tube and the inversion the fact that direct and indirect sound operate on opposite sides of the ear-drum. The result is that sound amplitude measured on the combined signal varies with sound direction in an approximately cardioid function.

The implemented circuit is mounted on top of the robot. The two microphones face forward and their exact separation can be varied. In the experiments below it was set at eighteen millimeters, approximately one-quarter the wavelength of 4.7 kHz sound, which is the carrier frequency of Gryllus bimaculatus song. The circuit is programmable so that the relative delay between the ears and gains of the combined signal can be altered. In the experiments below it was set to a fifty-three microsecond delay—the time for sound to propagate one-quarter wavelength of 4.7 kHz, and gains of one were used.

An important feature of this system is that the tuning of the ears separation and the delay result in the circuit being most directional for a particular signal frequency and providing progressively less directionality as the frequency increases or decreases. Thus behavior, such as turning to the sound, that depends on the directionality, should become progressively worse as the carrier frequency of song is altered from the ideal. Although the system as described has no direct frequency filtering, the behavior will nevertheless appear frequency selective.

Experiments on the robot demonstrated that this does in fact occur. Full details are given in Lund, Webb and Hallam (1997) but in summary, the robot would approach cricket sounds or a synthesized signal with a 4.7 kHz carrier frequency, would ignore a 9.4 kHz carrier frequency, and had a raised threshold for taxis to a 2.35 kHz signal. Moreover the robot was able to "choose" a 4.7 kHz signal over a 6.7 kHz signal when played simultaneously.

The Robot's Neurons

The model neurons implemented are a simplified version of the Scutt-Dampner (Scutt and Dampner 1991, Scutt 1994) model, which has previously been used in a phonotaxis simulation (Scutt and Webb 1997). Implementing such a model on the robot produced strong constraints. While it was considered essential to retain the dynamic membrane potential (and spiking) elements of the neurons, it was also necessary that the model run at real time speed (e.g. spiking at up to two hundred to three hundred times a second, or at least three to five times during a cricket's fifteen to twenty millisecond syllable) on the robot's microprocessor.

General Features of the Model

The implemented model uses a two-state system to describe neuron membrane potential, modeled as a single compartment. In the pre-firing state there is leaky integration of input. When threshold is reached a spike (rapid increase in potential) occurs and the neuron goes into a-post-firing state. In the latter state input is still added but there is also a rapid decrease in potential. While the neuron is above a recovery level it passes proportional activation via weighted synapses to other neurons. When it drops below this level it returns to the pre-firing state. The time-constant and the recovery level can be varied; to mimic specific properties of identified neurons.

Neurons are connected by "weighted synapses." During the post-firing (pre-recovery) state, a spiking neuron passes potential to those neurons with which it connects, the amount of potential dependent on the membrane potential of the neuron and the size of the weight of the connection. These synapses also exhibit depression, i.e. the efficacy is decreased after firing and takes time to recover. It is also possible for synapses to connect to other synapses, in which case they facilitate or inhibit that connection by altering its weight.

Neurons can be defined to have sensory input, in which case the signal is represented as a change in membrane potential; or motor output, in which case spikes in the neuron are interfaced with the motor control of the robot. The original model (Scutt 1994) included mechanisms for long-term alteration of connection weight, to model biological learning mechanisms. These and various other details have been stripped out of the code and it has been optimized as far as possible. The four-neuron model described below runs faster than a cycle/millisecond: one cycle updates all neuron membrane potentials including input and output functions.

The Phonotaxis Circuit

The current robot controller consists of only four neurons and four synapses (figure 1). The two input neurons are based on the identified "AN1" neurons in the cricket (Wohlers and Huber 1982), which are closely associated with taxis (Schildberger and Horner 1988). The amplitude signal from the auditory circuit is scaled-down by a factor of 4 and a "noise" constant subtracted. The resulting value is added to the membrane potential of the respective input neurons. If this is higher than the constant "leak," the potential will eventually sum to threshold. The AN1 in the cricket has spikes superimposed on a raised potential so recovery (i.e. ability to spike again) in the model neuron is set near threshold rather than near the resting level. This means that continued input will rapidly lead to further spikes for the duration of the stimulus (see examples in figure 2). The amplitude of the input will be represented both by the initial

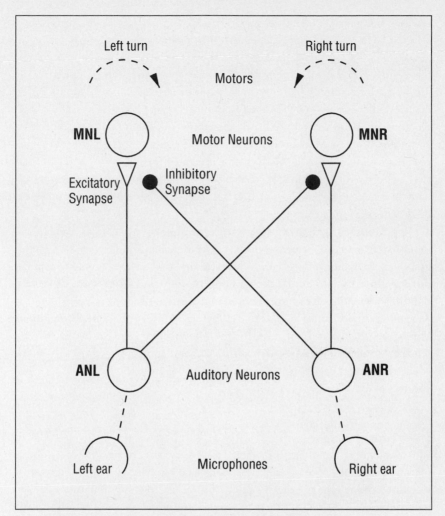

Figure 1. The four neuron model for phonotaxis.

Auditory neurons (AN) neurons have input from ears, excite an ipsilateral motor neuron (MN), and inhibit the opposite AN-MN connection. Both connections habituate. When an MN fires the robot turns in that direction.

latency to start spiking and the consequent firing rate. The time constant of this neuron is matched to the cricket neuron such that it decays half-way to resting potential after around ten milliseconds (Wohlers and Huber 1982). This gap appears to set a limit on the fastest temporal patterns that can be encoded in its spike pattern (Schildberger 1984).

In the cricket the AN1 send axons to the brain, but although a number of brain neurons involved in auditory processing have been identified (Schildberger 1984; Bohm and Schildberger 1992; Staudacher 1998) the circuit connectivity is not known. In the robot model each AN makes an excitatory connection to a motor neuron (MN) on the same side. Thus an initial spike raises the potential of the MN towards threshold. However the depression of this synapse means that immediately following spikes do not raise the potential significantly further. Only if there is a gap in the firing of the AN1, leading to recovery of the synapse, can a further spike in AN1 contribute sufficiently to MN to drive it above threshold. As MN also performs leaky integration, if the gap is too large, potential will have decayed too far below threshold for this to occur. Each AN1 also makes a further, inhibitory, connection to the opposite AN-MN synapse. This means that the AN1 firing first will suppress any effect of the opposite AN1 firing slightly later.

Each MN controls motor behavior in the following way. If it spikes, the robot makes a turn in the corresponding direction at a fixed speed and of a fixed duration. If another spike occurs before the duration elapses, it is extended. If the opposite MN fires during the duration the turn will be reversed. Currently the speed and duration of turns is set at approximately fifty-five degrees per second for one hundred fifty milliseconds Obviously this is a substantial simplification of the actual control of turns by a walking or flying cricket but in the absence of detailed information it was adopted as a simple approximation: most cricket behavioral data is reported in terms of body movement rather than leg control.

Experimental Variables

The robot can be run in several modes to facilitate the collection of data. First, the membrane potential of each neuron can be recorded at each cycle so that recordings of the spiking behavior can be produced. Memory limitations on the robot limit consecutive recordings to around four hundred cycles worth of data (less than half second) but as the relevant input patterns vary at thirty Hz this is sufficient for most purposes in which such a detailed record is required. Second, the motor behavior can be recorded. The default forward speed of the robot can be selected, altering how fast it moves, towards the speaker or in other directions. This speed can be set at 0 so that instead of moving towards the sound source, the robot rotates in a fixed position, generating data directly comparable to that collected from crickets walking on a treadmill. The rate of recording motor position can be varied but is generally set at around ten Hz, allowing up to sixty seconds worth of data to be collected consecutively. Finally the robot can be run in "nonrecording" mode in which case it performs the behavior without breaking off to download data.

Results

The data below comes from a series of tests run in "treadmill" mode, i.e. with the robot turning in response to MN spikes but not moving closer to the sound. Using recordings of the neurons and the motors, the behavior was examined with both recorded cricket songs and artificial stimuli.

Turning to Sound

The graphs below (figure 2) show how this circuit controls turns towards the sound source. The stimulus is recorded cricket song (fifteen millisecond bursts of approximately 4.7 kHz sound), looped to repeat the syllables continuously, and the robot is initially facing about forty-five degrees to the right. The output of the auditory circuit is thus much stronger for the left ear than the right ear; in fact the right ear is initially below threshold. It can be seen that each syllable of sound in the left ear produces a ramp in potential in the left AN followed by four spikes, and then a slow decrease towards resting level once the syllable has ended. The first spike of each group increases potential in the left MN, but due to synaptic depression, the immediately following spikes have little effect. MN potential decays between syllables but slowly enough such that after two or three syllables it exceeds threshold and produces a spike.

The spikes turn the robot left, towards the sound, as can be seen by the increase in input amplitude for the right ear and decrease in the left. The right AN begins to spike, but close comparison will show that it takes longer to reach threshold and spikes later than the left AN. This means that the left AN activity will have inhibited the connection between the right AN and MN, so the right MN does not yet fire, while the left AN continues to do so.

Selectivity for Syllable Rate

The turning response can be made selective to a bandpass of syllable rates by tuning the time constants. The first critical factor is illustrated in figure 3, which shows the neural response on one side of the circuit to syllables faster than normal—this is a synthesized signal consisting of 4.7 kHz tone bursts of ten millisecond duration with ten millisecond gaps. The time constant of AN is sufficiently slow that it is unable to code this pattern clearly, but instead continues to fire almost constantly. This means that the MN-AN synapse is depressed and never gets an opportunity to recover, so MN does not receive sufficient input to fire, and no turn is made even though the direction of sound is clearly represented in the input.

Figure 4 shows the same neurons when the synthesized syllables are doubled to last twenty milliseconds with twenty millisecond gaps. Note that these gaps

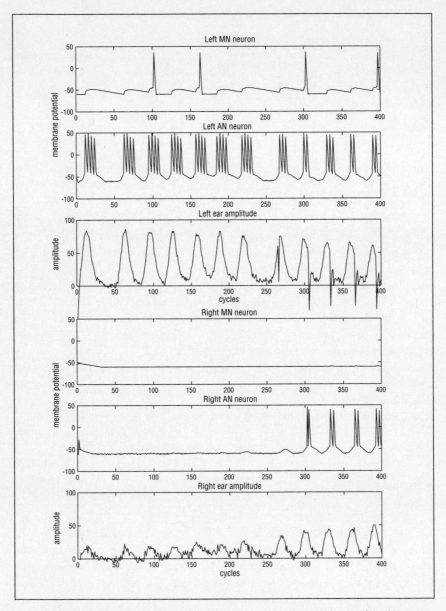

Figure 2. The model neuron response to cricket song—15 millisecond bursts of 4.7 kHz tone.

At the start, only the left input is strong enough to cause spikes AN, and these sum to a spike in MN every two or three syllables. This means the robot turns towards the sound. The right ear amplitude increases, but it is still lower than the left. Thus the right AN spikes after the left AN, which has inhibited its connection to MN. Note that the amplitude and membrane potential are arbitrary units, cycles refer to processor cycles of average duration just under one millisecond.

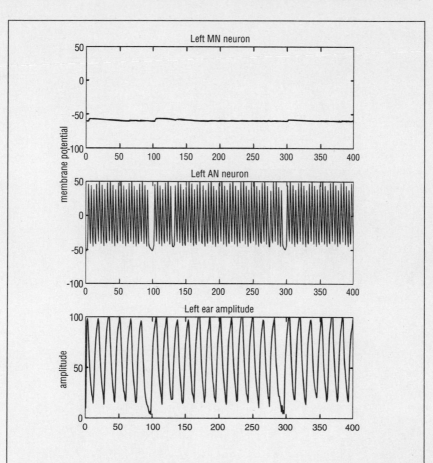

Figure 3. Response to fast (ten millisecond) syllables (left side only).
The AN neuron does not recover between firing to each syllable, so the AN-MN connection remains inhibited and the robot does not respond to the sound.

are about the same length as those in the cricket song stimuli in figure 2. In this case the AN firing clearly represents each syllable with a burst of spikes. The first spike in a burst produces an increase in potential in MN. The gap is long enough for the depression of the AN-MN connection to recover, so that the following burst again increases MN potential. Though MN potential decays in the gap, each increase brings it closer to threshold, and MN fires after two or three syllables, producing turns towards the sound source.

When the length of syllables is increased further the circuit becomes less effective at locating sound as shown in figure 5. Here each syllable and gap lasts 40 milliseconds Though these gaps are long enough to allow the AN-MN connection to recover, they are also long enough for the MN potential to decay

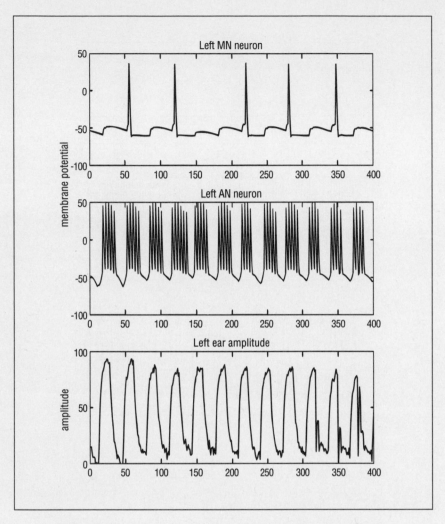

Figure 4. Response to medium (twenty millisecond) syllables (left side only).
As in figure 2, every two or three syllables produces a spike in MN. The robot responds quickly to sound

most of the way back to threshold, hence more syllables are needed to produce a spike in MN.

The ability of the robot to locate sounds of different syllable rates was tested behaviorally by adopting the treadmill paradigm used by Thorson, Weber, and Huber (1982). The robot starts facing between two speakers that are at ninety degrees separation, right and left. The signal is produced in one speaker, switched to the other after about ten seconds, and switched back again after a

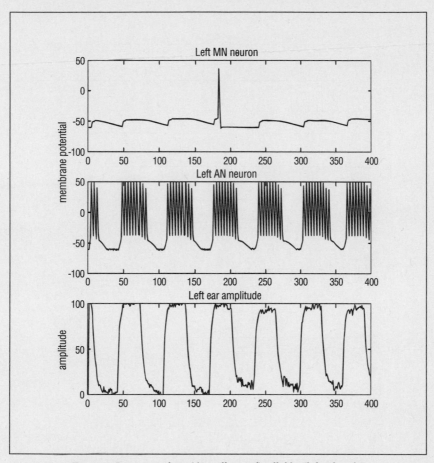

Figure 5. Response to long (40 millisecond) syllables (left side only).

MN potential decays further in the longer gaps between syllables and thus is less likely to reach threshold. The robot is slower to respond to sound.

further ten seconds. Crickets performing phonotaxis show a characteristic oscillation around the speaker direction and follow the switch between the speakers, provided the signal has the "preferred" temporal properties.

The results are shown in figure 6. For continuous sound the robot does not move, and at ten milliseconds one turn occurs when the sound is switched back. At fifteen milliseconds the robot actually turns the wrong way although it produces some periods of oscillatory behavior. At twenty and thirty milliseconds the robot tracks the sound in the characteristic fashion and quickly follows the shift in direction. The tracking at thirty milliseconds shows slightly larger oscillations. At forty milliseconds, slower oscillation around the sound direction occurs, and the robot fails to follow the switch between the speakers.

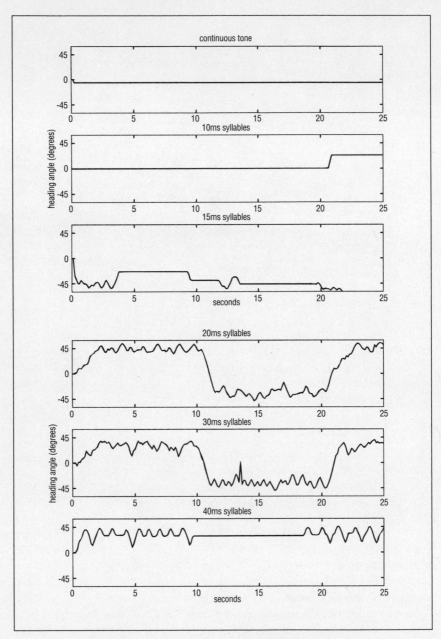

Figure 6. Behavior of the robot with different syllable rates.

Sound is switched from +45 to—45 degrees after approximately ten seconds and switched back at twenty seconds. The robot successfully tracks the switch only for syllables of twenty to thirty milliseconds.

Recognition and Choice?

As a further test of the capabilities of the implemented circuit the following additional tests were performed. Crickets have been shown to perform nondirected oscillation behavior to a sound broadcast directly above them that they presumably can't localize, and this has been taken as evidence of independent recognition of the signal (Weber and Thorson 1988). In the same study, crickets presented with two sound sources are shown to track one of them rather than confusing the direction, and this is taken to mean the female cricket can choose between males if more than one is calling (Hedrick and Dill 1993). In figure 7 three trials using recorded cricket song are shown. In the first, the robot successfully tracks and switches between speakers. In the second, faced with two sounds, the robot briefly oscillates between them then turns towards and tracks one sound. In the third, initial silence, producing no turning behavior from the robot is replaced after about ten seconds by a sound directly above. The robot begins to oscillate as though it had "recognized" the nondirectional signal.

Discussion

The robot cricket described here demonstrates a plausible, simple mechanism by which crickets may carry out selective phonotaxis. It raises a number of interesting issues for understanding of this system. More generally it reveals the complex neural/behavior interactions that can emerge from even a simple model circuit. Finally, the methods described can be used to support models of alternative hypotheses and other sensorimotor systems.

Implications for Cricket Phonotaxis

The four neuron circuit implemented on the robot demonstrates the complexity of behavior that can result from the dynamic properties of neurons embedded in a real sensorimotor device. It can be usefully considered as a "minimal" model of phonotaxis, that is, it represents (probably) the simplest neural circuitry that can actually support the observed behaviors: tracking of sound sources, selectivity for specific frequencies and syllable rates, and tracking behavior without directional input or with competing sounds.

So how might this relate to the actual circuitry in the cricket? More than four identified neurons have been associated with auditory processing and taxis behavior. Our strategy has been to include the connections and properties of neurons in the model only when they appear to be functionally demanded in attempts to reproduce the behavior. For example, it might prove useful to include the mutually inhibitory ON1 neurons that appear to increase the difference in

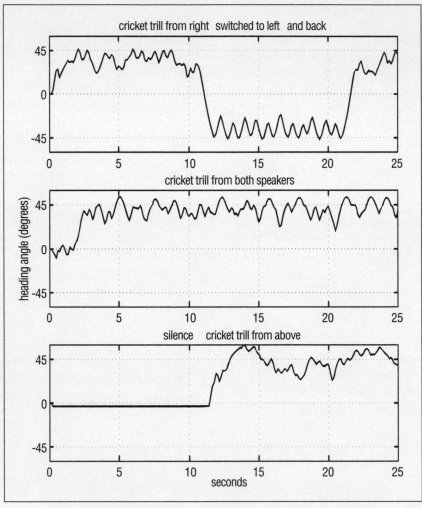

*Figure 7. Behavior of the robot with (top) recorded cricket song switched
between speakers (middle) song simultaneously from both speakers and
(bottom) song from a speaker above the robot.*

The ability to track one speaker out of two and to make phonotaxis like turns when there is
no directional information have been taken as evidence of independent "recognition" in the
cricket, but the simple robot circuit can reproduce these behaviors.

firing of the AN1 neurons (Horseman and Huber 1994). This additional suppression of firing of the wrong side may solve some of the problems caused in
the current circuit by the latter firing sufficiently long after the right side to
cause a motor spike in the wrong direction.

An important implication for cricket neurophysiology of the model is that more caution should be exercised in assuming that spike rates provide sufficient information about the function of neurons, and that operations on spike rates directly control the behavior. The time scale and temporal patterning of the signal already suggest that changing firing rates may not provide the best "information." More subtle interactions of the timing of spikes can be employed successfully to control behavior. And firing rates that correlate with the behavior—in particular the evidence of a brain neuron that appears to fire most to the syllable rates preferred by crickets (Schildberger 1984)—do not necessarily imply a functional role for those firing rates. In the current model, the MNs in the four-neuron circuit show the same correlation of firing rate to preferred syllables (i.e. they spike most frequently to the correct syllable rates), but this is simply a side effect, not a clue to their function.

The minimal model given here thus provides one plausible answer to the question—what neural mechanism underlies phonotaxis? It suggests a number of directions for further investigation of this system, including:

- What relative role is played by the inherent frequency tuning of auditory neurons versus the frequency limitations of directionality in the auditory system?
- Are time differences in AN firing alone able to cause turns? For example if a short syllable on one side preceded a normal length syllable on the other, then latency and number of spikes would suggest opposite directions of movement.
- Can recognition be disambiguated from localization in neural responses? Many experiments fail to allow this distinction to be drawn.
- How should female choice studies be interpreted? The results here suggest that a simple sensory bias hypothesis may suffice to explain the fact that females can directly approach the sound more like the correct calling song. However better experiments on both crickets and the robot are needed to follow this up.

Further Work

Although the robot described has been used to implement a particular hypothesis about phonotaxis, an important feature of the design is that it can easily be used to test alternative hypotheses. The neurons and connections can be specified independently of the general processing mechanism so various circuits can be tested in the same robot device. Further, it is quite plausible to add different sensory and motor capabilities to the robot (there are already light sensors, camera inputs and gripper controllers implemented on the same robot base by other research groups) and interface these to the neural circuitry. This means that various other neuroethologically investigated systems could be explored, for example escape behavior.

What the system provides is a tool for thinking about the problem of sensorimotor control in terms of the dynamics of neural interaction and real-world constraints. This can produce alternate theories to the standard functional decompositions and information processing accounts. One hope is that a "toolbox" of circuit ideas may accumulate allowing the design of more complex neural processors, in a manner analogous to analog electronic circuit design. Even better would be to develop a formalism for this kind of processor: however this is likely to be a difficult task as a balance must be continually maintained between abstraction to enable mathematical tractability and realism so that important low-level properties of neurons are included. An alternative route is to adopt the "neuromorphic" approach of building explicit electronic circuitry to model neural processes rather than using software. This would offer advantages of speed and parallelism but perhaps at the cost of flexibility.

Acknowledgments

The ears circuit was built under EPSRC grant GR/K 78942 at the University of Edinburgh, designed by John Hallam and Andrew Haston and implemented by Henrik Lund. The neural model is based on collaborative work with Tom Scutt.

2

Environmental Information, Animal Behavior, and Biorobot Design
Reflections on Locating Chemical Sources in Marine Environments

Frank W. Grasso

There are two uses of biorobots. They can be employed, first, as tools to aid biological research, and second, as the end products of biological research that perform useful tasks with an efficiency that approaches that of animals. My focus is primarily on using them as aides to developing a deeper understanding of animal behavior and its physiological substrates. The idea of producing useful robots along the way, while desirable, is a secondary consideration.

In the study of biological systems there are two broad areas in which biorobots contribute. First, they allow for the direct test of biological hypotheses themselves. If an appropriate implementation of a theory fails to replicate the biological process it is intended to explain, that failure constitutes strong grounds for rejecting the hypothesis. I shall return to this point in detail later. A second application for biorobots is exploring the constraints of the world of an animal. The behavior produced and data collected from a properly scaled autonomous robot in the natural environment of the animal it emulates are about as close as we can come to experiencing the world of another species. I shall reflect on both these applications of biorobots in detail in this chapter.

To produce useful robots, one must have a well-defined problem and a workable solution to that problem. Certainly animals can be found with capabilities that are desirable in robots. Researchers who aim is to implement animal algorithms and hopefully approach animal efficiency in these areas add to their labors the burden of having the animal solution in hand before they begin construction. The extent of this self-imposed burden depends upon the vagueness with which the builder is "inspired" by the natural system. Future designers of practical biorobots will rely on understanding of the model animals gleaned from biological research. For such an understanding to be adequate it will most likely have one foot on traditional biological research and the other foot on previous generations of biorobots used as tools of biological research.

Three Issues

As a result of my experiences in the study of robots and animals, three issues have been promoted to high relief in my thinking about projects involving biorobots:

1. What constitutes a sufficient understanding of the organism to ensure that a biorobotic implementation will lead to useful results?
2. What constitute good measures of robot performance?
3. What is the proper control algorithm(s) to represent a biological function in a robot—more specifically, how does one decide the relative importance of environmental cues and internal representations?

These are good questions for researchers to ask themselves in the early planning phases of a biorobotic project, regardless of whether they are planning on using robotics to understand biological phenomena or are interested in the development of practical robots based on biological inspiration. The answers—even partial answers—to these questions, obtained from the perspective of a particular task or biological system, are more useful to have in hand at the start of a biorobotics project than they are as "discoveries" at the end of one. In this chapter I will review the results of studies exploring the nature of lobster chemo-orientation with our autonomous underwater biorobot, RoboLobster and use them to illustrate the effect answers to these questions have on the biorobotic approach to understanding biological phenomena and the production of useful robots.

The RoboLobster Experiments

The RoboLobster experiments and design specifications have been described in previous publications. In this section I summarize the key features of that work that illustrate the general points. The reader interested in the details of the robot and chemo-orientation is directed to those papers (Consi, Atema, et al. 1994; Consi, Grasso, et al. 1995; Grasso, Dale, et al. 1996; Grasso, Dale, et al. 1997; Grasso, Basil, et al. 1998; Grasso, Consi, et al. 2000).

Three Lines of Attack

Marine species appear to have evolved a variety of strategies to deal with chemo-orientation in the sea (Dodson and Dohse 1984; Moore, Scholz, et al. 1991;

Dunsenberry 1992; Weissburg and Zimmer-Faust 1994; Zimmer-Faust, Finelli, et al. 1995; Baird, Johari, et al. 1996; Cox, Hunt, et al. 1997; Dale 1997; Moore and Lepper 1997; Barbin 1998). The spatial dynamics of the fluid medium and the animal's speed of locomotion appear to dominate the strategy each species uses. Some—and probably many species not yet studied under multiple conditions—appear to have evolved multiple strategies that they can switch on and off depending on context (Dunsenberry 1992; Oliver, Grasso, et al. 1996; Beglane, Grasso, et al. 1997; Mjos, Grasso, et al. 1999).

The aim of the RoboLobster project was to evaluate alternative hypotheses of lobster chemo-orientation in the American lobster, *Homarus americanus*. RoboLobster was one component of three parallel lines of research aimed at explaining lobster chemotaxis. The other two components involved understanding the animal behavior and understanding the environment of the plume-tracking lobster. Our efforts with RoboLobster would have been a tangle of free parameters without these two sources of constraints.

In the following sections, I will review studies of the chemo-orientation behavior of lobsters under conditions of turbulent flow and the physics of chemical distribution under the action of turbulence before turning to the implementation of chemo-orientation algorithms in RoboLobster.

The Animal

In the case of the American lobster, it is clear that—at least for the plumes so far studied—they use two chemo-sensors to inform their chemo-orientation strategies. They perform more efficiently (i.e., they take straighter, less convoluted paths) when they use both lateral antennules, but they can still track a plume to its source with one (Devine and Atema 1982; Beglane, Grasso, et al. 1997). Although it is not possible at this time to exclude the possibility that animals using one antennule are employing a degraded form of the two antennule strategy, it appears that the lobster is capable of using at least two strategies. The following paragraph will illustrate why multiple strategies are likely.

Lobster behavior suggests that they might actually be using the turbulence-induced spatial-temporal structure of the odor plume to track odors to their source (Moore, Scholz, et al. 1991; Basil 1994). In contrast to the predictions of other strategies such as odor-gated rheotaxis (Kennedy 1986), the closeness of the lobster's direction of travel (heading angle) to the direction of the source increases as the lobster progresses through the plume (see figures 1 and 2). This unequivocally demonstrates that the animal is extracting some form of information about the direction of the source that is distinct from the direction of mean flow on which odor-gated rheotaxis is based. If the lobster were to approach the source along a line parallel to the direction of mean flow (the definition of Rheotaxis) its heading angle would increase unless it were walking a parallel directly downstream from the source. The likely source is the pattern of intermit-

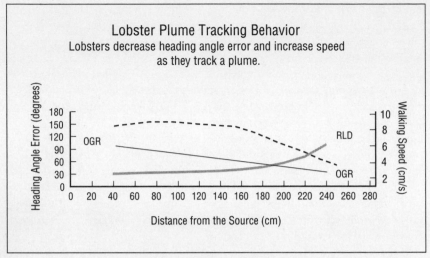

*Figure 1. The pattern of lobster behavior that indicates the
extraction of guidance information during tracking.*

Solid lines are plots of heading error angle versus distance from the odor source as predicted from
odor-gated rheotasis (OGR), and from representative lobster data (RLD). Dashed line is a plot of
lobster speed versus distance from odor source from representative lobster data. Summary of the results obtained from Moore, Scholz, and Atema (1991) and Basin (1994).

tent odor patches produced by turbulence source (Moore, Scholz, et al. 1991;
Basil 1994).

If we accept the conclusion that lobsters are extracting and using some plume
information beyond mean flow, the natural question is, what information is the
lobster using? Recordings of these intermittent odor patches encountered by
plume-tracking lobsters indicate that they make turning decisions on the 2-4
second time scale (Grasso, Basil, et al. 1998). This is much too rapid an interval
for an accurate estimate of the average odor concentration. Neurophysiological
studies of the response dynamics of the chemo-receptor neurons on the lobster's
lateral antennules indicate that these cells are capable of following the temporal
fluctuations of turbulence-influenced concentration signals (see next section)
(Gomez, Voigt, et al. 1992, 1994a, 1994b; Gomez and Atema 1996a; Gomez
and Atema 1996b). Simulation studies based on this data indicate that the temporal filter properties of these neurons selectively preserve this information
(Grasso, Voigt, et al. 1998).

The Environment

To understand the task an American lobster faces as it tracks an odor plume to its
source, we must place ourselves in the lobster's situation. In practical terms, diffu-
sion is too slow to cover distances of more than a few millimeters in the time that

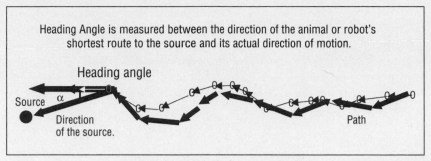

*Figure 2. The method of extracting heading
angle (α) from a digitized path as viewed from overhead.*

The heading angle may be computed from any pair of position measurements along this hypothetical path.

a lobster walks a number of meters distance. The lobster places its lateral antennules above the viscous sublayer (the sheet of water nearest the substrate) up into the flowing medium that lies above it to sense these passing chemicals (as perceived chemicals known as odors that can be individual compounds or mixtures of chemicals). The lobster can sense this passing flow and sample the chemicals that are carried within it. The lobster obtains a frame of reference to evaluate the relative motion of the flow-borne patches of odor through its contact with the substrate. Turbulence produced by physical features that effect the motion of the seawater generates spatial patterns of flow, and therefore spatially heterogeneous distributions of chemical. Thus, what can be thought of as confusing noise to a concentration-tracking strategy may provide guidance cues to help the lobster track the chemical to its source using a feature detection-based strategy.

Studies of chemical distribution in turbulence in the field and in the laboratory provide insights into the nature of the signal environment that animals actually encounter (Moore and Atema 1991; Murlis, Elkinton, et al. 1992; Finelli, Pentcheff, et al. 1999). The period of time required to obtain a statically stationary estimate of concentration depends on the magnitude of the turbulence. In our seawater conditions, the time scale for such estimates is typically several minutes. On purely physical evidence, these studies demonstrate that the idea that animals (or at least lobsters and similar-sized crustaceans) track chemicals to their source by ascending the concentration gradient in environments that contain even moderate levels of turbulence ($Re > 1 \times 10^2$) is untenable.

Studies of the dynamics of the concentration signal have revealed features (such as characteristic rates or patterns of change) that could provide the lobster (or other animals) with guidance cues for certain plumes (Dittmer, Grasso, et al. 1995; Dittmer, Grasso, et al. 1996; Finelli, Pentcheff, et al. 1999; Moore and Atema 1991; but see Hanna, Grasso, et al. 1999). Examples of cues extracted from the concentration signal include peak height (the maximum value of a pulse of odor), peak slope (the rate of change of concentration in time on the rising phase of an odor pulse), and interpeak-interval (the delay between the passing of one peak and the arrival of the next at a sensor). There are many others that have been studied. Such cues might provide the information lobster behavior indicates they are using to decrease their heading angles during chemo-orientation (figures 1 and 2).

The Robot

The constraints supplied from the physics of odor plumes and the behavior of lobsters provided a suite of testable hypotheses on how lobsters locate odor sources in turbulence. They also provided suitable constraints for the construction of a robot that could be used to test those hypotheses.

Why a Robot?

Hypotheses of chemo-orientation mechanisms are difficult to test in animal behavior experiments because measures of the cue stimuli are very difficult to obtain—and harder still from a freely moving animal. The viscosity of water guarantees that the effects of physical perturbations from obstacles or changes in the shape of the channel persist far downstream from the agents that produce them. Once a perturbation is introduced (say from a plume-generating device or the animal itself), it evolves in a way that is only predictable in a stochastic way that requires large numbers of repetitions before statistical stationarity is achieved. This makes the construction of apparatus for testing lobster reactions to specific features highly problematic (if not technically impossible) for two major reasons: First, the control of flow through a stimulus delivery device to produce odor pulses of a predetermined duration, slope, or other character is exceedingly difficult, and second, good methods are not yet available to reproduce arbitrary patterns. This would suggest a restrained animal preparation that would allow tight control of the stimulus delivery to the chemo-sensors. However, this approach also removes the possibility to observe natural behavioral responses from the animal. Sequential effects would also be very difficult and time consuming to extract from such a preparation.

At first glance, simulation studies appear to be a means to circumvent these difficulties. An artificial plume environment constructed from calculations within a theoretical framework would provide the experimenter with perfect control of the environment. Such direct numerical simulation (DNS) methods exist in the field of fluid dynamics, but they come with serious caveats for the biologist or biorboticist. First, they describe long-term average behavior of fluid dynamics systems; the second-by second spatial structure of the signals encountered by the animals is not available from such simulations. Second, the computational load of DNS that approaches the appropriate spatial scale is so great as to practically prohibit the large repetitions required for evaluation of orientation algorithms in a reasonable amount of time (Belanger and Willis 1996).

We have implemented a number of algorithms in simulation, with "playback" plumes. These plume simulations are based on the playback of data recorded from actual odor plumes rather than the theoretical approach described in the previous paragraph. These simulation studies have identified guidance features, which are available to the lobster through its peripheral chemoreceptors. The use of these features speeds up the simulation's orientation by an order of magnitude compared to concentration-averaging techniques (Grasso, Gaito, et al. 1999). Such studies are useful as a means of screening algorithms and tuning parameters prior to biorobotic studies, but they cannot, for reasons discussed above, completely capture a number of important environmental features such as the effect of the robot or lobsters hydrodynamic shadow on the guidance cues. This is a problem that must be solved in all simulation studies of behavior.. The results of the simulation study are only as good as the simulation of the task environment. In the case of chemo-orientation in turbulence, a robotic implementation is a critical and unequivocal test of the quality of an orientation algorithm.

By constructing an artificial lobster and placing it into the same environment as the biological lobster, we had a method for testing hypotheses of chemo-orientation that circumvented these difficulties. Tom Consi, Jelle Atema, David Mountain, and I undertook a series of experiments to test simple hypotheses of lobster chemo-orientation (Consi, Grasso, et al. 1995; Grasso, Dale, et al. 1997; Grasso, Basil, et al. 1998; Grasso, Consi, et al. 2000)

There is an additional advantage to a biologist who has a biorobot in his or her tool-kit. By placing a scaled surrogate of the animal under study in the exact environment, the biologist can view the sensory world of a given species. Data from sensors with spatial and temporal sampling scales matched to that of the animal could be logged to on-board data-storage media. (This was the case in Robolobster.) Offline analysis of these logs can be of great value in evaluating the reasons for an algorithm's failure to reproduce animal behavior. By suggesting alternative hypotheses for testing of the animals, such data closes the loop between robot and animal experiments.

Bio-Mimetic Scaling

The first biorobot we used to study lobster chemotactic strategies—dubbed RoboLobster—was designed and built by Tom Consi and Cliff Goudey who were then working at the Massachusetts Institute of Technology's AUV lab (Consi, Atema, et al. 1994). It had wheels instead of legs and was not intended to mimic lobster biomechanics or morphology (figure 3). Instead it incorporated those features essential for the evaluation of the chemotactic hypotheses: RoboLobster was built to the proportions of the American lobster and had two chemo-sensors that can be positioned at the same height and separation as the lobster's two lateral antennules.

Figure 3. RoboLobster with a standard dye-tinted plume.

The robot is inside a ten meter by two meter flume in seawater forty-four centimeters in depth. The robot is designed to serve as a platform to carry chemical sensors, visible above the front end of the robot, through an odor plume. *(Photo courtesy Tom Consi and Margorie Steele.)*

In addition to scaling the hardware we also shaped the control software to scale the robot's performance to that of the lobster. The RoboLobster's chemo-sensors acquired sensor data at rates that were much higher than those that could possibly operate in the American lobster's nose. We used software to scale the data acquisition rates to match those that we knew from lobster-chemoreceptor neurophysiology. Similarly, RoboLobster's motors could propel and turn the robot at speeds and angular speeds exceeding those of the lobster. We programmed lobster-scaled speeds into the algorithms controlling behavior during trials.

What RoboLobster Allowed Us to Do

Our ultimate aim was (and remains) tests of the feature-based chemo-orientation strategies mentioned above. First however, with Ockham's razor in mind, we tested a set of simpler algorithms. Our thinking was that if these simpler algorithms were adequate to provide a satisfactory explanation of lobster plume-tracking behavior, our conclusion would put feature-based algorithms into question. We decided to focus on what seemed the simplest dual-sensor strategy: tropotaxis. *Tropotaxis* is an orientation strategy based on an instantaneous estimate of the local gradient of a cue derived from two sensors (Fraenkel and Gunn 1961).

The major result of these studies was a solid demonstration that tropotactic concentration-sensing algorithms could not explain the plume tracking behavior lobsters—at least not in the type of plume that we tested (Moore and Atema

	Overall Length (cm)	Speed (cm/s)	Sensor Height & Separation (cm)	Chemo-sensor ampling Rate (Hz)
Lobster	~30.0	~9.0	9.0 & 3.0	~2.5
Robot	24.0	~9.0	9.0 & 3.0	2.0 – 5.0

Table 1. RoboLobster's critical points of biomimetic scaling.

1991; Dittmer, Grasso, et al. 1995). As a consequence, we are forced to consider other biologically reasonable algorithms in search of a reasonable explanation.

The negative result was significant because the conditions of the series of experiments were carefully constructed to succeed if and only if the plume structure supported the algorithm. The plume structure failed to do so in an interesting way. The behavior of the robot as it tracked the plume showed two statistically distinct patterns of locomotion in two regions of the plume using the same algorithm. In the downstream region, the robot did not make significant progress toward the source. In the upstream region, where progress toward the source was possible with a tropotactic algorithm, the paths produced showed little resemblance to those of lobsters (figure 4). Thus RoboLobster revealed to us something about the lobster's world that we had previously only suspected: the need to switch tracking strategies between different regions of the plume.

In one series of experiments we systematically varied the intersensor separation. Since tropotaxis relies on an instantaneous estimate of the gradient, the increased distance between the sensors should have improved performance. This was the case in the upstream but not the downstream regions of the plume. These experiments, which varied one of the biologically derived constraints of the robot, represent a type of evolutionary experiment in that they test the sensitivity of an algorithm to architectural variation. They place the question of why the lobsters possess the intersensor separation that they do (other species have both greater and less separations) in high relief and open the door to further experiments that can explore the relationship between environment and evolutionarily derived structure.

Sufficient Description for
Biorobotic Algorithm Implementation

A biologically meaningful biorobot cannot be created de novo from first principles. A good practical robot might arise from first principles but not a biorobot. There must be a sufficient descriptive database available to provide appropriate constraints for the design parameters. Without this set of constraints one who

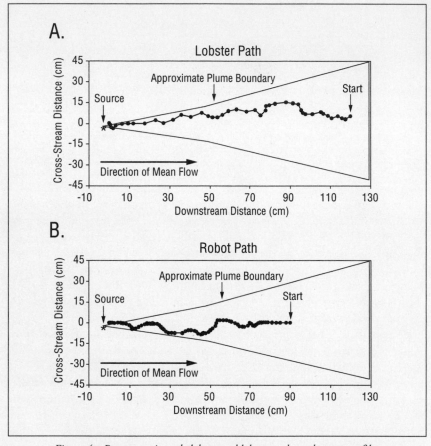

Figure 4a. Representative robolobster and lobster paths and sensor profiles.

These particular paths were chosen because they show the closest similarity between lobster and robot paths obtained. Panels A and B show the paths. The lobster's path in panel A contrasts that of the robot in Panel B. Robolobster, running a simple tropotactic algorithm makes a series of sweeping counter-turns as it approaches the source (marked by an *).

sets about building a loosely constrained biorobot will, unless very lucky, produce neither a practical robot nor good biology. They would also probably never finish building the robot.

These statements might appear to pose a paradox. If the biological system is so sufficiently well understood that a biological replica can be built, why bother building it as a tool to study the biology? If the biology is imperfectly understood how does one proceed with the development of a robot? This reduces to the old question of judging the dividing line between essential facts and irrelevant details. The basis for the experimentor's determining the relevance of particular features of the description of the system should be strong theoretical in-

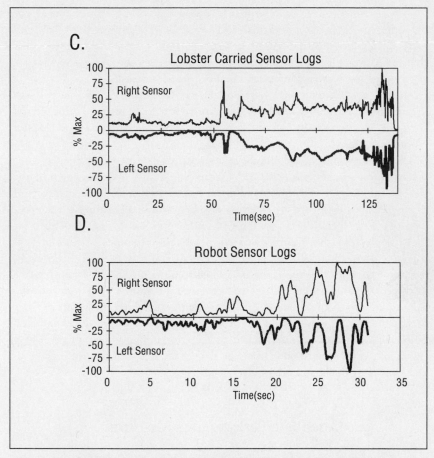

Figure 4b. Representative robolobster and lobster paths and sensor profiles.

These particular paths were chosen because they show the closest similarity between lobster and robot paths obtained. Panels C and D the corresponding sensor logs. Panel C shows dopamine concentration profiles recorded with a pair of electrochemical electrodes mounted on the back of the lobster and positioned in the olfactory sampling area of the lobster. Dopamine was used as a tracer in the food odor plume the lobster tracked. Panel D shows concentration signals taken from the robot's sensor logs. Both C and D are expressed as percent of maximum signal. RoboLobster's counter turning near the source is evident in the sensor log.

ference (Platt 1964). That is, do they fulfill the requirement that the included features are both necessary and sufficient to explain the system under study?

In our studies with RoboLobster, we made an effort to explain the observation that lobsters reduce their heading-angle error as they progress through the plume. Based in part on the observation that lobsters perform well with two antennules, we formulated a chemo-tropotaxis model as an explanation. This framework allowed us to suppose that legs were not essential for our robot but that appropriate speed was essential. It allowed us to determine the spatial and temporal resolution of the sensors so that we could be reasonably certain that the information that the robot used for guidance was comparable to that are available to the lobster. Plume signals above five Hz frequency and below the size of the lobster's antennules were not allowed to inform the tropotactic algorithm. These and similar constraints were sufficient to allow us to critically test the concentration-based tropotaxis hypothesis as an explanation of lobster plume-tracking behavior.

This is the essence of the biorobotic strategy: Construct a robot that is competent to test a hypothesis or set of hypotheses that have been suggested by the biology and then allow the robot's behavior to inform you of the acceptability of that hypothesis. If you are in possession of the biological algorithm you can proceed to the production of practical robots and hypothesis testing is not an issue. If the algorithm is not known one need include only those constraints that are required to test the hypothesis under consideration. I assume here that one undertakes a robotic study to answer a biological question only if it is not possible or too costly to obtain the answer directly from the animal. Constraints or design features that are not required to test the hypothesis (in our case legs, for one example) are likely to cloud the scientific issues and make for greater technical difficulties. In other words a sufficient database for a biorobotic implementation is one that leaves at most one or two, preferably no, free parameters in the model suggested by the hypothesis to be evaluated.

Adequate Performance Measures

If the aim of the biorobot is hypothesis testing, then the performance measures must be sufficiently well understood in the biological system for a meaningful comparison to be made between the robot and the animal. As with constraints on robot design, the hypothesis being tested delineates the relevant and irrelevant features of the biological behavior in an adequate description of performance. Performance measures should be derived from descriptions of the biological behaviors that are adequate to permit the determination that the algorithm under study is or is not operating.

In our case, it was essential to have a good description of the animal behavior. We measured a number of descriptors of the paths RoboLobster took as it traversed the plume. These were measured using exactly the same methods and under exactly the same conditions as those used in lobster studies.

The trials where RoboLobster "missed" the source must be due to failures of the implemented algorithms. We cannot be certain, however, that the same is true for the lobster. Motivation makes the "hit" rates of the lobsters difficult to contrast with RoboLobster because the robot is programmed to always seek the source, while the lobster may not be driven by a single motivation. Thus we used a finer-grained performance measure. We digitized the paths taken by the robot at intervals that are shorter than the variation in lobster locomotor performance. From these, we were able to measure, in both the lobster and the robot, the distance from the source, time to various points from the source, locomotory speed, and the path tortuosity (a measure of the deviation of the path from a straight line). These parameters allowed us to make direct, quantitative comparisons between lobster and robot performance with specific relevance to the tropotactic hypothesis.

This narrow view of the performance measure has a cost, however. Given that the performance matches some reasonable criterion of the biological system, there is no guarantee that the function implemented in the robot is *the* strategy used by the animal. It merely constitutes evidence that the two are consistent. The narrowing of the performance measures to just those that are adequate to evaluate the hypothesis may mask inconsistencies in other aspects of performance. In contrast to the robot design, performance measures should be chosen to at least permit testing the hypothesis. A discrepancy in some aspect of performance that is unessential for the hypothesis points to a limitation of the model (maybe the hardware, maybe the software implementation, or maybe the theory itself) that is in need of explanation.

Control Algorithm Selection and Internal Representations

The choice of the sophistication of the algorithms to be tested in an experimental biorobot is also of importance. The biorobot could be designed with elaborate internal representations of the world that it will encounter, and detailed contingency mechanisms that are activated when certain conditions are met. Alternatively, it could be designed so that its behavior is driven by the stimulus world.

In a biorobot intended to evaluate a biological hypothesis, it is likely that actual algorithms will fall between these extremes. With the exception of simple unicellular animals (Berg and Purcell 1977), most animals produce behaviors that suggest they plan their actions, make use of environmental features, remember past tribulations and successes, and use this information to adjust their behaviors accordingly. These information-use strategies suggest some form of internal representation. Biorobotics is an ideal tool to explore such hypotheses. On the other hand, it is possible to generate quite complex behaviors from a relatively simple algorithm if the environment is complex (Braitenberg 1984, Kennedy 1992). Whichever side one chooses, the implications of this assumption must be considered.

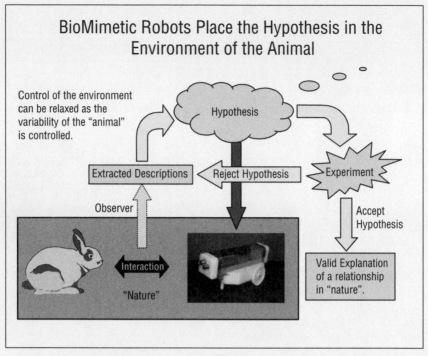

Figure 5. The role biorobots can play in basic biological research.

The environment, through evolution or ontogeny, plays a critical role in shaping the behavior of an animal. By placing the robot in the natural environment the contribution of the environment to behavior can be disassociated from that of the animal.

We applied the principle of parsimony in choosing our algorithms. In our biorobotic studies with RoboLobster we could have assumed a large amount of data stored in the lobster's brain to support chemo-taxis. Instead, we started with very simple chemo-orientation strategies that assumed a minimum knowledge of the lobster's world. The failures of simple algorithms to explain lobster behavior justify our implementation of more complex algorithms, since we are left with no simpler alternatives.

This is the principle of Ockham's razor—and it seems as useful a heuristic in the evaluation of biologically-relevant hypotheses with biorobots as it does in the rest of science. This approach also highlights one of the major advantages of biorobots in biology. The biorobot offers a way of systematically evaluating the contribution and influence of environmental structure on behavioral patterns and a justification of the use of more complex devices and systems (such as these that include internal representations) in models as the simpler explanations are demonstrated to be untenable (figure 5). By placing the biorobot in the same environment as the animal, we are, in reality, placing the hypothesis directly into the environment.

Summary

Recently, Vogel (1998) has strongly argued against the common prejudice that biological solutions to problems are necessarily optimal. He points out that evolution has shaped biological systems to be adequate to ensure the survival of the individual animal until it can reproduce. In this, optimality is not required—merely adequacy. At the same time, biological solutions exist (to problems such as chemo-orientation in turbulence) that are superior to our present ones. The animals themselves are existence proofs of such superior solutions. Biorobots are a powerful tool that can aid our efforts to uncover these natural strategies.

To achieve this however, we must acknowledge that the science of biology, with its own brand of methods and logic, must be at the center of any such effort. The performance measures, hypotheses, and design parameters must be biologically meaningful and not merely biologically inspired if we are divine nature's solutions to difficult problems.

Acknowledgements

The experimental work summarized here has been previously published. Nevertheless I must acknowledge the contributions a number of people. The work was conducted in the laboratory of Jelle Atema and rests largely on the many years of lobster research conducted in that laboratory in earlier years. Tom Consi and David Mountain were also central to the RoboLobster project. I must also thank Jennifer Basil for generously the supplying the lobster data in figure 4. Jonathan Dale, Paul DiNunno, Kevin Dittmer, Diana Ma, and Rainer Voigt all made significant technical contributions to the project. Steve Gaito, Megan Mahaffy, Christina Manbeck, and Christian Reilly made significant contributions to the development and study of theoretical chemo-tactic algorithms. Photocredit for figure 3 goes to Tom Consi and Marjorie Steele. This work was largely supported by two NSF grants to Jelle Atema—BES-9315791 and IBN-9631665.

3

Insect Strategies of Visual Homing in Mobile Robots

Ralf Möller, Dimitrios Lambrinos,
Thorsten Roggendorf, Rolf Pfeifer, and Rüdiger Wehner

Animals of many species are impressive navigators. Especially insects such as bees or ants solve demanding navigation tasks, despite their tiny brains. Desert ants of the genus *Cataglyphis* (see figure 1), for example, unfailingly return to the nest from foraging excursions that took them several hundred meters away (Wehner 1987). Unlike other ants, *Cataglyphis* can not use chemical cues for navigation, since no marker substance would endure long enough in the heat of its desert habitat. Experiments revealed that the ants instead, besides using path integration, rely on visual information about landmarks in their environment (Wehner and Räber 1979; Wehner, Michel, and Antonsen 1996).

The limited brain size of insects restricts the complexity of the mechanisms that could underlie their navigational capabilities. Hypotheses about these parsimonious and yet efficient navigation strategies can serve as a guideline for the development of navigation strategies for mobile robots. Vice versa, in a process of "synthetic modeling," the understanding of a natural system can be improved by constructing an artificial agent that mimics some aspects of its behavior, and observing the behavior and internal states of the artificial agent, preferably in environments similar to the habitat of the biological agent. Synthetic modeling is an indispensable complement to computer simulations, and will especially be used in cases, where the agent-environment interaction is too complex to be simulated with sufficient accuracy.

The work presented here focuses on modeling the *visual homing capabilities* of insects with mobile robots. Two navigation models—the "snapshot model" and the related "average landmark vector model," which both widely explain the navigation behavior observed in bees and ants—were implemented and tested on mobile robots. The snapshot model was tested in a software implementation on the mobile robot Sahabot 2, while the average landmark vector model was

Figure 1. The desert ant Cataglyphis *bicolor (courtesy R. Wehner).*

implemented in analog hardware on a robot with fully analog control (called "analog robot" in the following).

The section "Visual Homing of Insects" briefly outlines the experiments that have been done with insects to analyze their visual homing strategies. The snapshot model and the average landmark vector model are presented in the section "Navigation Models." The section "Robot Implementation" describes, how the navigation models are implemented on the two mobile robots. The experimental setups and the results of the robot experiments are presented in the section "Robot Experiments." The "Discussion" section provides a discussion of the experimental results and relates the study to other work in both the fields of synthetic modeling and visual robot navigation. It also provides first experimental results of an application of the average landmark vector model to navigation in indoor environments.

Visual Homing of Insects

Desert ants of the genus *Cataglyphis* are solitary foragers that have to return to important locations in their environment, which can be either food sources or

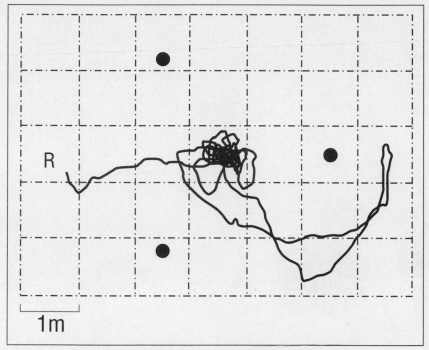

Figure 2. Landmark navigation experiment with Cataglyphis.

Ants were trained to locate the center of an array of three landmarks (black cylinders, depicted as circles). The figure shows the trajectory of a single ant that was displaced to a test area
with an identical landmark configuration. *R* marks the release point (adapted from Wehner,
Michel, and Antonsen [1996]).

the nest entrance. Experiments revealed that the ants resort to three different
navigation strategies: path integration (dead reckoning), visual landmark navigation, and systematic search (Wehner, Michel, and Antonsen 1996). Path integration guides the animal to the vicinity of the target location, but is subject to
cumulative errors that limit the precision of this strategy. Ants that by means of
path integration returned to a target location that is not surrounded by landmarks have to start a systematic search around the expected goal position. However, their behavior is completely different, if landmarks are visible: in this case,
the ants precisely pinpoint the goal (Wehner, Michel, and Antonsen 1996).

The typical experimental procedure to analyze the visual homing strategies
that was used for experiments with both ants (Wehner and Räber 1979;
Wehner, Michel, and Antonsen 1996) and bees (Cartwright and Collett 1983)
is depicted in figures 2 and 3. In a training area, landmarks are positioned
close to a target location, e.g., the nest entrance. When the animals have
learned to locate this goal, they are displaced to a test area with another landmark configuration, where their search path is recorded. The place where the

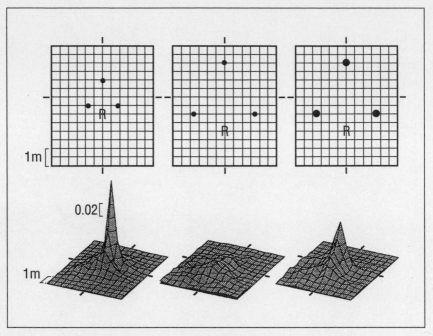

Figure 3. Search density profiles of Cataglyphis *ants trained to the
landmark array shown in figure 2.*

R marks the release point of the ants. *Left:* Test in the training situation. *Center:* Test situation
with landmarks separated by twice the training distance. *Right:* Test situation with landmarks
of twice the training size and in twice the training distance (adapted from Wehner, Michel,
and Antonsen [1996])

animals search most densely is assumed to be the position where they expect
to find the target.

By varying the landmark configuration in the test area with respect to the
training configuration and observing the changes of the search peak position,
properties of the insects' navigation strategies can be unveiled. From experiments like the one depicted in figure 3 it can be concluded that the visual memory of the insect contains a rather unprocessed two-dimensional "snapshot" of
the visual scene. When returning from the excursion to the vicinity of the snapshot position, the insect moves in a direction where the discrepancy between the
snapshot and the current view is reduced, until the two views match (Wehner,
Michel, and Antonsen 1996). Which aspects of the two views are actually compared was derived from experiments with bees, where size and position of the
landmarks were varied. The results suggested that no more than the apparent
size and the bearing of the landmark are considered (Cartwright and Collett
1983); bees also use distance cues, but the effect of distance is negligible compared to apparent size (Cheng et al. 1987).

Navigation Models

Several models have been devised to explain the visual navigation abilities of insects. These models differ in the information that is assumed to be stored about the target location, and in the mechanisms used to derive a home direction from currently available and stored information. An early algorithmic model was suggested by Anderson (1977) and studied in computer simulations. He supposed that bees consider the overall "Gestalt" of a landmark configuration—specifically the "surroundedness" by landmarks—rather than remembering the landmarks around the goal pictorially. However, this concept was later given up based on evidence from the experiments by Wehner and Räber (1979) and Cartwright and Collett (1983) in favor of a pictorial matching process. The corresponding algorithmic description is the "snapshot model," studied in computer simulations by Cartwright and Collett (1983). Recently it could be shown that the Gestalt concept and the snapshot model are actually closely related; the bridge between the two domains is established by the "average landmark vector model" (Lambrinos et al. 1998, 2000). While the snapshot model is already considered parsimonious, the average landmark vector model turns out to be extremely cheap, both with respect to the memory capacity and computation required. The algorithms of both the snapshot model and the average landmark vector model are described in the following subsections.

Snapshot Model

Cartwright and Collett (1983) proposed an algorithm of the snapshot matching procedure that reproduces some aspects of the behavior observed in bees; figure 4 (left) visualizes the matching process of this model. It assumes that the views on which the matching process is operating are horizontal images comprising dark and bright sectors corresponding to the landmarks and the gaps between them, respectively. These views are supposed to be aligned with an external compass direction. A pairing between sectors in the two views is established by searching the closest sector of the same type (dark or bright) in the current view for each sector in the snapshot. Each pair of sectors contributes two vectors to the final home vector: a tangential vector pointing from the snapshot sector towards the paired sector in the current view, and a radial vector that points centrifugally from the snapshot sector, if the apparent width of the current view sector is smaller than the width of its counterpart in the snapshot, and vice versa. A movement in the direction of the tangential vector reduces the difference in bearing of the paired sectors; a movement in the direction of the radial vector reduces the difference in their apparent size. The model could also take into account differences in apparent height, though this was not considered in the original snapshot model. Averaging all contributions gives a home vector point-

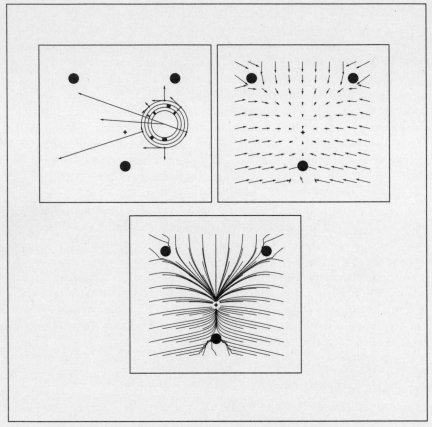

Figure 4. Simulation of the snapshot model (version with proportional vector contributions) for a configuration of three landmarks (black circles).

Top left: A snapshot (inner ring) taken at the nest position marked with a cross is matched with a current view (middle ring) visible from the position in the center of the ring diagram. Each pair of matched sectors (both landmarks and gaps) contributes a radial and a tangential vector (attached to the outer ring in the diagram). The home vector (originating from the center) is obtained by averaging the contributing vectors. *Top right:* A home vector can be assigned to each point of the plane. *Bottom:* Trajectories running tangentially to the home vectors. Most trajectories end at the snapshot position, some trajectories run into one of the landmarks.

ing approximately to the position of the target (figure 4, top right); a trajectory following these home vectors that are attached to each point of the plane will approach the location where the snapshot was taken (figure 4, bottom).

Despite this rather simple procedure, homing is highly reliable even for more complex landmark configurations like the one shown in figure 5. As can be seen in the center image and in the view trace on the right, the algorithm tolerates the occlusion of landmarks and the fusion of landmark sectors.

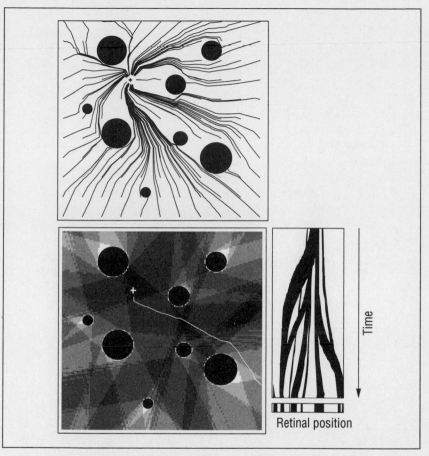

Figure 5. Simulation of the snapshot model (with proportional vector contributions) for a configuration of eight landmarks (black circles).

Top: Trajectories running tangentially to the home vectors. *Bottom left:* Number of landmark sectors visible from each point; darker areas correspond to higher numbers of visible sectors. A selected trajectory is depicted with a white line. *Bottom right:* Transformation of the current view over time (upper part) towards the snapshot (lower part) for the trajectory depicted in the center image.

Average Landmark Vector Model

Surprisingly, there is an even more parsimonious method, the "average landmark vector (ALV) model," which can be derived mathematically from the snapshot model (Lambrinos et al. 1998, 2000). In this model, views are characterized by two-component "average landmark vectors," which are computed as the average (or sum) of unit vectors pointing towards the selected image features; see figure 6. Instead of a snapshot image, only the average landmark vector of the target

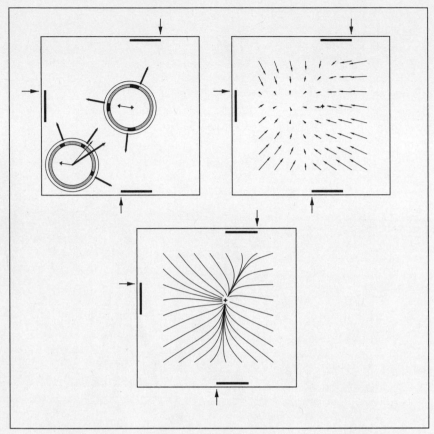

Figure 6. Simulation of the ALV model. Black bars depict landmarks, of which the edges marked with an arrow serve as landmark cues for the algorithm.

Top left: Each gray ring depicts the view as visible from the center of the ring. A unit-length landmark vector is assigned to each detected edge (vectors attached to the outer ring). At the target location (cross), an average landmark (AL) vector (wide head, originating from the center) is computed as the sum (or average) of all landmark vectors. In the current location (lower left diagram), another AL vector is determined in the same way (thin vector, small head, originating from the center). The difference of the two AL vectors is the home vector (thick vector, originating from the center. *Top right:* AL vector field. *Bottom:* Trajectories for the target position marked with the cross.

location has to be stored. An image matching procedure as in the snapshot model is not required; in the ALV model, this step is simplified to a subtraction of the average landmark vectors of the current and the target location. Like the snapshot model, the ALV model presumes that the vectors are aligned to the same global reference system. For the analog implementation of the ALV model, it is advantageous that only a vector has to be rotated and not an image as in the snapshot model, which would require more hardware effort.

Robot Implementation

The snapshot model and the average landmark vector model were tested on two different robots and in two different types of implementations. The snapshot model was conventionally implemented in software on the mobile robot Sahabot-2 and tested in setups comparable to those used in navigation experiments with desert ants. In principle, the average landmark vector model could have been implemented and tested in the same way. However, the extreme parsimony of this model made it possible to implement it completely in analog electronic hardware (without processors or even digital components). Since analog hardware and biological nervous systems share a number of processing principles, an analog implementation provides additional insights in the neural architecture that may underlie insect navigation capabilities (see the Discussion section).

Implementation of the Snapshot Model

Hitherto, the snapshot model has only been tested in computer simulations. For the test on a mobile robot, the model had to be adapted and linked with the information provided by the robot's sensors, as described in the following. Modifications of the algorithm were necessary in order to find a termination criterion for the robot experiments. The representation required by the snapshot model had to be extracted from the visual information obtained from the camera image. An additional sensor was incorporated to provide the compass information necessary for the view alignment in the snapshot model.

Modifications of the Model

In the original model presented by Cartwright and Collett (1983), all contributing vectors have unit length. For the robot experiments described below, these unit vectors have been replaced by vectors with a length proportional to the difference in bearing or apparent size of the paired sectors. This modified method was also used in the simulations shown in figures 4 and 5. As demonstrated in figure 7, this modification facilitates the use of the length of the home vector as a measure of discrepancy between current view and snapshot, called "disparity" here, which also relates to the distance from the goal. This is not possible with the original unit vector model, since the disparity does not decrease while approaching the snapshot position; it would only become zero if a perfect match between snapshot and current view was achieved. Using proportional contributions, the robot runs can be stopped when the disparity falls below a threshold. Moreover, the proportional vector model enables the reduction of speed while approaching the target, which can be used to improve the precision of homing. For the weighting of tangential and radial contributions, the same ratio of 1:3 as given by Cartwright and Collett (1987) was used.

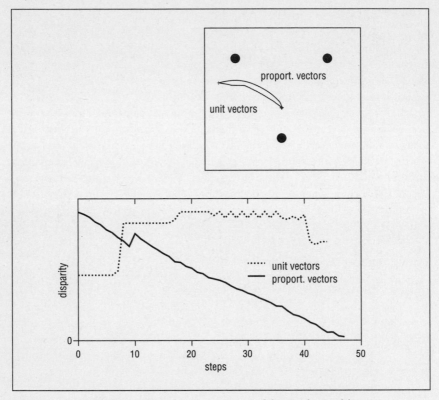

Figure 7. Simulation of two versions of the snapshot model.

Bottom: Time course of the disparity (length of the home vector) in a simulation of the original snapshot model using unit vector contributions, and of a version where vector contributions have a length proportional to differences in bearing and apparent size of sectors. *Top:* Corresponding trajectories running towards the snapshot position in the center (see also figure 4, bottom.

Robot Hardware

Figure 8 shows the robot Sahabot 2 that was used for the visual homing experiments. It has two propeled wheels in the front (differential steering) and two caster wheels in the rear end. All computation is done on-board using a PC/104 embedded PC and a 16 bit micro-controller. The sensor arrays in the rear part and at the sides of the robot are part of a "polarized light compass" that is used for the alignment of snapshot and current view (see the section "External Compass Reference").

Visual input comes from a 360 degree camera system mounted above the center of the front wheels' axis. It consists of a digital CCD camera and a conically shaped mirror in the vertical optical axis of the camera (see figure 9). The opening angle of the cone was determined so that the visual field extends ±10

Figure 8: The mobile robot Sahabot 2.

degrees around the horizon. In order to reduce the total light intensity, a neutral density filter was mounted between camera and mirror. An additional infrared filter was necessary to prevent an influence of thermal radiation on the camera image.

Image Processing

Figure 10 illustrates the image processing steps that transform the camera image into a horizontal view with black and white sectors as required by the matching mechanism described in the section "Snapshot Model." The same processing steps were applied to both snapshot and current views. In the first step, the camera image (obtained from a situation similar to the one shown in figure 13) is transformed into an azimuth-altitude representation. A mean gray value is determined from the transformed image and used to adjust the brightness parameter of the camera in a way that the mean gray value of this image is kept constant. This is indispensable for the subsequent thresholding operation separating dark and bright regions. The final one-dimensional horizontal view is obtained by counting the number of black pixels within a part of each pixel column (limited by the two lines shown in the thresholded image) and applying a threshold of 50 percent.

External Compass Reference

An important prerequisite of the matching procedure between snapshot and current view is the alignment of both views with respect to an external compass

Figure 9. Detailed view of the 360 degree camera system of the Sahabot 2.

The 360 degree camera consists of a camera with vertical optical axis (within the case) and a conical mirror that is aligned with the axis of the camera and mounted within an acrylic glass tube. The axial alignment and the distance between mirror and camera can be adjusted. An infrared and a neutral density filter are mounted between camera and mirror.

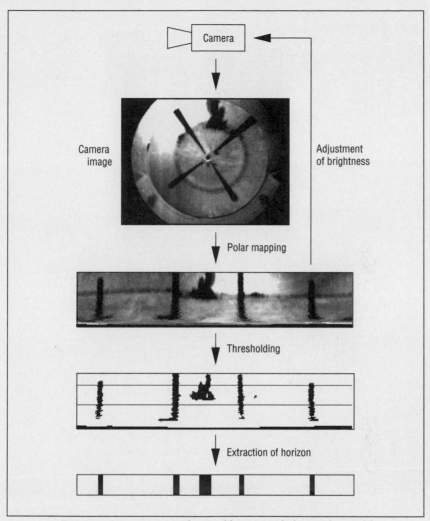

Figure 10. Image processing for visual homing with the snapshot model.

The image from the 360 degree camera (160 x 120 pixels) is transformed into a polar view (351 x 56). After applying a threshold to each pixel, the segmented horizon (351 x 1) is extracted from the area within the two lines; a pixel in the horizon will be black, if more than 50 percent of the pixels in the corresponding column are black. The landmark extracted in the center belongs to equipment in the vicinity that was removed for the experiments.

reference. Without proper alignment, the number of mismatches between sectors—sectors in the two views that are paired, but do not correspond to the same landmark or gap—will increase significantly, resulting in an erroneous home vector. *Cataglyphis* ants, as other insects, gain the compass direction from celestial cues, mainly from the polarization pattern of the blue sky (Wehner

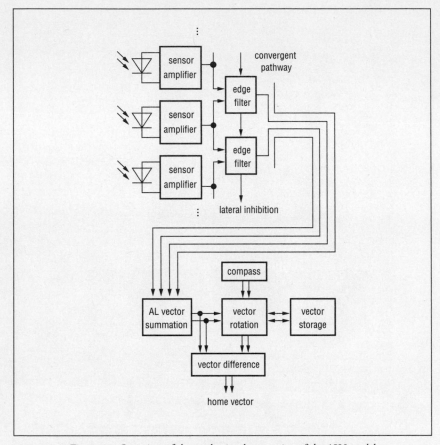

Figure 11. Overview of the analog implementation of the ALV model.

1994). The Sahabot 2 is equipped with a special "polarized light compass" (see figure 8), which is based on the same principles that insects use to derive compass information from the polarization pattern. In the experiments described below, directional information provided by this compass was used to align the current view with the stored snapshot. The construction of the polarized light compass and methods for extracting compass information are described elsewhere (Lambrinos et al. 1997, Möller et al. 1998, Lambrinos et al., 2000).

Implementation of the ALV Model

The implementation of the ALV model is based entirely on discrete analog components. Most of the active components are operational amplifiers that are used in standard circuits (as amplifier, comparator, adder etc.). The sensors, the

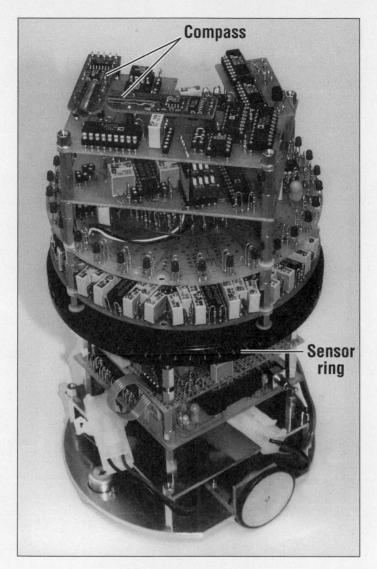

Figure 12. The analog robot (height 22 centimeters, diameter 12.8 centimeters).

The black ring in the center contains thirty-two photo diodes, the boards above implement the ALV model, the boards below belong to the motor control circuitry. A magnetic compass is mounted on the top of the robot.

boards implementing the ALV model, and the also fully analog motor control boards are mounted on a small robot base (see figure 12).

An overview of the ALV circuit is given in figure 11; technical details are presented in Möller (1999, 2000). Visual input comes from a ring of thirty-two photo diodes (see figure 12) mimicking the portion of ommatidia of both insect eyes facing the horizon. The angle between two neighboring diodes is $\beta = 11.25$ degrees.

An aperture in front of each diode restricts the opening angle to $\alpha = 8$ degrees. The signals of the photo diodes are amplified. Edges of one polarity (clockwise black-to-white) are used as landmark cues; they are detected by thresholding the difference of the signals of two neighboring sensors. Unidirectional lateral inhibition between neighboring edge filters ensures that only one pixel per edge becomes active; this is a prerequisite for the operation of the ALV model. For opening angles smaller than the inter-sensor angles, and for sharp visual edges as they are used in the experimental setup, lateral inhibition can be restricted to immediate neighbors.

From the outputs of the edge-filters, which deliver binary signals (high constant voltage for an active edge, or 0 V), the robot-centered AL vector is computed. A radial landmark vector is assigned to each edge pixel, and all landmark vectors are added simultaneously. This can be achieved in a simple way by encoding the two components of each landmark vector in two resistors that are connected to the input of two adder circuits ("convergent pathway" in figure 11).

The home vector is the difference of the AL vector of the current location and the AL vector of the target location, with both vectors relating to the same coordinate system. Before the target AL vector is stored in two capacitors, it is rotated to world coordinates using a circuit with four analog multipliers. The orientation of the robot in the global reference system is determined by a magnetic (fluxgate) compass. In the return phase, the stored vector is rotated back to robot coordinates according to the current orientation of the robot, and subtracted from the current AL vector, which gives the home vector in robot coordinates.

The robot uses differential steering. Each of the two motors can be directly controlled by one component of the home vector, if the robot coordinate system is rotated by forty-five degrees with respect to the front of the robot, so that the vector (1, 1) points to the front. The component of the axis on the left side determines the speed of the right motor and vice versa. This arrangement will stabilize a home vector in the frontal direction; if the home vector is pointing to the rear, the robot will automatically turn around, since the opposite direction is unstable. As in the proportional vector model, the length of the home vector of the ALV model corresponds to the distance from the goal. Since the home vector components determine the speed of the motors, the robot automatically slows down when it approaches the target location, which avoids oscillations around that location.

Figure 13. Example of a landmark array used for the experiments with the Sahabot 2.

Robot Experiments

Snapshot model and average landmark vector model were tested in setups with comparable complexity; however, while the Sabahot-2 experiments on the snapshot model were done outdoors under varying conditions of illumination, the analog implementation of the average landmark vector model is so far restricted to a laboratory setup. Both series of experiments, described below, aim at demonstrating the applicability of the models under real-world conditions. As a quantitative criterion, the precision of homing achieved in the experiments and factors influencing the precision are analyzed.

Experiments with the Sahabot 2

Experiments with the Sahabot 2 were done in one of the habitats of *Cataglyphis* in the Tunisian part of the Sahara desert. The experimental field was a sandy salt-pan flat. A grid was painted on the desert ground to simplify the alignment of landmarks and robot as well as the registration of the final points. Figure 13 shows a typical setup. Black cylinders were used as landmarks; the same type of landmarks was also used for the ant experiments.

Before each experiment, the robot was placed at the starting position within the landmark array. The landmark array used for the experiments shown in figure 14 consisted of three black cylinders with a height of eighty centimeters and a diameter of thirty centimeters, forming an equilateral triangle with three-me-

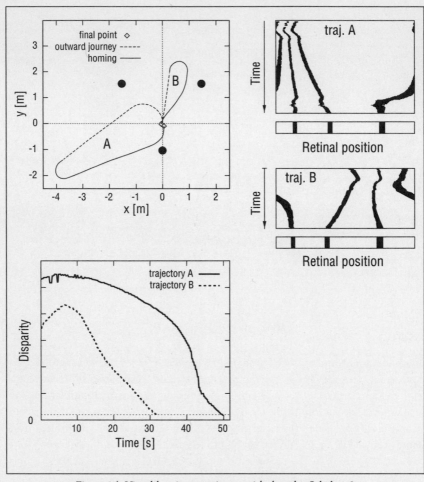

Figure 14. Visual homing experiment with the robot Sahabot 2.

Top left: Two typical trajectories of the robot in an array of three landmarks (circles). From the end of the preprogrammed outward journey (dashed line) towards the target position (0,0) the robot is guided by the visual landmark navigation algorithm (solid line). *Top right:* Transitions of the rotated current view over time towards the snapshots (images underneath each trace) for the two trajectories. *Bottom:* Time course of disparity between snapshot and current view for the two trajectories. The dashed line depicts the threshold used for terminating the runs.

ter side length. The starting position was situated on a symmetry line of this triangle in a distance of one meter from one of the landmarks. The same setup was used in the simulation presented in figure 4.

Data from two of the experiments are visualized in figure 14. At the beginning of each experiment, a snapshot was taken at the starting position, processed as described in the section "Image Processing," rotated by the angle obtained from the polarized light compass, and stored in the form of black and white sectors (figure 14, top right). After taking the snapshot, the robot had to follow a certain direction for a certain distance (four meters for trajectory A, two meters for trajectory B; see figure 14, top left) corresponding to a short foraging journey (it could also have been displaced manually). At the end of this outward trip, control was handed over to the homing algorithm that accomplished the extraction of a sectorized horizontal view from the camera image, the alignment of this view according to the compass direction, and the computation of the home vector by matching the aligned view to the snapshot, using the proportional vector model described in the section "Modifications of the Model." Transitions of the rotated current views are shown in the center of figure 14. The resulting home vector was used to set the direction of movement. As soon as the disparity became lower than a threshold, the experiment was stopped (figure 14, bottom).

Eight runs (including trajectories *A* and *B* in figure 14) with different angles and distances of the outward journey were executed with this landmark configuration and the same starting point; the final parts of the eight trajectories are shown in figure 15 (bottom). The deviation between final and initial position of the camera axis was between seven and twenty centimeters. However, this deviation does not reflect the maximal precision that can be obtained with this homing mechanism, since the final points are locations where the disparity reached the termination threshold, but not locations with minimal disparity. For a visual evaluation of the data, those points on the trajectory are marked, where the disparity dropped below 1.5 *x* threshold. For comparison, the upper part of figure 15 visualizes the disparity for points in the vicinity of the snapshot location; two iso-disparity curves obtained from this simulation are overlaid to the experimental data in the left part. The final points as well as the points where 1.5 *x* threshold was passed are located on two different iso-disparity bands around the snapshot position, with the band of the final points lying inside the other. Since these bands are not overlapping, noise induced to the disparity from the sensor signal seems to be in a range below the termination threshold. Therefore it can be assumed that a lower termination threshold will bring the final points even closer to the snapshot location. This will require a modified control algorithm for the final phase of the approach enabling the robot to locate the target point more precisely.

Experiments with the Analog Robot

The experiments with the analog robot were done in a one meter by one meter arena with white walls (30 cm high) and floor; see figure 16. Three black pieces of paper (21 cm x 29 cm) attached upright to the walls served as landmarks. Light came from the ceiling lamps of the room. Figure 17 (left) shows the AL vector voltages measured (using multimeters with computer interface) while the

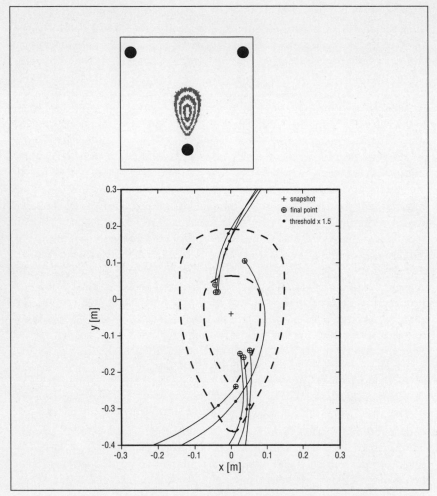

Figure 15. Analysis of homing precision.

Bottom: Zoom into the target region showing the final parts of 8 homing trajectories (for the configuration in figure 14, including trajectory A and B shown there). All points relate to the position of the camera axis. Large cross-circles (⊕) mark the end points of the trajectories. Small dots are placed on the trajectories at points, where the disparity dropped below a value of 1.5 x termination threshold. Two iso-disparity curves from the right figure are overlaid (dashed lines). *Top:* Disparity in the vicinity of the snapshot location. Gray regions are restricted by iso-disparity curves with equi-distant disparity values; disparity decreases when approaching the snapshot position.

robot was placed at 64 locations on a grid and aligned with the world coordinate system; compare this field with the AL vector field obtained from the computer simulation in figure 6 (top right) where the same setup was used.

Figure 17 (top right) shows a home vector field obtained for the target posi-

Figure 16. Arena used for the experiments with the analog robot.

tion marked with the cross-circle in the same setup. The robot was first placed at the target location, and the AL vector of that location was stored. Then the robot was rotated by sixty degrees (to test the vector rotation system) and moved to sixty-four positions on a grid, where the two voltages of the home vector were measured. Evidently, all home vectors point approximately to the target location; their length decreases in the vicinity of the target.

For the homing experiment presented in figure 17 (bottom), the robot was first placed at the target location, where the AL vector was registered, and then moved to different starting points close to the walls of the arena. A pen was mounted in the center of the robot between the two wheels. After some seconds, a time switch released the motors and the robot started to move. The trajectory was drawn by the pen on paper covering the floor of the arena; the trajectories were afterwards digitized from a photo of the paper (this method causes the small distortions of the diagram). The V-shaped parts in some of the trajectories result from changes in the movement direction of the robot from backwards to forward (see the section "Implementation of the ALV Model"). In the upper left trajectory, the robot temporarily lost sight of one of the landmarks, which caused a short disruption.

On average, the final points of the trajectories shown in figure 17 (bottom) deviated from the target point by 58 ± 17 millimeters. The experiment was re-

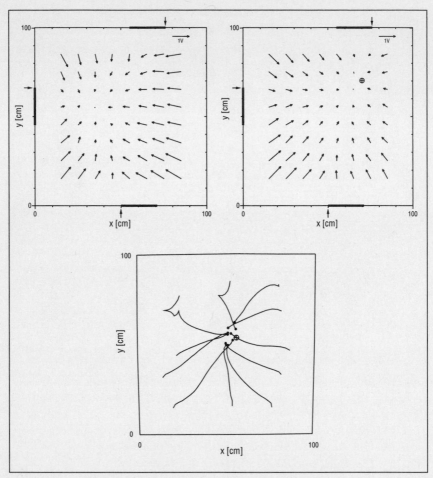

Figure 17. Visual homing experiment with the analog robot.

Three landmarks (depicted by bars) where attached to the walls of the arena. The detectable edges are marked by an arrow. *Top left:* Average landmark vector measured for 64 positions on a grid. The vector scaling is shown in the upper right corner (1 V). *Top right:* Home vector field for the target location marked with the cross-circle. *Bottom:* Robot trajectories. The cross-circle marks the target location where the AL vector was stored. The final positions of the robot are depicted by dots.

peated nine times with different target locations; the mean deviation over all 99 runs was 68 ± 35 millimeters. The deviations in this and other experiments can almost entirely be explained as an effect of the low visual resolution of the robot. In a relatively large area around the target point, the edge-filtered view perceived by the robot is constant. Consequently, the target location can not be located with higher precision. This "iso-view" region has been constructed geometrically for the experiment in figure 18. The view sector of each active edge pixel, which

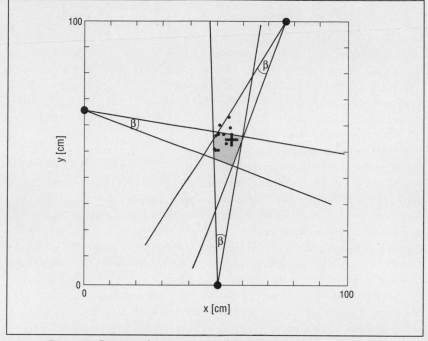

Figure 18. Geometrical reconstruction of the region where the perceived view does not change (hatched area) for the experiment in figure 17 (bottom).

Dots on the margins depict the position of the detectable edges, the cross marks the target position, and the small dots show the final points of the robot trajectories. β = 11.25 degrees is the intersensor angle.

has an angular size equal to the inter-sensor angle β = 11.25 degrees, was attached to the corresponding landmark; the cross section of all view sectors gives the iso-view region (hatched area). Depending on the orientation of the robot, different edge detectors are activated, which results in iso-view regions with similar size but different shapes; in the geometrical reconstruction, the orientation was chosen in a way that the shape of the iso-view region was in accordance with the final points of the trajectories obtained in the experiments. Apparently, an iso-view region could be found where the final points are located close to the margin or inside the region.

Discussion

Mobile robot experiments proved to be useful tools for testing hypotheses about information processing in biological agents, especially in the field of visual navigation. Franceschini, Pichon, and Blanes (1992) constructed a vision system for a robot based on the motion detection circuits in the compound eye of the housefly. Elementary motion detectors of insects have also been modeled in several analog VLSI implementations (see chapter 1). Visual dead-reckoning evidently performed by honey bees was tested on a mobile robot by Srinivasan, Chahl, and Zhang (1997). Mechanisms of path integration using a polarized light compass that mimics the celestial compass found in certain insect species have been reproduced with mobile robots by Lambrinos et al. (1997, 2000) and Möller et al. (1998). An overview of projects in biomimetic robot navigation is given by Franz and Mallot (2000).

The investigations presented here focus on synthetic modeling of visual homing strategies of insects. It was demonstrated that the snapshot model—which was only tested in computer simulations before—works under real-world conditions. The experiments with the mobile robot Sahabot 2 have shown that the deviations of the final points of the robot's return journeys from the target position are in the range of ten centimeters. From this distance, the nest entrance should be visible for the ant. Therefore it is justifiable to assume that the precision of the visual homing is comparable to the precision achieved by desert ants. To directly compare the homing precision of ants and robot is legitimate, since the visual processing is not affected by differences in body size and propulsion. Moreover, the high precision of homing could be achieved with a relatively low visual resolution, which is in accordance with animal data—the resolution of the camera image along the horizon is approximately 2 degrees, whereas a resolution of 3 degrees was determined for the horizonal belt of the *Cataglyphis* eye (Zollikofer, Wehner, and Fukushi 1995). The robot could successfully cope with sensor noise in the visual system and in the polarized-light compass that was used for the view alignment required by the snapshot model.

In the robot experiments, the same type of artificial landmarks were used as in experiments with *Cataglyphis* ants. Attempts have been made to use those landmarks that are relevant to the ants in their natural habitat. However, whereas the ant's eyes are about 0.5 centimeter above ground, the mirror of the robot's visual system is at 27 centimeter height. Objects like small shrubs or stones that stick above the horizon of the ants and are therefore visible as a skyline against the bright sky as background are usually below the horizon seen by the robot. From its higher perspective, the frequent shrubs in the vicinity of the test field form a single band around the horizon, which can not be separated into distinct landmarks. For the setup with artificial landmarks, only very few and simple image processing steps were necessary to link the visual input to the representation required by the navigation method, since the landmarks are clearly distinguishable from the background. In more complex environments, however, the effort required for the extraction of landmark cues may increase (see the section "Application for Robot Navigation").

The experiments with the analog robot have shown that insects might employ an even simpler navigation method, the ALV model. Snapshot model and ALV model are closely related and it is known that a version of the snapshot model and the ALV model even yield identical home vectors in the vicinity of the target location (Lambrinos et al., 2000). There are also versions of the ALV model, where the apparent size of the landmarks is considered (Lambrinos et al., 2000). With the experimental procedures described in the section "Visual Homing of Insects" it is therefore difficult to decide which strategy is actually used by the insect. Only experiments, where bees had to decide between two different landmark arrays, provide some evidence that it may actually be a picture that is stored in the animal's brain (Cartwright and Collett 1983, figure 15).

The homing precision achieved in the experiments with the analog robot seems to be limited only by the very low visual resolution (11.25 degrees). However, also the precision of the compass is critical for the homing precision; a redesign of the compass system was necessary, since the original, less precise system entailed large position errors. With the successful operation of the analog implementation of the ALV model it is possible to define a lower limit of complexity for visual-homing mechanisms: the apparently computationally complex task can be realized in a very simple analog electronic circle (the current implementation contains ninety-one operational amplifiers, eight analog switches and twelve analog multipliers).

The analog implementation also adds plausibility to the ALV model as a model of insect navigation, since analog electronic circuits and biological nervous systems share a number of information processing principles. The processing in both architectures is analog, continuous in time, inherently parallel, and the same operations are easy to realize (like weighted addition of signals) or difficult (like shifting an array of data). It therefore seems likely that the analog circuit has a close biological counterpart, which may not be the case with a system relying on digital computation (where, for example, the shifting of an array can be done by changing a single pointer variable, while weighted addition is a time-consuming process with considerable underlying hardware effort). The first processing steps from the sensor information to the robot centered AL vector are widely compliant with the architecture of biological nervous systems, since they are mainly based on weighted addition of signals and thresholding operations. Differences will occur in the part for rotation and storage of the AL vectors, where precision analog components were used that are unlikely to have direct correspondences in biological neural systems. Starting from the architecture of the analog implementation, it may be possible to interpret the responses of biological neurons that are involved in the navigation system; neurons that encode the AL vector, for example, would be identified as large field neurons with a specific sinusoidal response over the horizon. From the simplicity of the analog implementation and the fact that the largest part of the circuit (sixty-four of the ninety-one operational amplifiers) is organized in a retinotopical manner it may be concluded that visual homing capabilities are implemented in the peripheral parts of the insect's visual brain.

Application for Robot Navigation

Besides approaches that employ mobile robots for the "synthetic modeling" of animal behavior, a growing number of approaches in robotics get inspiration from the navigation capabilities that insects show despite their diminutive brains. Related to this, there seems to be a shift from "computational," "quantitative" towards "qualitative" methods. Traditional approaches in visual robot navigation are based on determining the metric position of the robot using accurate geometrical two-dimensional maps or CAD-like three-dimensional world models (reviews can be found in Kuipers and Byun 1988, Kortenkamp 1993, and Bartlett et al. 1995). Typically, the amount of required computation and information that has to be stored about the environment by far exceeds the limits that can be assumed for insects.

Recent changes in the robotics paradigm towards "cheaper" methods affect both world models and navigation strategies. Concerning the type of world models, there is a transition from the aforementioned topographical to topological maps that only represent "interesting places" in the environment and relate these places by notions of order, proximity, or instructions for the transition between them. This idea is appealing, since it eliminates the problem of dealing with movement uncertainty in mobile robots (Kortenkamp 1993).

Many of the "cheap" navigation strategies that currently replace the "computational," position-based methods regard "homing" as the basic navigation ability. In particular, homing methods are used in conjunction with topological maps (Kuipers and Byun 1988; Franz et al. 1998a). There are two different approaches to image-based homing, called "local" and "associative" homing (Hong et al. 1992). Local homing methods gradually align a current view with a snapshot stored at the target position by deriving a direction of movement from the differences between the two images (Hong et al. 1992; Franz et al. 1998b). Associative homing methods associate stored scenes with movement vectors pointing towards the goal (Gaussier et al. 1997; Cassinis, Grana, and Rizzi 1996; Nelson 1989). The method presented in this study belongs to the local homing methods. It is a disadvantage of the associative approaches that they require an exploration phase and some external means like path integration to determine the home direction associated with a scene.

Local homing methods have to cope with the problem what features to use as landmarks for the comparison of images, and how to establish the correspondence between features in the current and the stored view (an exception is the "warping" approach suggested by Franz et al. 1998b). The computationally most expensive part of these methods is the correlation of image regions (Gaussier et al. 1997; Hong et al. 1992). An alternative is the approach presented here, which is based on the snapshot model (Cartwright and Collett 1983). Only a small set of features, like two different types of edges, has to be extracted from the images. To establish the correspondence, the closest features in the two views are paired with each other, without identifying the features as belonging to the same landmark. Whereas the neural apparatus required to perform a correlation of image regions will be rather complex, it could be shown that a neural architecture realizing the matching procedure of the snapshot model is actually very simple (Möller, Maris, and Lambrinos 1999). The "average landmark vector model" is even cheaper: only a reliable detection of landmark features is necessary, but no correspondences have to be established between features in the two views.

The two robot implementations described here are restricted to artificial setups. The detection of landmarks in the desert experiments with the Sahabot 2 relies on the fact that the dark artificial landmarks can be separated from the bright background using a simple thresholding mechanism. The analog implementation uses a very simple feature detection mechanism (threshold and lateral inhibition) that only works under room light conditions and in the artificial setup with its sharp contrast edges. While the navigation methods themselves are very parsimonious, it still has to be investigated, how much effort has to be invested for a reliable detection of landmark cues in more complex visual environments without artificial landmarks and under changing light conditions.

First experiments in an indoor environment provide some evidence that actually relatively simple image processing steps might be sufficient for an extraction of landmark cues. An album of images was taken with the camera of the Sahabot-2 in an area of 3 meters x 4.5 meters on grid positions with a spacing of 30 cm; the light conditions were constant for all images of the album. Figure 20 shows the environment, an entrance hall, which was left unmodified for the registration of the album. All images are aligned in the same direction. Figure 19 explains the image processing steps that were afterwards applied to extract landmark vectors for the ALV model. A stripe above and including the horizon was extracted from the camera image. The gray values in the columns of this image were averaged. The resulting one-dimensional image was low-pass filtered. Landmark vectors point to those pixels, where the low-pass filtered view crosses a threshold.

The threshold is adjusted automatically in the following way: In the low-pass filtered image, regions with small absolute value of slope were detected (dots on the curve). The corresponding gray values were marked in a table of the 256 possible values (right diagram). The gray value in the center of the largest unmarked region (bracket) was used as threshold. This method increases the stability of the detected features when the robot is displaced from the target position. Small changes in the gray values of the low-pass filtered image will not add or remove detected landmarks; this directly affects the size of the region of attraction. After the threshold has been determined for the target location, it is stored together with the AL vector and kept constant during the return to this location.

The home vectors obtained with this method are visualized in figure 21. In

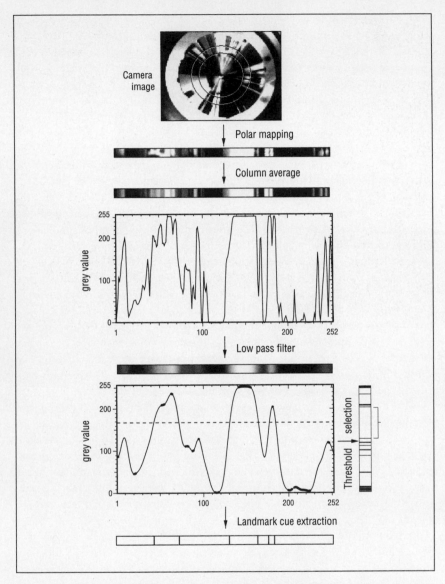

Figure 19. Image processing for visual homing with the ALV model in indoor environments.

80 of in total 150 grid points, the same landmarks as in the target location were detected. Trajectories starting from 98 of the grid points converge to the target point, which corresponds to a region of attraction of 8.8 meters^2 . This result shows that a large region of attraction may be obtained based on few simple image processing steps. The issue of changing light conditions, however, is still un-

Figure 20. Indoor environment where the image album was taken.

resolved, as is the problem of the compass—magnetic compasses are unreliable indoors and should be replaced by landmark-based compass information.

Finally it shall be mentioned that from the application perspective it may also be interesting that a cheap analog implementation could be found for the ALV model. Analog circuits have considerably lower power consumption than digital computers, are extremely fast due to the inherent parallelity, simplify control tasks since processing is continuous in time, and have a better fault tolerance than digital computers (changing an analog value will only gradually impair the performance, while a single flipped bit in a digital computer can cause a total breakdown). The trade-off for these advantages is the lack of flexibility of analog systems.

Conclusion and Future Work

Two parsimonious visual-homing algorithms—the snapshot model and the average landmark vector model—have been implemented on mobile robots and shown to operate successfully in the real world, however in simplified experimental setups. This suggests that the two models are plausible models of insect navigation. Additional support for the ALV model is gained from the fact that it

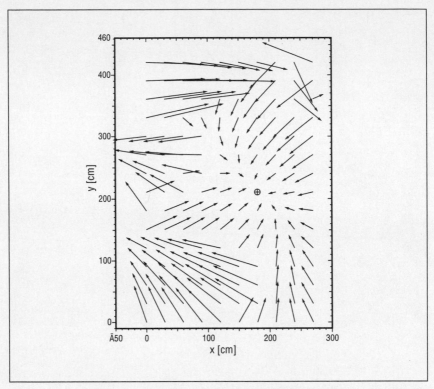

Figure 21. Home vectors computed for the indoor album.
The cross-circle marks the target location.

was implemented in analog hardware that shares a number of information processing principles with nervous systems. The results also indicate that the parsimonious strategies of insect navigation can provide a guideline for robotics research. Future work will try to adapt the mechanisms to environments with more complex visual features and to integrate multiple snapshots in topological maps.

Acknowledgments

This work was supported by grants from the Swiss Federal Office for Education and Science (VIRGO TMR network), the Swiss National Science Foundation, the Human Frontier Science Program, by a personal grant from the Kommission zur Förderung des akademischen Nachwuchses der Universität Zürich to R.M., and by Rosys AG (Hombrechtikon). Many thanks to Christian Gfeller, Koh Hosoda, Hiroshi Kobayashi, Thomas Labhart, Lukas Lichtensteiger, Marinus Maris, and the workshop of the Physics department for their contributions and the fruitful cooperation.

Aerial Minirobot that Stabilizes and Tracks with a Bio-Inspired Visual Scanning Sensor

Stéphane Viollet and Nicolas Franceschini

The present study was carried out in the context of our previous studies using a biologically-inspired minimalistic robotic approach, which were based on the idea of reconstructing natural visuomotor processes in order to better understand them. Here we show that an elementary visual sensor composed of only two pixels is able to accurately detect contrasting features within its visual field, provided it uses a particular scanning mode, such as that recently discovered in the compound eye of flies. This low-complexity, low-weight, low-power, low-cost scanning sensor was found to deliver an output that is (1) quasi-linear with respect to the angular position of a contrasting object in its field of view and (2) largely invariant with respect to the distance to the object and its level of contrast.

The most novel feature of this visual sensor, which differs from other systems based on *scanning at constant angular speed* and *pulse-scanning*, is that it scans the visual field at an angular speed that varies gradually with time (*variable speed scanning*). The sensor's output then becomes a graded function of the position of a contrast feature within its visual field, with the interesting consequence that if this sensor is incorporated into a visuomotor control loop, it is able to stabilize a robot such as a micro air-vehicle with respect to the environmental features.

In the first part of this chapter, we simulate the pure rotation at a variable speed of two photoreceptors in front of a stationary contour (a light-to-dark edge) and show that the processing of the apparent motion yields a signal that gradually varies with the angular position of the edge in the visual field. On the basis of our simulation results, we then describe the structure of a miniature scanning sensor coupled with an elementary motion detector (EMD), the principle of which was again derived from the fly compound eye. Finally, we describe a miniature twin-engine aerial robot, which stabilizes in yaw by means of a visual feedback loop based on the scanning sensor. The latter picks up an error signal, which is used to drive the two propellers differentially, causing the "seeing robot" to reorient and adjust its line of sight so as to remain visually locked onto a nearby or distant contrasting target.

Contrary to the kind of yaw stabilization, which can be achieved with a gyroscope having similar low-weight and low-cost characteristics, the one described here is not only stiff but also devoid of drift. Some examples are given below, where the (tethered) aircraft either tracks a slowly moving dark edge or maintains fixation onto a stationary target for seventeen minutes.

The scanning visual sensor and the visuomotor control loop we have developed are appropriate for: detecting low speed relative motion between a craft and its environment; rejecting environmental disturbances by maintaining visual fixation onto a nearby or distant target, regardless of its contrast and distance within a given range; and stabilizing the attitude of a craft optically with respect to environmental features.

Scanning at a Variable Angular Speed

In this section, we simulated the concerted rotation of two photoreceptors at a variable angular speed in front of a light-dark brightness transition (an edge) (see figure 1a). Each photoreceptor can receive light only within a small field of view characterized by the angular sensitivity function.

Photoreceptor Model

The angular sensitivity of a lens-photoreceptor combination is usually approximated by a bell-shaped function. In the present case, we use a Gaussian function, the bottom part of which is truncated below the threshold s_0.

The angular sensitivity $S(\varphi)$ of photoreceptor i is therefore given by:

$$S(\varphi) = \left(\frac{abs(G_i(\varphi) - s_0) + (G_i(\varphi) - s_0)}{2} \right), \tag{1}$$

with

$$G_i(\varphi) = \exp\left[-\frac{\varphi^2}{2\sigma^2} \right] \tag{2}$$

$S(\varphi)$ is characterized by its total angular width Lv and its angular width at half height $\Delta\rho$. Both parameters can be expressed with respect to σ as follows:

$$\Delta\rho = 2\sigma\left[2\ln\left(\frac{2}{1+s_0}\right)\right]^{\frac{1}{2}}$$ (3)

$$Lv = 2\sigma\left[2\ln\left(\frac{1}{s_0}\right)\right]^{\frac{1}{2}}$$ (4)

Variable Angular Speed

As sketched in figure 1a, we have simulated the concerted rotation of two photosensors, 1 and 2, separated by a constant angle $\Delta\varphi$, called the interreceptor angle, in front of an elementary panorama consisting of a single segment AB. The pair of photosensors is assumed here to rotate clockwise at an angular speed Ω that decays exponentially with time. The angle ψ is given by figure 1b:

$$\psi(t) = A\left(1 - \exp\left(-\frac{t}{\tau}\right)\right)$$ (5)

Hence the angular speed Ω(t) is:

$$\Omega(t) = \frac{A}{\tau}\exp\left(-\frac{t}{\tau}\right)$$ (6)

The position of the segment is defined by the points $A(x_1, y_1)$ and $B(x_2, y_2)$ with $y_1 = y_2$.

At any time, the output $R_i(t)$ from photoreceptor i is obtained by integrating the angular sensitivity $S(\varphi)$ weighted by the intensity $I(\varphi)$:

$$R_i(t) = \int_{-Lv/2}^{Lv/2} I(\varphi)S(\varphi)d\varphi$$ (7)

Processing the Photoreceptor Signals

To calculate the output signal from each photoreceptor, we used a discrete version of equation 7. The signal sampled, $R_i(kT)$, with T in seconds, results from a convolution of the light intensity I with the Gaussian mask $S(kTs)$ (Ts in degrees). In other words, at each value of ψ, $R_i(kT)$ results from the filtering of I by a filter with a Gaussian-shaped impulse response. In all these calculations, the Gaussian mask $S(kTs)$ based on equation 1 was processed with a spatial sampling step Ts equal to 0.004 degrees. $R_i(kT)$ is maximal and equal to 1 when a black segment ($I = 10$) covers the whole visual field Lv and it is null when the black segment is completely outside the visual field ($I = 0$).

In order to show that the time lag between the two photosensors varies with the *position* of the contrast feature, we refer to the scheme of figure 1a, in which we put the dark edge at 3 positions (1, 2, 3) along the x axis. For each of these

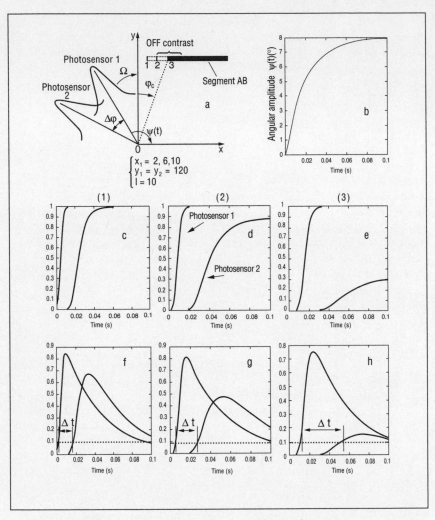

Figure 1. Simulated response of two adjacent photosensors.

(a) Simulated response of two adjacent photosensors rotating clockwise at a variable angular speed Ω, and encountering a dark edge placed at various positions 1, 2, 3 (a). (b) Variation of angle $\psi(t)$. (c, d, e) Output from photoreceptors 1 and 2, depending of the position of the dark edge (1, 2, 3). (f, g, h) High-pass filtered version of (c, d, e) (cut-off frequency : 2Hz) and thresholding of the output signal from each photoreceptor. $\Delta\rho$ = 2 degrees , $\Delta\varphi$ = 4 degrees , Lv = 5.2 degrees , s_0 = 0.01, A = $2\Delta\varphi$, τ = 20 milliseconds, T = 0.01s

stationary positions, figures 1(c, d, e) give the output from photosensors 1 and 2 as they turn clockwise at a variable angular speed Ω. In figures 1(f, g, h), the output from each photosensor was passed through an analog high-pass filter with a cut-off frequency of 2Hz.

Figure 1(f, g, h) shows that the time lag Δt between the differentiated and thresholded outputs of the two photosensors indeed varies gradually with the angular position φ_c of the contrast edge within the visual field. Moreover, it should be noticed that the angular separation (1.8 degrees) between each position (1, 2, 3) of the dark edge is smaller (by about 50 percent) than the inter-receptor angle $\Delta\varphi$. This leads to the expectation that scanning at a variable angular speed can lead to subpixel accuracy in target location.

The Elementary Motion Detector (EMD)

The elementary motion detector (EMD) — is an analog circuit yielding an output signal that decreases gradually when the time lag Δt between its two inputs increases. Like many insect motion detecting neurons, the analog EMD is directionally selective. The EMD we used here detects only light-to-dark transitions ("OFF contrasts") when the scanning direction is clockwise. The use of the derivative in the first EMD processing step is essential, as it makes it possible to eliminate the DC level of the photosensors and discriminate between positive (ON) contrasts and negative (OFF) contrasts.

A block diagram of the EMD is shown in figure 2.

The signal output V_0 results from multiplying an exponentially decaying pulse by a delayed fast pulse. V_0 varies inversely with Δt and hence grows larger with Ω. We originally designed this scheme for an analog motion detector on the basis of our electrophysiological findings on flies, and we patented it in 1986. We used an array of motion detectors of this kind in 1991 onboard a visually guided autonomous robot capable of avoiding obstacles at 50 centimeters per second. A similar EMD principle (called "facilitate and sample" scheme) was discovered independently by authors at the California Institute of Technology in 1996, and patented in 1998.

It can be predicted from the simulations shown in figure 1, that if an EMD is driven by a pair of photosensors rotating at a variable angular speed, its output V_0 will vary gradually with the angular position φ_c of a dark edge in the visual field of the scanning sensor.

The Scanning Sensor

In the previous sections, we have shown that scanning plus motion detection can lead to position sensing. We now present the construction and test of a miniature scanning sensor with only two pixels that scan the environment locally at a variable angular speed.

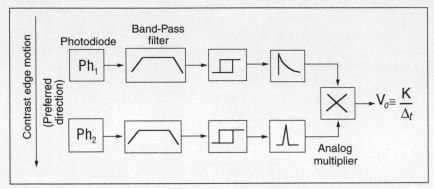

Figure 2. Structure of the EMD.

The Scanning Sensor

We built a miniature scanner, the components of which are sketched in figure 3. A dual photosensor and a lens (focal length: 8.5 millimeters), mounted opposite each other on a blackened perspex drum (diameter 15 millimeters), form a miniature "camera eye," which is driven by a DC micromotor (diameter 10 millimeters). The angle of divergence $\Delta\varphi$ between the visual axes of the two photoreceptors ("interreceptor angle") is:

$\Delta\varphi = 4$ degrees

The angular position of the drum (and hence, that of the sensor's mean line of sight) is monitored by a *magnetoresistive sensor* responding to the angular position of a micromagnet glued to the hub of the drum. This sensor is part of the loop of an accessory position-servo, which controls the eye so that it will follow any imposed signal.

This servo-eye is positioned by a composite periodic signal at 10 Hz (cf figure 4a), which eventually leads to two scanning phases (cf figure 4c). During the first phase (duration: 25ms), the angular speed Ω of the eye is made to decrease quasi-exponentially with time. During the longer "return phase" (duration 75 ms), the eye is made to return to its original position at a quasi-constant speed. The amplitude $\Delta\xi$ of the scan is expressed in terms of the interreceptor angle $\Delta\varphi$ by means of the scanning factor α:

$$\alpha = \frac{\Delta\xi}{\Delta\varphi}$$

The EMD has a preferred direction such that it responds only during the first part of the scan (short phase), delivering an output that varies in a graded manner with the position of the contrasting edge within its visual field. Imposing a slow and constant angular speed during the return phase improves the robustness of the scanning sensor, making it responsive to environmental features far beyond the simple edge considered here.

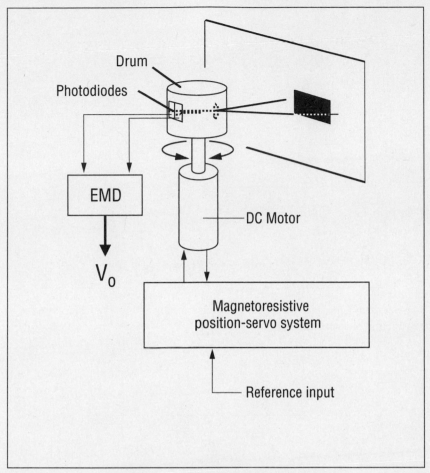

*Figure 3. Sketch of the complete visual scanning sensor
in front of a dark object posted up on the wall.*

Sensor Output Versus Contrast and Distance

The complete scanning sensor was mounted vertically onto the shaft of a re-solver and a 16-bit resolver-to-digital converter was used to accurately deter-mine the angular orientation of the sensor. The two photoreceptor outputs were connected to an EMD via soft microwires. We varied the orientation of the scanning sensor manually and at each orientation recorded the voltage output V_o from the EMD and the angular position φ_c of the sensor.

The object was a contrast step (an edge) made of grey paper that stood out from the background. The contrast m was determined by measuring the relative illuminance of the paper (I_1) and its background (I_2) and calculating:

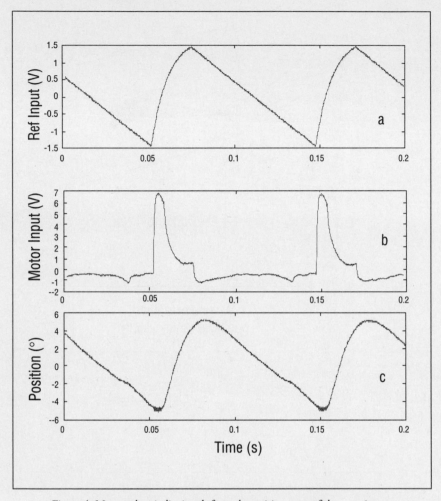

Figure 4. Measured periodic signals from the position servo of the scanning eye.

(a) reference input voltage imposed upon the position servo. (b) actual motor input voltage. (c) resulting orientation of the "eye" as monitored by the magnetoresistive sensor

$$m = \frac{I_1 - I_2}{I_1 + I_2}$$

Contrast was measured *in situ* with a linear photo device having the same spectral sensitivity as the dual photosensor used.

Figures 5(a, b, c) show that the sensor output varies with the position of a contrasting edge within its visual field, as predicted on the basis of the simulation results shown in figure 1. The responses are quasilinear with respect to

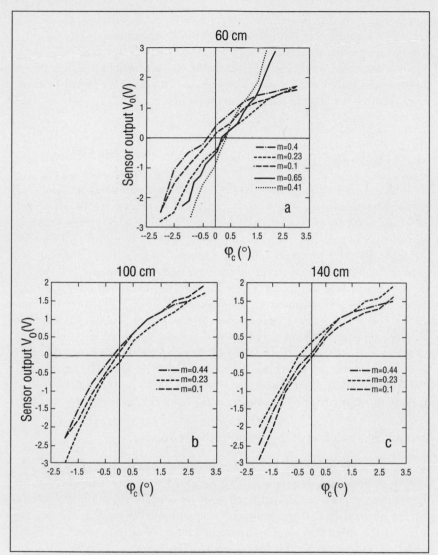

Figure 5. Voltage output V₀ from the scanning sensor (cf figure 3) as a function of its orientation φ_c and the contrast m of the pattern.

Accuracy: ± 50mV. (a) response at D = 60 centimeters with respect to a dark edge (solid) and a dark stripe 10 millimeters in width (dotted). (b) response at D = 100 centimeters to a dark edge of various contrasts. (c) response at D = 140 centimeters to the same dark edges. (Δφ = 4°, α = 2).

the yaw orientation of the scanning sensor and largely invariant with respect to the contrast m and the distance D of the dark edge. Subtracting a reference signal $r = 5.5V$ from all the data gives an odd function, which is a useful feature for incorporating the scanning sensor into an optomotor loop. Moreover, invariance with respect to the distance—within a limited range—is an important feature for the dynamics of an optomotor loop of this kind, because it does not introduce any gain variations liable to cause instability. The sensor was designed to be robust against any spurious modulations caused by neon room illumination (100Hz intensity modulations).

Visual Control of a Miniature Twin-Propeller Robot

We built a miniature aerial robot equipped with its scanning sensor described in the previous section. The robot is made of carbon, wood, fiberglass, and EPS (figure 6a). Its total weight is 100 grams, including the engines, scanning sensor, gyroscope, and the complete electronics. The onboard battery (LiMnO$_2$, 9V-0.8A.h) weighs another 54 grams and gives about one hour autonomy. In order to minimize the inertia around the yaw axis, the DC engines are positioned close to the axis of rotation and transmit their power to their respective propellers (diameter 13 centimeters) through a 12 centimeter-long carbon fiber shaft and bevel gear (reduction ration 1/5). The SMD electronic components occupy five decks of printed circuit boards interconnected via miniature bus connectors. Each board (diameter 55 millimeters) is dedicated to a particular task: (a) power conditioning and (b) 433 MHz RC receiver and PWM motor controller for each propeller, (c) EMD circuit, (d) optomotor analog controller circuit (e) servoloop controller of the scanner.

Dynamical Modeling of the Twin-Propeller Robot

We analyzed the dynamics of the twin-propeller system around its yaw axis from its response to a step input.   We mounted the robot onto the shaft of the resolver, which was selected because of its negligible friction and inertia. The 16 bit resolver-to-digital converter was then used to measure the angular speed of the robot in yaw. This tachometer has a scale factor of $2.27.10^{-3}$ V/°/s, a scale factor error of ten percent and a bandwidth of 125Hz.

In order to convey a step input voltage to the autonomous plant, we designed a remote control system operating at 433MHz (1,000 bauds). At the transmitter, the throttle and yaw commands were adjusted by means of "digital" joysticks. Onboard the robot, these signals were received by a miniature receiver and dispatched to two digital potentiometers via a PIC16F84 microcontroller. These potentiometers (8-bit digital-to-analog converters) generated a differential signal u_d to adjust the yaw and a signal u_c to adjust the common throttle (figure 7). In order to make sure that the two thrusters reached the same nominal speed (i.e., the same "operating point") during each experimen-

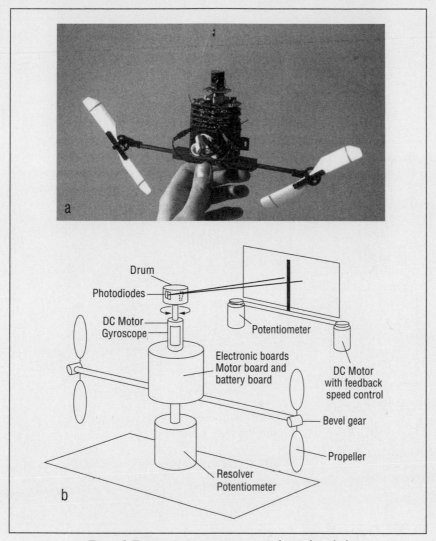

Figure 6. Twin-engine autonomous minirobot and test-bed.

(a). Twin-engine autonomous minirobot equipped with its scanning visual sensor. The robot's body has a diameter of 55 millimeters and the robot weights 100 grams, including all the electronic signal processing, motor control systems, radio throttle control, and start and kill switches. The robot is usually tethered to a 100 μm wire secured to the ceiling. The robot controls its yaw orientation by performing visual fixation and tracking, even in the presence of pendulum oscillations. The robot's heading direction is the same as the mean eye axis.

(b) Test-bed used to characterize the robot and identify its dynamics. Instead of being suspended, the robot is here mounted onto a low-friction resolver to assess its dynamical properties or to a low-friction potentiometer to measure its orientation in yaw. The visual pattern (here a dark bar) can be moved in front of the robot to test its tracking ability.

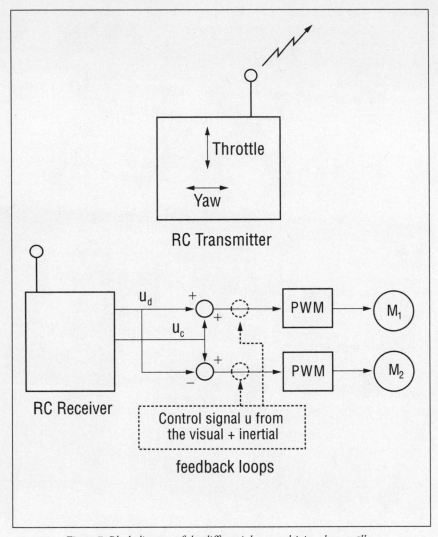

Figure 7. Block diagram of the differential system driving the propellers.

tal run, the DC level u_c was memorized in the microcontroller flash memory and called back via a third remote control channel.

The open loop model G(s) of the robot obtained from its step response is as follows:

$$G(s) = \frac{\theta_a}{U_d} = \frac{2700}{(0.026s^2 + 0.232s + 1)} \quad ,$$

where $\dot{\theta}_a$ is the angular speed (°/s) of the robot and U_d is in volts.

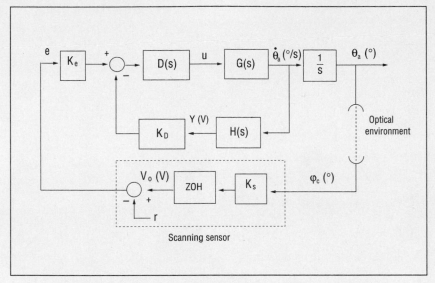

Figure 8. Block diagram of the closed-loop visual control system incorporating the scanning visual sensor (outer loop) and a gyroscope (inner loop).

The Visual Inertial Feedback System

The complete position feedback system we have designed is shown in figure 8.

The scanning sensor is modeled by a simple gain $Ks \cong 1 V/°$ (cf figure 5), and its output signal was maintained by a zero-order hold (ZOH) until the completion of each scan (T = 100 milliseconds). Since the transfer function from the controlling yaw input to the yaw angle has three main poles, we incorporated a velocity feedback using a miniature piezo gyroscope. The latter was modeled by the following transfer function $H(s)$:

$$H(s) = \frac{Y}{\theta_a} = \frac{6.7.10^{-3}}{(0.0032s + 1)}$$

The gain K_D = 5 was chosen so as to give a closed loop step response with a settling time of 100 milliseconds with a minor overshoot. The lead compensator $D(s)$ was chosen so as to raise the phase margin further, thereby increasing the damping and reducing the settling time to 100 milliseconds. The transfer function of D(s) is given by :

$$D(s) = 0.3\left(\frac{0.08s + 1}{0.014s + 1}\right),$$

and Ke = 6.10^{-2}

The frequency response of the open-loop transfer function

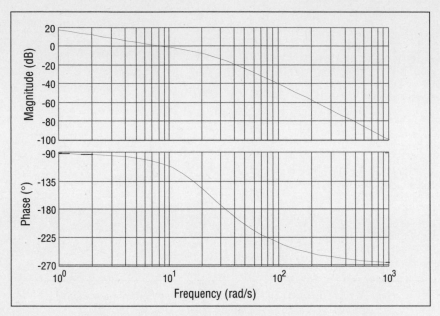

Figure 9. Frequency response of the complete system (figure 8) obtained with Matlab. In this Bode diagram, the visual scanning sensor is modeled as a simple gain.

$$B_o(s) = \frac{V_o(s)}{(s)}$$

is shown in figure 9.

Target Tracking and Visual Fixation

We assessed the performance of the visual-inertial feedback system on the testbed described in figure 6b. Both the angular position of the dark edge (input) and the angular orientation in yaw of the robot (output) were measured with miniature servopotentiometers, as depicted in figure 6.

Figure 10 illustrates the actual tracking performance of the robot with respect to a sinusoidal variation of the position of a dark edge in the visual field of the scanning sensor.

The response was found to lag behind the command by about 100 milliseconds, i.e., by hardly more than the scan period, which turned out to be the main limiting factor. The maximum linear speed of the dark edge that the aerial robot was able to track was about twenty-five centimeters per second at a distance of one meter (i.e. 14°/s). The histogram in figure 11 shows that the robot steadily controls its two propellers so as to gaze steadily on a stationary target during a long (seventeen minute) experiment.

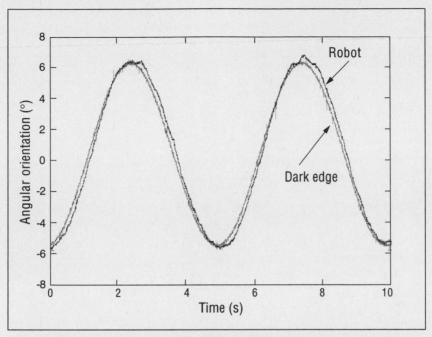

Figure 10 Dynamic performance of the overall twin-propeller robot (cf figure 6) tracking a dark edge (contrast m=0.2) located at a distance of 1 meter in front of the eye and oscillating at 0.2 Hz perpendicularly to its line of sight. r = 5.5V.

Conclusion

We described a low-level, low complexity, miniature sensor designed to provide a micro-air vehicle with visual stabilization and tracking possibilities. We established that a hundred gram twin-propeller robot equipped with this miniature scanning eye can track an object with various levels of contrast (down to ten percent) at various distances (up to 1.5 meters), using its onboard electronics and energy in a completely autonomous manner.

The aim here was not to achieve a high performance closed-loop system such as those based on a CCD camera that recognize a target and track it at high speeds. Such systems rely on more complex control laws, which require larger, heavier, and more consuming computational systems. Our low-level visual system is not based on any "understanding of the environment," and consequently cannot detect and track a specific target among many others. Yet this moderately complex, inexpensive ($\cong$ 400 USD) system can be used to stabilize a micro air vehicle around a given axis of rotation, where the time-constant is small (the small time-constants of micro air vehicles make it difficult for them to be stabilized by a human operator); to replace a gyroscope by maintaining an angular

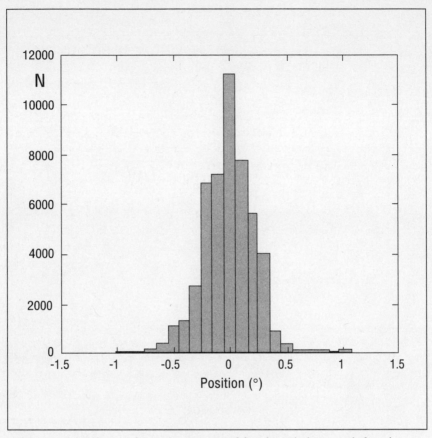

Figure 11. Distribution of the yaw orientation of the robot, which constantly fixated a stationary dark edge (contrast m=0.2) for seventeen minutes.

Number of samples = 50000 Acquisition time = 1000s Standard deviation σ = 0.22 degrees .

position with respect to environmental features, for a long time and with no drift; and to track a target visually with relative insensitivity to shape, contrast, and distance, using a single pair of photoreceptors scanning concomitantly.

It is worth noting that the optical position-servoing method we have developed is based on a *position sensor* that actually relies on a *motion sensor*.

An essential message of this chapter is that a simple, low amplitude scanning of two adjacent photoreceptors with motion detection can provide positional information to an accuracy far better than that expected from their angular sampling basis, hence leading to *subpixel accuracy in target localization and tracking*. Extending these results to a 1D or 2D photoreceptor array will retain this most interesting property while enlarging the sensor's field of view.

Acknowledgments

We thank M. Boyron for his expert technical assistance and I. Daveniere and J. Blanc for improving the English manuscript. This research was supported by CNRS (Life Sciences, Engineering Sciences, and Program on Microsystems) and EEC (IST/FET program). S. Viollet received a predoctoral fellowship from Ministry of National Education and Scientific Research (MENRS). The content of this chapter is largely based on a paper entitled "Visual Servo System Based on a Biologically Inspired Scanning Sensor" by S. Viollet and N. Franceschini, appearing in *Sensor Fusion and Decentralized Control in Robotic Systems II* edited by G. T. McKee and P. Schenker, SPIE Volume 3839, pp. 144-155. Bellingham, Washington: International Society for Optical Engineering, 1999.

Motor Systems

Construction of a Hexapod Robot with Cockroach Kinematics Benefits both Robotics and Biology

Roger D. Quinn and Roy E. Ritzmann

T he goal of this project was to demonstrate the advantages of careful biological emulation in robot design. The robot would be used as a platform on which both biologists and engineers could test hypotheses about posture and locomotion. We did not intend to build a robot with all of the remarkable locomotion capabilities of the cockroach. The state of actuator and power source technology precludes this. Therefore, we limited the locomotion goals of Robot III to walking, turning, and climbing in a manner similar to a cockroach. To determine the aspects of the insect's legs and their control that are critical to those behaviors, we made detailed kinematic and neurobiological observations of the animal while performing those tasks.

In this chapter we first describe the biological observations that were made, providing detailed kinematic data on cockroaches running on a treadmill and climbing over barriers. We then describe how those data were incorporated into a dynamic simulation that predicted motor and structural loads that were used in design of the robot. Finally, we describe the construction of the robot and development of its posture controller. The posture controller is an important part of the locomotion controller that is currently under development.

Biological Observations

In order to collect the necessary data on the mechanics of cockroach walking, our first task was to build a walking platform that would allow us to monitor the movements of all leg joints as the animal performed real walking movements. Considerable work had been done in the past on cockroach walking

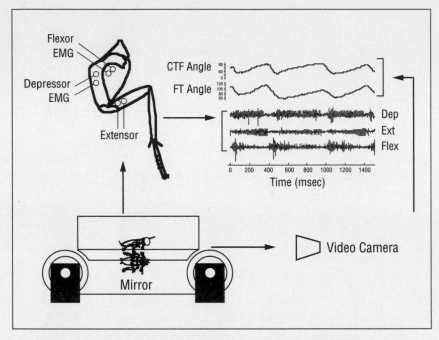

Figure 1. Schematic showing data collection methodology.

The leg in the upper left corner shows the placement of insulated wires for EMG recording. The record in the upper right corner shows joint angle data from a rear leg (trace 1 from the coxa-trochanter-femur (CTF) joint and trace 2 from the femur-tibia (FT) joint) combined with three electormyograms (trace 3 from the trochanter depressor, trace 4 from the tibial extensor and trace 5 from the tibial flexor).

(Pearson and Iles 1970; Delcomyn 1971; Pearson 1976; Spirito and Mushrush 1979; Delcomyn 1985). However, most of that work focused upon the timing of foot contact with the ground (i.e. footfall patterns). In order to provide accurate information on leg movements and on the control of leg movements, we had to move beyond footfall patterns to monitor individual joint movements.

Fortunately, advances in high-speed video systems made these observations possible. However, an important problem had to be overcome. Insects make complex leg movements in three-dimensional space. Because of the inherent problems associated with viewing a three dimensional movement projected onto a single plane, any single view could readily generate false data on joint movement. In order to accurately determine joint kinematics, we had to view leg movements from two orthogonal directions, measure the joint angles and then reconstruct the true three dimensional movements from those data (Biewener and Full 1992). To accomplish this task, we constructed a miniature transparent treadmill that allowed us to view the animal simultaneously from the side and from the ventral surface (underside), via a mirror positioned at a forty-five degree angle under the belt (Watson and Ritzmann 1998a) (figure 1). Video images were taken at either two hundred or two hundred and fifty frames per second. The videotape was then played back frame by frame so that we could digitize specific landmark points on the legs. The digitized data from both views were entered into a custom program along with measurements of the actual dimensions of each leg segment. The program then reconstructed the true angles of the leg joints in three dimensions as the animal moved along the treadmill.

Each cockroach leg is divided into several segments (figure 4a). Although the segments are reproduced in each of the three pairs of legs, their dimensions are very different in the front, middle and rear legs. The leg segments from the most proximal to the most distal segment are called the coxa, trochanter, femur, tibia and a series of foot joints collectively called the tarsus. The joint between the body and coxa is made of two plates with soft tissue between them. The complex musculature coupled with complex mechanics confers upon this joint three degrees of freedom much like that of a ball and socket joint (Laurent and Richard 1986). The distal joints are for the most part more straightforward. The joints between the coxa and trochanter, between the trochanter and femur, and between the femur and tibia are simple one degree of freedom joints. The joint between the trochanter and femur makes only a small movement and has often been referred to as fused. However, our observations suggest that because of the 45° orientation of the joint coupled with its proximal location on the leg, even the small movement of the trochanter femur joint allows the animal to rotate the tibia and tarsus relative to the ground. This movement is important to the actions associated with several movements, especially climbing. The tarsal joints each have several passive degrees of freedom making for agile foot placement. Finally, a claw located on the end of the tarsus can be raised or lowered to engage the substrate during locomotion on slippery surfaces for climbing (Frazier et al. 1999).

We also have an interest in the control of the leg joints. Thus, we combined our kinematic analysis with electrophysiological recordings of motor activity (figure 1). Neuromuscular activity can be readily monitored in a freely behaving animal by recording the electrical currents in the muscle extracellularly (Watson and Ritzmann 1998a). The resulting records are referred to as electromyograms (EMGs). In insects, this technique is particularly useful because, unlike vertebrates, each arthropod muscle is typically innervated by relatively few motor neurons. For example, the muscles that are believed to provide most of the action in extending the femur of each leg during walking are innervated by only two motor neurons, the fast and slow depressors (Df and Ds respectively) (Pearson and Iles 1971). Moreover, muscle records from these two motor neurons are readily distinguished based upon the size of their related EMG potentials. Thus, activity in the muscle can be directly related to activity in specific motor neurons.

In order to make a useful robotic vehicle, we wanted it to be able to walk through complex terrain and interact with its environment in three dimensions. Specifically, the tasks that we wanted the robot to be capable of performing in-

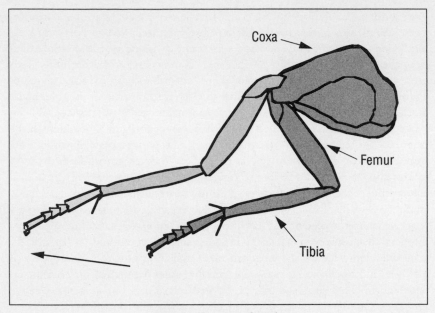

Figure 2. Movement of rear leg.
Equal movement of the coxa-femur joint and the femur-tibia joint results in a powerful rear directed movement.

cluded efficient walking, turning and climbing over objects. We, therefore, set out to study the leg movements and joint control in horizontal walking at various different speeds, as well as during turning and climbing.

Horizontal Walking

Even in our initial observations, it was clear that the movements of the three pairs of legs were not similar. The typical gait during most speeds of walking is an alternating tripod gate (Delcomyn 1971). In this movement the front and rear right legs move in synchrony with the left middle leg forming a tripod that alternates with the tripod that is made up of the remaining three legs. Although the feet of the three legs move in synchrony, the joint movements of the front, middle and rear legs are distinct. Each leg's joint movements are specialized for unique roles played by each pair of legs. This observation is consistent with data on ground reaction forces indicating unique patterns of behavior for each pair of legs (Full, Blickhan and Ting 1991).

The rear (metathoracic) legs are specialized for producing power to accelerate the animal forward. The movement of the two joints that are responsible for extending the leg, coxa-trochanter-femur (CTF) and femur-tibia (FT) joints extend in synchrony moving through approximately the same excursion in both joints (Watson and Ritzmann 1998a) (figure 1). As a result, the tarsal segments are driven directly backward in a line essentially parallel to the animal's long axis, providing powerful forward propulsion on the body (figure 2).

In the middle (mesothoracic) legs, the two joints also move synchronously, but the FT joint goes through a smaller excursion than the CTF joint (Watson and Ritzmann 1998a). This movement, along with the orientation at the body coxa joint, results in a sweeping movement, which first decelerates and then accelerates the animal (Full et al. 1991). Other observations described below suggest that the middle legs are particularly important in turning the animal and in climbing movements.

The front (prothoracic) legs are the most unique. To form a functional tripod movement, the tarsus of these legs must extend forward during swing and then be pulled rearward while the middle and rear legs of a given tripod extend rearward. To do this the front leg must make much more use of the body-coxa joint to swing the coxa forward than is seen in the middle and rear legs. With the forward swing of the coxa and the required forward movement of the tarsus, the CTF and FT joints must come out of synchrony to make the appropriate foot placement. Indeed, in some cases these two joints actually move in antiphase (Tryba and Ritzmann 2000). Although the movement made by the prothoracic legs is complex, it can be at least partially visualized by realizing that, unlike the other two pairs of legs, the front legs are extended during swing. Then during the stance phase, they are drawn back toward the body and then extended again. The first part of the stance movement is accomplished by flexing the FT joint while extending the CTF joint and rotating the coxa backward. As the tarsi are drawn under the body, the FT joint stops flexing and the CT joint continues to extend pushing the tarsi rearward. During swing the process is essentially reversed, while the leg is lifted off the ground.

Also unlike the middle and rear legs, the movements of the front legs are somewhat variable. Indeed, the forward projection and variability of the prothoracic leg movements are reminiscent of human arms, suggesting that they may be used as sensori-motor appendages for investigating the local environment.

The different joint movements found in the three pairs of legs should be associated with equally different motor activity. This was found in the related EMG records (Watson and Ritzmann 1998a). In the rear legs, activity in the slow depressor motor neuron (Ds), which controls extension of the CTF joint occurs in near synchrony with activity from the slow extensor of the tibia (SETi), which controls extension of the FT joint (figure 1). In the middle legs the two motor neurons are also in synchrony, but SETi is active at a lower frequency consistent with the smaller movement at the FT joint in that leg. In the prothoracic legs, activity in Ds and SETi are not in synchrony (Tryba and Ritzmann 2000). Rather, SETi fires before Ds to produce the initial FT Flexion. After the FT flexion and as the CF joint is extending, there is a second lower frequency burst in SETi. This occurs as the leg is passing under the animal's body. It is consistent with a hypothesis that, at this point, the front leg is being loaded and a small amount of tension is required in the FT joint to prevent collapse of the leg. This burst could result from a reflex initiated by sensory receptors called campaniform sensilla (Zill 1990; Zill and Seyfarth 1996) that are located in the leg's cuticle and detect cuticular strain such as would occur during loading.

Change in Walking Speed

In order to walk faster, the cockroach increases the velocity of joint movement, in particular in the stance phase (depression and extension of joints). This change is accomplished by increasing the rate of activity in the slow motor neurons that control movement of those joints (Watson and Ritzmann 1998a). In fact there is a linear relationship between the firing rate of Ds and SETi and the related joint velocity. At very high speeds, the second motor neuron that controls each of these joint movements is recruited. These neurons are called the fast depressor (Df) and the fast extensor of the tibia (FETi). They are easily distinguished from the slow motor neurons because they generate much larger muscle potentials in the EMG records (Watson and Ritzmann 1998b).

In response to activity in Df, the CTF joint appears to become much stiffer (Watson and Ritzmann 1998b). The joint rebounds more rapidly from swing to stance thus shortening the transition time. Timing of activity in Df comes at the right time for this change in transition duration to occur. Stiffening of the CTF joint appears to be an important event for walking at any speed. The Df potential occurs at the same time in which Ds normally fires a high frequency burst. Thus, it appears that at this time of transition it is very important for the joint to become stiff in expectation of the increased load during foot touchdown, regardless of walking speed. A similar high frequency burst has also been found at the onset of extensor activity in cats (Gorassini, Prochazka, Hiebert and Gauthier 1994). Finally, joint stiffening at touchdown was found to be a critical problem that has to be overcome in walking movements of Robot III. This observation is just one example of where hurdles that have to be overcome in Robot III point to an explanation for universal properties of legged locomotion in animals.

Turning

In order to turn, the cockroach must create a mismatch in joint movement in the right and left legs that at any given time are generating forward-directed force. This can be accomplished by altering the velocity of movement in the middle leg relative to the activity of the rear leg of the same tripod. For example, to turn to the right the animal would increase the activity in the left middle leg relative to the right rear leg. However, if the alternate tripod is on the ground it would turn towards the middle leg by decreasing activity in the right middle leg relative to the left rear leg. Observations of animals turning on the treadmill indicate that this does, in fact occur (Watson and Ritzmann 1998b). Thus, the middle legs play an important role in turning the animal. They are also critical to changes in body attitude during climbing.

Climbing

In order to climb over a barrier, the cockroach first appears to measure the height of the object. It then pitches its body up and finally extends its legs forcefully to push it up and over the obstacle. We have very little information on how the insect measures the height of the object. However, we are confident that such a measurement is done, because in over half of the climbs that we observed, the front legs are precisely placed on top of the barrier without bumping into the side of the object. Reasonable sensory devices for making the measurement include the compound eyes and the antenna. They may in fact be acting in tandem to make the calculation.

In order to alter the attitude of the body in preparation for the climb, the middle legs are rotated so that the tibia is more nearly perpendicular to the substrate (figure 3) (Watson, Tryba, Ritzmann, and Zill 1997). Once this is done, extension of the middle leg will pitch the animal up in preparation for the climbing movement. The rotation of the tibia occurs via a combination of movements at the body-coxa (BC) and trochanter-femur (TF) joints. Both the TF joint and the BC joint of the middle leg are located at an angle, so that movement of the BC joint will rotate the leg segments distal to the joint. Because both of these joints are located proximally on the leg, relatively small movements at the BC joint can result in large rotations at the tibia and tarsus. The contraction of the BC joint rotates the coxa along its long axis. This movement is very different from the movement that occurs in the front and rear legs where contraction of that joint causes the coxa to rock forward increasing the angle between the coxa and body as viewed from the side. In fact during the climb the side view angle of the coxa and body do not change significantly from what occurs during walking. Nevertheless, the coxa rotation will swing the tibia to a more perpendicular position.

The movement of the TF joint is subtle. In fact, this joint was previously thought to be fused. However, we have found that a small flexion does occur and that such a flexion can contribute to the rotation of the tibia relative to the substrate. Indeed, when we did fuse the TF joint with staples or pins through the tendon, we found that the rotation of the tibia during climbing was significantly reduced, and the animal had difficulty executing the climb.

Once the animal has reared up, it can then extend its rear legs forcefully to push it up and over the barrier (Watson et al. 1997). It does this by activating Ds at a particularly high frequency to generate greater force and push the animal upward. We are currently performing experiments to test whether this increased activation is yet another example of a reflex adjustment initiated by the campaniform sensilla, which serve as strain detectors in the cuticle.

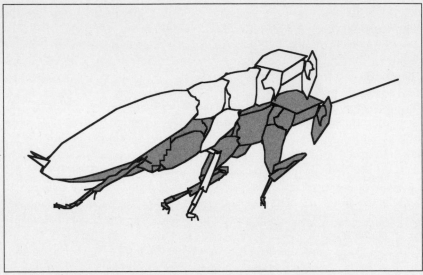

Figure 3. Diagram of a cockroach moving from a standing position (dark shading) to an elevated position (light shading) in preparation for climbing.
The critical movement is a rotation of the middle leg that redirects the
extension of that leg to lift the animal upward.

Summary of Biological Data

The biological data described above provides the essential parameters for design of the robot. By incorporating the insights that were gained in those experiments it was possible to create an agile hexapod vehicle with the potential to walk and run at various different speeds, turn and climb over barriers. We found that the most efficient way to incorporate these data into the design of the robot was to use a dynamic simulation tool that could utilize the digitized kinematic data to generate appropriate dynamic properties and then scale those factors up to the size of the actual robot.

Dynamic Model of *Blaberus*

We developed a dynamic model of the *Blaberus* cockroach to help us understand the biological data and to aid in the design of the robot (Nelson and Quinn 1995; Nelson 1995). The model is based upon a quasicoordinate formulation developed in the Biorobotics Laboratory that can be used to accurately model any legged animal or vehicle (Nelson and Quinn 1996). The model has a total of thirty-six degrees of freedom, three translations and three rotations of the body, and five actuated degrees of freedom in each of its six legs.

Each cockroach leg has ten segments and seven degrees of freedom. Six of these segments are in the tarsus (foot) and are actuated by a single muscle group. We found that the majority of the locomotion data of interest could be modeled using the three major segments (coxa, femur and tibia) and five degrees of freedom in each leg (Nelson and Quinn 1995). In the interest of limiting actuation, this ignores for the time being the relatively small movement of the TF joint. We believe that we can capture that action in climbing by making adjustments to the BC joint. The BC joint has three degrees of freedom and the CF joint and FT joint are each modeled with one degree of freedom.

The inputs to the simulation include the lengths and inertia of the leg segments and the body and joint angle trajectories from the behavioral studies discussed in the previous section. These joint angle trajectories were used as equilibrium point trajectories in the simulation. The joint torques are computed using a proportional-derivative control law:

torque for a joint = $(\theta actual - \theta desired) \; k + (d\theta actual/dt - d\theta desired/dt) \; c$
where $\theta actual$ is the actual angle, $\theta desired$ is the desired angle, and k and c are constants.

The joint torques caused the model's legs to move and when they contacted the ground they caused the body to move. The foot-ground interaction was modeled using a spring in parallel with a viscous damper and slip was permitted using a Coulomb friction model. Two sets of walking data were used, one for a tripod gait and one for a slower gait. In both simulations, the model walked similarly to the animal.

The outputs from the simulation include the joint torques, the body motions, the ground reaction forces and the structural bending moments in the leg segments. The body motions of the model are not input and therefore, are a good measure of the success of the simulation. Because the mechanical properties of the model are similar to the insect, the joint torques are good predictions of those used by the cockroach. This information is useful for the biologists because joint torques are difficult to measure in a walking animal and can be related to EMG data. The ground reaction forces are also a measure of the success of the simulation. Our predicted ground reaction forces qualitatively agree with measured data (Full 1993). The ground reaction forces and structural bending moments can also be used in robot design to choose materials and size the components.

A Robot based on Biological Observations

We designed the robot to be 17 times larger than the animal to ease the robot's development and to make use of commercially available actuator technology (Bachmann et al. 1997; Nelson et al. 1997). It is convenient to construct and work with a robot that it is desktop size, about 1-3 feet in length. It is also easier to visualize its motions and conduct locomotion studies. We chose a length of 30 inches because we wished to use commercial air cylinder actuators. For this robot size the actuators are readily available.

Pneumatic piston actuators were chosen because their power to weight ratio is much higher than standard DC motors and they offer the possibility of passive spring-like properties. It has been shown that the passive spring-like properties of muscles are important for efficient locomotion of animals (Alexander 1988). Our previous robots, Robot I and Robot II (Quinn and Espenschied 1993; Espenschied et al. 1995; Espenschied et al. 1996; Beer et al. 1997), used DC motors that are good for slow locomotion as observed in stick insect, but they are not energetic enough for the complex locomotion goals of this robot.

We wished to reduce the number of degrees of freedom of each leg as much as possible to further simplify the robot design. The joint angle trajectory from the biological data for the modes of locomotion of interest showed that two of the three degrees of freedom in the BC joint in the rear leg exhibited small excursions. Furthermore, one degree of freedom in the BC joint in the middle leg was found to move only slightly and could be eliminated (Nelson et al. 1997). We also felt that one degree of freedom in the body-coxa joint in the front leg could be eliminated even though all five degrees of freedom of that leg showed significant excursions.

The dynamic model of the cockroach discussed in the previous section was scaled up seventeen times in length and used to test the reduced degrees of freedom design: three degrees of freedom in the rear legs, four degrees of freedom each in the middle and front legs (Nelson et al. 1997). The middle and rear legs functioned similarly with or without the eliminated degrees of freedom for both walking gaits. However, the front legs did not reach forward as far with the four degrees of freedom configuration. We could have changed the joint trajectory input to try to compensate for this or we could have returned to the five degrees of freedom design.

The choice between these two strategies was influenced by our original goals. The goals of the robot include climbing and turning as well as walking. As discussed above the animal propels itself forward with its rear legs and this can be performed using the three degrees of freedom configuration. The middle legs pitch the body for climbing and yaw the body for turning. The four degrees of freedom configuration for the middle legs is sufficient for these functions. However, as described above, the cockroach uses its front legs as sensori-motor "arms" as it reaches and climbs over barriers. This function requires these legs to be the most dexterous pair and for this reason we chose to design the robot's front legs with five degrees of freedom (figure 4b).

The robot was designed to be energetic and mechanically robust (Bachmann et al. 1997). Our dynamic simulation was further used as a design tool for sizing actuators and structural members. Each leg was designed to be capable of withstanding 1.5 times the robot's weight in its most extended configuration because

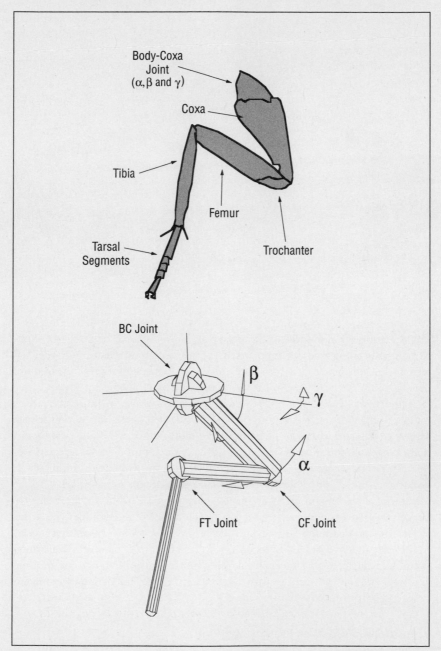

Figure 4. Cockroach front leg.

(a). Cockroach front leg diagram with segments labeled. (b) Schematic of front leg design showing five degrees of freedom.

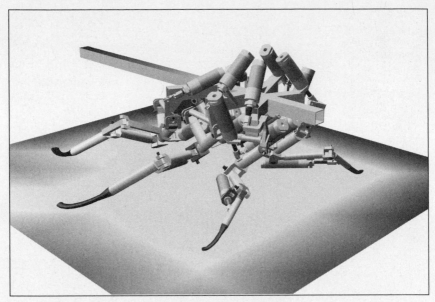

Figure 5. CAD model of Robot III.

in simulation it was found that a ground reaction force could be that large. Also, structural bending loads were predicted for the case where the robot model was dropped from a height of 1 inch onto three legs. Predicted torques during simulated locomotion were used to size the pneumatic actuators.

The range of motion of each degrees of freedom is just as important as the number of degrees of freedom in the legs. The desired range of motion for each degree of freedom was determined from the biological data. Where possible the joint ranges of motion are 110 percent of the desired minimum values. Actuator placement and actuator attachment points affected the mechanical limits of the joint range of motion. These further affected the actuator moment arms, which determined the maximum joint torque possible for a given actuator size. In many cases two actuators were used for a given degree of freedom to balance the force input and permit a larger range of motion of the joint. This design process was clearly iterative and CAD (figure 5) was essential to visualize the leg configurations and determine mechanical interference and joint ranges of motion. Three prototype legs were constructed before the final leg designs were determined (Bachmann et al. 1997).

Construction of Robot III's Physical Plant

The robot is 30 inches long and its structure, constructed mostly of aluminum, weighs 6.9 pounds (Bachmann et al. 1997) (figure 6). Its leg segments are made of hollow aluminum tubes and its joints are fabricated of machined aluminum

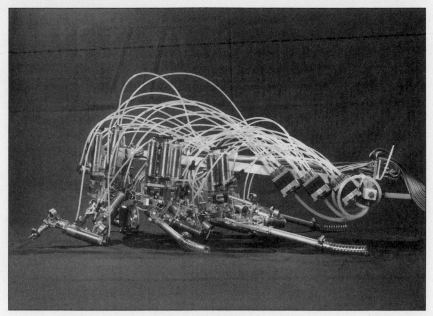

Figure 6. Side view of Robot III.

with roller bearings and hardened steel shafts. The tarsi are made of flexible plastic hoses clamped to the distal ends of the tibias. The hose material was chosen for its stiffness and frictional characteristics. Coil springs are inserted inside the plastic tarsi of the middle and rear legs to increase the stiffness of these load bearing legs. This construction models the passive stiffness of the animal's tarsi in a simplified manner and the friction is necessary to support horizontal loads in the stance legs.

The robot's total weight is 29.5 pounds including thirty-six double-acting air cylinders, forty-eight air valves (six blocks of eight valves), air hoses, and wires. The air valves are located on the robot's "abdomen" such that the fore-aft location of its center of mass is at the body-coxa joints of the rear legs as it is in the animal. A potentiometer is mounted at each joint to measure joint angles and a strain gage is mounted at the proximal end of each tibia to measure loading of the legs. These play the roles of chordotonal organs that monitor joint angle and campaniform sensilla that monitor cuticular strain in the animal (Zill 1990).

The robot has twenty-four active degrees of freedom. The minimum number of valves to control the robot is forty-eight three-way valves, one valve on each side of a double-acting air cylinder (or pair of cylinders). In this configuration the valve is always either pressurizing the one side of a cylinder or exhausting it and no air storage is possible. Unfortunately, the inability to store air eliminates the potentially useful property of passive stiffness.

The valves on the robot have a maximum frequency of about 200Hz and are controlled using pulse-width-modulation (PWM) at about 50Hz. Before choosing pneumatic cylinders to actuate the robot, we tested the control system using a prototype leg with four degrees of freedom and proportional control of individual joints (Nelson et al. 1997). The system was demonstrated to have the necessary smoothness, path following and repeatability characteristics for locomotion.

The biological data show that the rear legs typically operate with the CF and FT joints coupled, in-phase, and moving through equal excursions (figures 1 and 2). This provides the powerful piston-like motion that drives the animal forward. We designed the robot with three degrees of freedom in its rear legs in case all 3 were later found to be important, but we left provisions for a linkage to be attached to reduce it to two degrees of freedom. We now have installed a four-bar, parallel linkage mechanism on the rear legs and therefore have reduced the rear legs to two degrees of freedom. This mechanism simplifies the control of the robot because it stiffly couples the CF and FT joints, thereby reducing wobble in the posterior of the robot.

At thirty inches in body length, the robot is seventeen times larger than a typical adult *Blaberus* cockroach. Its leg segment lengths are also scaled to be seventeen times larger than those in the animal. The rear legs are large and powerful and have two degrees of freedom, the middle legs are smaller and have four degrees of freedom and the front legs are smallest and have five degrees of freedom.

Design of Robot III's Posture Controller

Posture control is the control of body motion in three translations and three orientations. Biological data on mammals suggest that robust posture control is essential for locomotion (Horak and Macpherson 1995). Furthermore, these studies have shown that the higher centers of the nervous system are important for posture. Although decerebrate mammals are fully capable of moving their legs in a pattern reminiscent of walking, they cannot stand on their own. Thus, normal posture requires an interaction between local reflex circuits in the spinal cord and computational centers in the brain. These centers process various kinds of sensory data such as leg position, head orientation and visual cues and then act through the local circuits in the spinal cord to actively control posture in a task and context dependent fashion. Insects have a more sprawled leg design that could require less attention to active posture control. Nevertheless, our own preliminary observations indicate that even in insects, information from the brain is critical to maintaining balance during active behavior. A cockroach that has experienced a lesion of both neck connectives demonstrates grossly extended leg joints and has a strong tendency to overturn with any rapid movements. Although some of these problems are reversed with time, the animal does not recover its agility even after a period of almost two months. Our conclusion from these observations and those on mammals is that posture is more than local reflex interaction. It appears to be the orchestration and tuning of reflexes in lower regions of the central nervous system according to some desired behavior. Robot III's posture controller reflects these ideas (Nelson and Quinn 1998; Nelson et al. 1998): It is a centralized controller based on the virtual model approach (Raibert et al. 1986; Pratt 1995; Pratt et al. 1997).

There are no sensors on cockroaches to directly measure their total body position or orientation, but there are many proprioceptors that monitor joint angle, strain on the cuticle, and position in extreme flexion. Total body posture can be calculated within the central nervous system from those proprioceptive measurements. In Robot III, body posture is also measured indirectly using proprioceptive data: from potentiometers on the stance legs. Even in humans, proprioceptive data are very important for posture control. Patients who have lost proprioceptive input to the brain have difficulty remaining upright even though their vestibular system is functioning normally (Horak and Macpherson 1995).

The input to the robot's posture controller is the desired body position and orientation. The desired forces F (in the x, y and z directions) and moments M (about the x, y and z axes) on the body required to cause this motion are calculated based on the robot being modeled as a body attached to six springs, one for each of the body's six degrees of freedom, for example:

$$F_i = K_i \, (actual_i - desired_i)$$

where *actual_i* is the actual body position in the i direction, *desired_i* is the desired body position in the i direction, and the subscript i denotes any of the three directions **x**, **y**, or **z**.

The posture control problem then is one of assigning the load bearing responsibilities to the stance legs such that their summation causes F and M to be exerted on the body. As the robot walks, the stance legs typically number from three to six. Therefore, the number of equations needed to solve this load distribution problem varies with the gait and the phase of the gait.

The problem is separated into a solution for the vertical force distribution (z direction) and a solution for the horizontal force distribution (x and y directions) (Nelson and Quinn 1998). The coordinates are further defined in figure 7. F and M are used to determine the desired center of pressure (COP) for the robot (figure 7). Equations are developed that constrain the sum of the vertical forces from the stance legs to equal F_z and the COP to be positioned as desired. Typically, depending on the number of legs in the stance phase, there are not enough constraint equations to solve directly for the vertical force required from each stance leg. Therefore, in addition to the constraint equations, an optimization problem is solved that encourages an equal sharing of vertical load among the stance legs. Note that normally the legs will not share an equal vertical load because of the enforcement of the constraint equations.

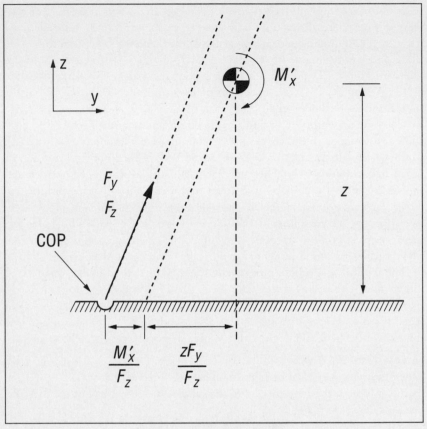

Figure 7. Desired center of pressure.

The desired center of pressure (COP) for the body can be found based upon the desired forces F and moments M. Note that z is the vertical direction, x is the heading direction and y is the lateral direction that follows for a right-handed coordinate system.

Independent constraint equations based on satisfying F and M on the body are formed to solve for the horizontal forces. Again, the problem is typically un-der-constrained and an optimization is used in the solution for the horizontal forces that encourages minimization of the joint torques in each leg. This has been shown to cause horizontal ground reaction forces directed in toward the body. A force distribution similar to this has been measured in walking cock-roaches (Full 1993).

With this posture controller the robot stands and resists large disturbances. When pushed from the side repeatedly while standing, it appears to exhibit a swaying reflex similar to that observed in animals (figure 8). To further demon-strate the posture controller and the robot's strength, we have shown that it can

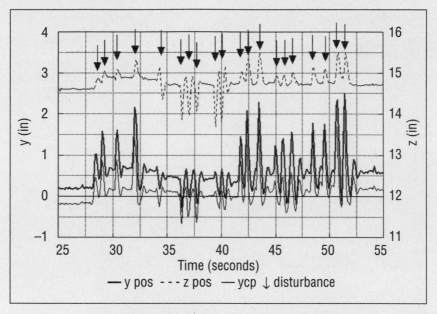

*Figure 8: Robot III's posture controller rejects disturbances
(reproduced from Nelson and Quinn 1998).*

The arrows indicate when the disturbance forces were applied. *ypos* and *zpos* are the *y* and *z* components of the position of the body and ycp is the y component of the position of the center of pressure.

perform push-ups while carrying a thirty pound weight (Nelson and Quinn, 1998; Bachmann et al., 1997).

The posture controller forms part of a locomotion controller. When the commanded body position is moved forward, the stance legs push the body forward. For the robot to walk, a gait controller must be added to encourage stance legs to lift and enter their swing phases in a coordinated manner. Also, a controller must be added to cause the legs to swing forward and transition to stance.

Conclusions

We have constructed a robot based strongly on the kinematics and behavioral observations of cockroach. Our strategy has been to use the animal's design and behavior as the default in the design and control of the robot rather than only using the biological design as inspiration to solve engineering problems. We resisted the urge to use a traditional engineering solution when the biological data suggested otherwise, even if it would appear easier. As a result, we have a robot

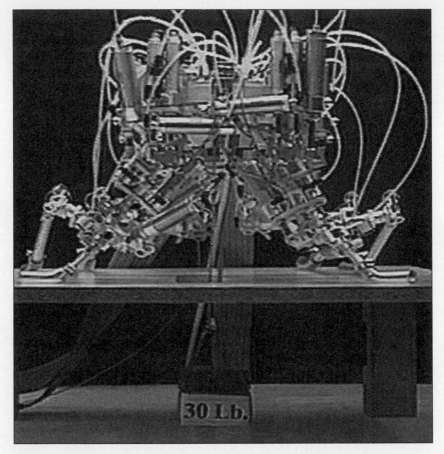

Figure 9. Robot III performing push-ups with a 30 pound payload.

that responds to disturbance in an animal like way and we believe will locomote in an animal like manner. An additional unforeseen payoff is that many of the problems that arise in controlling the robot lead to new understanding of the animal. These include the appreciation of the need for stiffening leg joints in anticipation of loading and the probable role of a sophisticated central control circuit that controls posture through interactions with local distributed circuits.

Robot III's leg designs capture the degrees of freedom, joint angle excursions and segment ratios that are necessary for walking and climbing in the animal remarkably well. This design is both a blessing and a challenge. In contrast, other hexapod robots, including Robot II, which was constructed by our group, have simpler leg designs (Beer et al. 1997). Typically, they include fewer degrees of freedom and all six legs are similar in construction. We believe that the leg designs for Robot III will ultimately make it behave in a more animal-like fashion, and this has been born out in the posture control. However, controlling the front legs has proved challenging because of their five degrees of freedom and relatively small inertia. A typical inverse kinematics approach such as that used in Robot II is difficult because of their kinematic redundancy. Even with these difficulties, there is benefit. The problems that we have encountered in controlling Robot III point to similar problems that animals face in controlling their legs, that if anything are even more complex. Thus, as a result of the close attention to biology in the design of this robot, the problems in control have led to insights in biology.

Although we are excited about the results of this project, we recognize that a detailed attention to biology is not necessary or desired in all biorobotics projects. Depending on the ultimate goals of the project, a group might be more inclined to use more traditional engineering methods and only look to biology for specific solutions. Indeed, in other projects that our group has undertaken, we are using this strategy. In deciding which strategy to take, a biorobotics group must first define the ultimate goals of the project. The goals of Robot III dictated a more detailed use of biology.

Acknowledgments

The work that is described in this chapter was supported by ONR grant N00014-96-10708 and NASA Marshall Space Flight Center grant NGT-52832. The work was carried out in the authors' laboratories. Our talented and diligent students and research associates, in particular James T. Watson, Andrew K. Tryba and Alan J. Pollack (biology) and Gabriel M. Nelson, Richard J. Bachmann, W. Clay Flannigan and Matthew C. Birch (engineering) played critical roles. A slightly different version of this chapter first appeared in 1998 in *Connection Science*, volume 10(3–4): 239-254. We are grateful to *Connection Science* for permission to reprint the paper.

6

Building Robots with a Complex Motor System to Understand Cognition

Holk Cruse

Could an ethologist be interested in building robots? At first sight, this seems to be implausible. The central interest of an ethologist is to understand how the behavior of an animal is controlled. To this end he or she observes the behavior of animals and performs experiments in order to search for information concerning the control principles underlying these behaviors. However, already quite simple control rules can produce unexpectedly complex behaviors, in particular when the loop through the world is taken into account (e.g. Braitenberg 1984, Brooks 1991a, Holland et al. 1994, Pfeifer 1996). This is because systems with recurrent information flow—in cases like the simple Braitenberg vehicles formed by the animat plus its environment—can have complex dynamic properties. If, in addition, the biological experiments indicate that several control rules cooperate in parallel within the brain of the animal, it becomes very difficult if not impossible to judge by intuition whether or not the observed behavior of the whole system can be traced back on these hypothetical rules. The only way to solve this problem appears to perform a simulation using these rules and by this way to test whether these rules form a sensible hypothesis. Typically such simulations are performed using digital computers. As the world usually represents an important part of the complete system, it is generally necessary to include some properties of the world into the simulation. This may prove difficult, in particular because some relevant properties of the world may be unknown to the programmer. A sensible way to overcome these problems inherent in such a "software" simulation is to use "hardware" simulations. This means to build a physical robot, or animat, which has to act in the real world. Such a hardware simulation has the advantage that the world no longer needs to be simulated, it is already there. Therefore, the above question has to be answered: yes, ethologists should be interested in the construction of animats.

Four Types of Animats

Real animals are, of course, far more complex systems than any animat yet built. Nevertheless, many researchers pursue the task of building simple animats in order to understand the principles underlying the construction of real animals, particularly the construction of their brains. So the question arises to what extent might such a reductionistic approach be sensible and helpful. To approach this question I will distinguish between four different types of animats. Many interesting investigations have been performed using the simple Braitenberg-type animats. These robots contain a simple sensory input (often two sensors), a simple motor output (usually two active, i.e., motor driven wheels) and a correspondingly simple connection scheme between sensor and motor units (e.g. Webb 1996, Scheier and Pfeifer 1998, Smithers 2000). Although of quite simple structure, these systems can show unexpectedly complex behavior, in particular behaviors that resemble considerably those observed in animals.

This type of animat can be made more complex when it is provided with more complex sensory input. This may either include different types of sensors like tactile and vision sensors (for example to be able to learn conditioned reflexes as in the work of Pfeifer and Verschure 1992) or may use only one type of sensor, often visual sensors, which form complex subsystems showing a sensory array with many pixels and many, possibly nonlinear, connections. Examples are the robots of Franceschini et al. (1992) exploiting visual movement detection for obstacle avoidance, or Mel's system (1997) for pattern recognition. The underlying schema is given in figure 1a (animat type 1). Because only feed-forward connections are considered here, these systems are strictly dependent on their sensory input and are therefore called sensory-driven or data-driven systems.

A major step to make the control structure of an animat more animal-like is to introduce internal recurrent connections (animat type 2, figure 1b). With an appropriate recurrent architecture such a system is no longer solely dependent on the actual sensory input, but can adopt internal states. When for example provided with an internal oscillator like a circadian rhythm generator, the response of the animat to a given sensory input might depend on the state of this oscillator. More complex versions are animats with a set of motivations (Maes 1991). Systems with internal states can also be considered as containing some kind of dynamic (short-term) memory. However, most of these animats still have a simple two degrees of freedom motor output. Although these recurrent systems are very interesting because they can show even more complex behaviors than do feed-forward systems, they have only rarely applied to the control of robots. One reason for this might be that the theoretical background of the dynamic properties of such recurrent systems is only poorly understood in most cases, which means that each individual version has to be separately studied in detail (see Beer [1996] for an interesting case study).

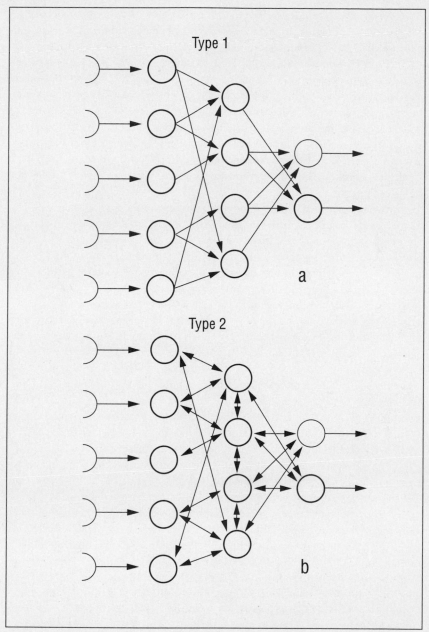

Figure 1. The control architecture of an animat with a—possibly—complex sensory input and a two degrees of freedom output.

a. A sensory-driven system using only feed-forward connections. b. A system with recurrent connections may have internal states.

Nevertheless, I would also like to argue that also these systems are still far simpler than real brains. In what respect? The general task of a brain is to control behavior. In the case of an animal, this means to control a high number of degrees of freedom, not just two. One reason for this is that there are no wheels in natural systems and locomotion is therefore very often based on the control of several articulated limbs. This is, of course, a more complicated task that requires an expansion of the control system. An obvious possibility to expand the system shown in figure 1b is simply to add a "motor system," which replaces the two wheels by, say, two legs, an articulated backbone, a neck, and maybe two arms. This motor system might consist of feed-forward connections only or it might be complicated by the introduction of recurrent connections as depicted in figure 2a (animat type 3).

The assumption that such a "bottleneck" architecture approximates the architecture of real brains might be intuitively supported by the qualitative observation that only an extremely small fraction of the rich sensory input passes our consciousness, and this small amount of information than seems to be used in a fan-out network to control our actions. Although probably nobody assumes that mammalian brains work that way, this idea still appears to guide our intuitions in some way. Many authors at least implicitly assume that insect brains may better be described by such bottleneck architectures. However, even in insects low-level activities, for example the activation of a leg muscle, appear to be represented in the head ganglia, too (Elsner 1994, Edwards et al. 1999). The existence of a high number of low-level reflexes clearly shows that also for insects a bottle neck architecture in the strict sense is only able to describe selected subsystems, but not the complete brain. Therefore, at least as far as mammalian brains are concerned, all knowledge indicates that a better approximation to the structure is given by the schema depicted in figure 2b (animat type 4), showing a massively parallel architecture including recurrent connections.

If a bottleneck structure was an appropriate description of a brain, the approach considering animats of type 1 or 2 (figure 1) is justified. But even if the holistic structure of type 4 (figure 2b) is a better approximation to reality, investigation of type 1 and type 2 animats can be helpful, in any case with respect to questions concerning application, but also with respect to brain research, because there might be cases where the brain is appropriately modularized making a reductionistic separation possible (e.g. the examples mentioned above). However, the strict concentration on only these types of systems precludes the investigation of possible "holistic" properties. By considering only animats of type 1, 2, or 3, the most interesting properties, and maybe the really essential properties of brains, might be completely neglected. This concentration on bottleneck architectures might mean more than just leaving out some modules. It rather might correspond to removing the essential part of the system. In an unpublished keynote lecture at the Conference on Simulation of Adaptive Behavior 1998, Zurich, Steven Grand formulated this as: "there is no such thing as half

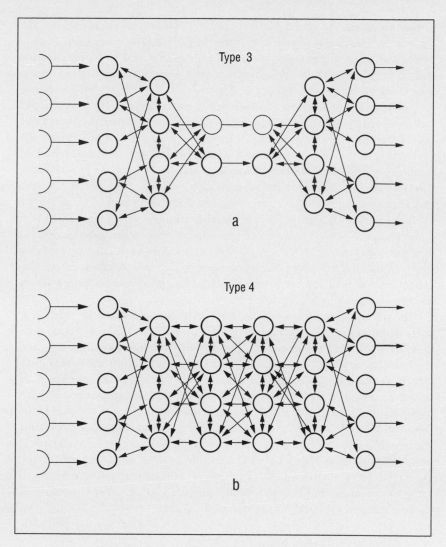

Figure 2. Two animats with complex sensory input and complex motor output.
a. A "bottleneck brain." b. A massively parallel holistic system.

an organism," which led him to the recommendation that we should "embrace complexity." Agreeing with this view, I would like to argue that investigation of only type 1, 2, or 3 animats comprises a, probably dramatic self-limitation when approaching the goal of understanding the function of brains. At the same conference, Keijzer (1998) argues along similar lines. He distinguishes two scales at which the animal and its environment can be coupled: the sensory-motor couplings for proximally guided behavior and perception-action couplings for distally oriented behavior. Concerning "wheeled behavior" he states: "wheels allow one to study distal behavior by simplifying the proximal mediating process: What if the proximal mediating mechanism is a much more central aspect of adaptive behavior than many tend to think?"

Two reasons may have caused researchers to stay away from studying complex recurrent systems. One is the lack of knowledge concerning properties of (massively parallel) recurrent systems. But there is also a more practical reason why researchers traditionally prefer to study systems with simple motor output as, for example, pressing a button or deciding between left and right etc. In such experiments the situation can be nearly completely controlled by the experimenter even when the input is arbitrarily complex, and the tools of classical systems analysis can well be applied. This is very different when studying systems with complex motor output. Already a simple stimulus may elicit a complex behavior and because of the autonomy of the system classical input-output analysis is not easily applicable. However, despite these problems, investigation of complex motor systems have to be performed in order to understand the principles underlying such autonomous systems.

The essential property of a brain is its capability of controlling behavior in the context of dealing with complex motor output, i.e., a high number of degrees of freedom. This, in general, means that the control system has to deal with the problem of redundancy, i.e., with situations in which the system has to choose between a number of possible solutions. The higher the number of degrees of freedom of the system the more intelligence, or autonomy, is required for its controller. It may not be by accident that in the domain of invertebrates, for example, those animals are considered as to be the most intelligent ones that have to deal with the most complex motor system, namely the Cephalopods, in particular Octopus. This leads to the conclusion that we should much more concentrate on the investigation of animals or animats that have not only complex sensory input, but also sufficiently complex body kinematics because the latter require a correspondingly complex motor control system.

Two Examples

Two examples presented below will illustrate—and propose solutions for—problems occurring when dealing with the control of nontrivial motor systems. The first example concentrates on an eighteen degrees of freedom system, namely a six-legged insect being able to walk on irregular substrate. This system is a comparatively simple case because it is organized in a modular way. The legs represent six quasi-parallel, mechanically coupled systems with three degrees of freedom—three active joints—each. As the body-ground distance is essentially fixed (one of the leg joints serves as a height controller) there remain twelve joints to be controlled.

How is the movement of these twelve joints organized to find a common solution? This task poses several major problems. It is not enough simply to specify a movement for each leg on its own: the mechanical coupling through the substrate means that efficient locomotion requires coordinated movement of all the joints of all the legs in contact with the substrate. However, the number and combination of mechanically coupled joints varies from one moment to the next, depending on which legs are lifted. The task is quite nonlinear, particularly when the rotational axes of the joints are not orthogonal, as is often the case for insect legs and for the basal leg joint in particular. A further complication occurs when the animal negotiates a curve, which requires the different legs to move at different speeds.

In machines, these problems can be solved using traditional, though computationally costly, methods, which consider the ground reaction forces of all legs in stance and seek to optimize some additional criteria, such as minimizing the tension or compression exerted by the legs on the substrate. Due to the nature of the mechanical interactions and inherent in the search for a globally optimal control strategy, such algorithms require a single, central controller; they do not lend themselves to distributed processing. This makes real-time control difficult, even in the still simple case of walking on a rigid substrate.

Further complexities arise in more complex, natural walking situations, making solution difficult even with high computational power. These occur, for example, when an animal or a machine walks on a slippery surface or on a compliant substrate, such as the leaves and twigs encountered by insects. Any flexibility in the suspension of the joints further increases the degrees of freedom that must be considered and the complexity of the computation. Further problems for an exact, analytical solution occur when the length of leg segments changes during growth or their shape changes through injury. In such cases, knowledge of the geometrical situation is incomplete, making an explicit calculation difficult, if not impossible.

Despite the evident complexity of these tasks, they are mastered even by insects with their "simple" nervous systems. Hence, there has to be a solution that is fast enough that on-line computation is possible even for slow neuronal systems. How can this be done? Several authors (e.g. Brooks 1991a) have pointed out that some relevant parameters do not need to be explicitly calculated by the nervous system because they are already available in the interaction with the environment. This means that, instead of an abstract calculation, the system can directly exploit the dynamics of the interaction and thereby avoid a slow, computationally exact algorithm. To solve the particular problem at hand, we propose to replace a central controller with distributed control in the form of local positive feedback (Cruse et al. 1998).

The positive feedback occurs at the level of single joints: the position signal of each is fed back to control the motor output of the same joint. How does this system work? Let us assume that any one joint is moved actively. Then, because of the mechanical connections, all other joints begin to move passively, but in exactly the proper way. Thus, the movement direction and speed of each joint does not have to be computed because this information is already provided by the physics. The positive feedback then transforms this passive movement into an active movement.

There are, however, several problems to be solved. The first is that positive feedback using the raw position signal would lead to unpredictable changes in movement speed, not the nearly constant walking speed that is usually desired. This problem can be solved by introducing a kind of band-pass filter into the feedback loop. The effect is to make the feedback proportional to the angular velocity of joint movement, not the angular position. In the simulation, this is done by feeding back a signal proportional to the angular change over the preceding time interval.

A second problem inherent in using positive feedback is the following. Let us assume that a stationary insect is pulled backward by gravity or by a brief tug from an experimenter. With positive feedback control as described, the insect should then continue to walk backwards even after the initial pull ends. This has never been observed. Therefore, we assume that a supervisory system exists that is not only responsible for switching on and off the entire walking system, but also specifies walking direction (for details see H. Kindermann 2001).

Compared to earlier versions (Cruse et al. 1995), this change permits the control of the stance movement to be radically simplified. In this way, an extremely decentralized, simple controller, based on a combination of negative and positive feedback at the joint level, copes with all these problems by exploiting the physical properties of the system, i.e. the mechanical connections between the leg segments.

As could be shown by a computer simulation, this extremely decentralized control system is able to solve straight and curved walking (figure 3a, 3b), walking over obstacles, and walking after a part of a leg has been cut. The system even showed the unexpected behavior of automatically righting up the body after a fall (figure 4).

One major disadvantage of this simulation is its pure kinematic nature that means that possibly important properties of the real world are not included. To test the principle of local positive feedback at least for straight walking, we have performed a dynamic simulation for the six-legged system under positive feedback control during stance. The basic software was kindly provided by F. Pfeiffer, Technical University of Munich. No problems occurred. Nevertheless, a hardware simulation of the walking situations is necessary and is currently being tested by M. Frik, University of Duisburg, using his robot TARRY II (Frik et al. 1999).

The second problem considered concerns the control of a mechanical chain of limbs that has extra degrees of freedom. When a leg is not in contact with the ground but is swung through the air to meet a given target's position, the trajectory of that leg (or likewise an arm) and its configuration at the endpoint could be

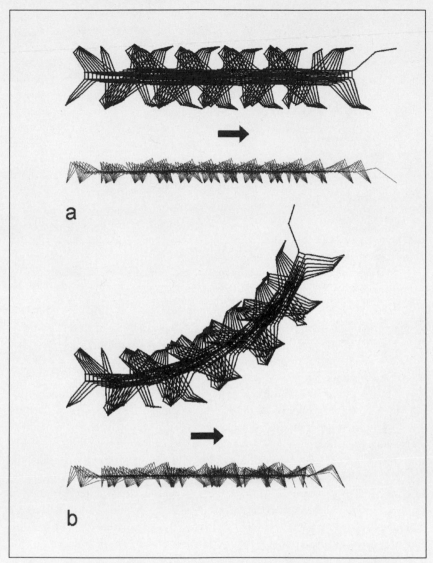

Figure 3. Simulated walk by the basic six-legged system with eighteen degrees of freedom.
Movement direction is from left to right (arrow). Leg positions are illustrated only during stance and only for every second time interval in the simulation. Each leg makes about five steps. Upper part: top view, lower part: side view. (a) Straight walking. (b) curved walking.

determined by a hardwired feed-forward network. This means that for a given starting configuration and a given target position the trajectory of the leg is fully determined. In this case the control system has no possibility to choose a different trajectory. However, in many cases, maybe not in insect walking but definitely in

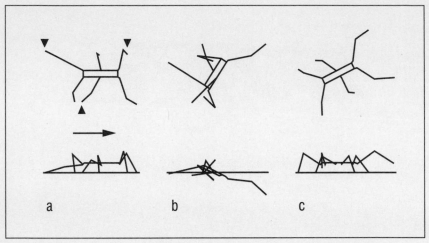

Figure 4. Righting behavior.

(a) By clamping the tarsi to the ground (arrowheads), the system is made to fall leading to dis-
ordered arrangement of the legs (b). Nevertheless, the system stands up without help and re-
sumes proper walking (c).

human grasping movements, an arbitrary selection of one out of all the geometrically possible solutions is possible. The number of possible solutions increases dra-
matically when the leg or arm has redundant degrees of freedom. For example,
consider the simple but generic case of a three joint arm moving in a two-dimensional plane. In this situation the control system has to choose in a continuous solution space (this is different to the above mentioned network of Maes (1991)
where a decision between discrete behaviors e.g. fight, flight, etc. has to be made
that can be done by using a WTA system, i.e., a special form of Hopfield network).

To solve this ill-posed problem in a way that does not use fixed, prescribed solutions (e.g. Brüwer and Cruse 1990), but that allow the control system to really
choose between all geometrically possible solutions, I see no other way then to
apply an internal representation of the arm, i.e., some kind of body model.

How could such a body model look like? Based on the "passive motion
paradigm" (Mussa-Ivaldi et al. 1988), a body model has been proposed in the
form of a relatively simple recurrent network (Steinkühler and Cruse 1998). A
linear version of this "mean of multiple computation" or MMC net is shown in
figure 5. This recurrent network can be used to solve the inverse kinematic
problem, the direct kinematic problem and any mixed problem. According to
the passive motion paradigm these problems can be solved in the following way.
Imagine that a mechanical model of the arm to be controlled is used and the
joints are provided with elastic springs. The inverse kinematic problem is solved
simply by pulling the endpoint of the mechanical model to the desired position.
During this movement the other joints automatically move to new angle values

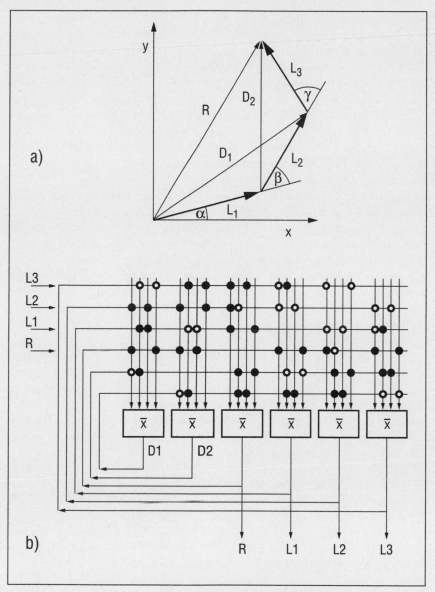

Figure 5. The MMC net for the three-joint planar arm.

a) The arm segments are represented by the vectors L_1, L_2, and L_3. Vector **R** describes the (e.g. visually given) position of the endpoint. The diagonals (D_1, D_2) are used as internal variables only. b) The recurrent network. Only the net for one spatial component is shown. Weights are 1 (closed circles) or −1 (open circles). The black triangles represent arbitrary weights that must, however, taken into account for the calculation of the weighted mean **x**. (see Cruse et al. 1998 for details).

and the final configuration of the mechanical model comprises a solution of the task. Now the angles can be read off the model arm and then be used to control the real arm. To solve another problem, one or more selected joints could be fixed before the endpoint of the mechanical model is moved. Then, of course, another solution is found (if it exists) that fulfills these additional constraints. The recurrent network proposed is a neuronal version of this mechanical model. As mentioned, it is not only able to solve these inverse kinematic tasks, but also the direct kinematic task and any mixed problem. Forming a holistic system, its internal structure does not have to be changed when switching between these tasks. This change is simply triggered by providing different input (see left hand part of figure 5b) to the network.

Figure 6a, and figure 6b shows an example of how the system behaves when relaxing from a given starting configuration to an end position defined by the coordinates of the end effector. The system always finds a solution for the inverse problem. The system is quite "tolerant" as it provides approximate solutions also to problems that cannot be solved exactly. Such a case is presented by the example in figure 6c, and figure 6d. Here, the coordinates of the endpoint cannot be reached by the manipulator because they specify a point outside its workspace. Nevertheless, the network tries to follow the desired coordinates as well as possible. The manipulator finally points in the direction of the desired endpoint coordinates.

This neuronal model can, as described, be used as a network to control movement, even in ill-posed situations. When disconnected from the motor output, it could likewise be used for motor planning. As Calvin (1996) argues, thinking is movement that has not yet taken place. Therefore, this internal body model could be regarded as being the basis for a simple form of thinking. This is in agreement with several researchers (e.g. Fuster 1995, Ito 1993) who argue that thinking is some kind of imagined movement.

Similarly, in a more general view this model can be considered as a neural system that is able to mentally deal with complex geometrical systems, a task similar to but more difficult than the mental rotation of geometrically fixed bodies (Shepard and Metzler 1971, Georgopoulos et al. 1989). In other words, the system can manipulate knowledge, in this case knowledge concerning the own body. This means that, according to the definition of McFarland and Bösser (1993), this network may be regarded as a basis for cognition.

Furthermore, the MMC net provides a solution for the problem of sensor fusion, occurring when different sensory inputs, for example visually or mechanoreceptively given input values, represent the same value. Using traditional feed-forward systems, because of limited exactness of these systems, in general numerically different results are produced for the same value. The holistic MMC network integrates the values and concatenates both the visual and the mechanoreceptively given spaces to form a common, dynamic representation.

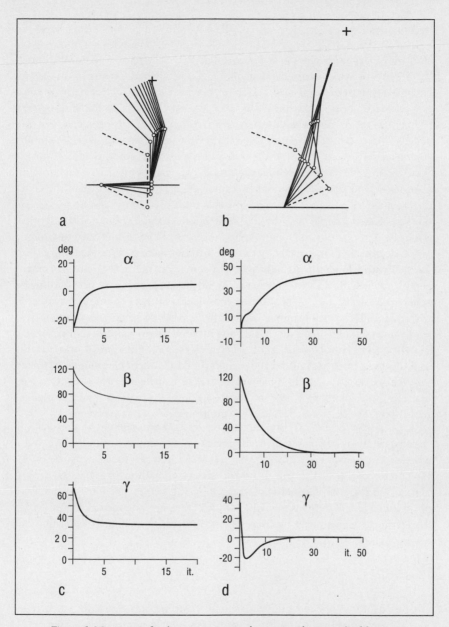

Figure 6. Movement of a three-joint manipulator using the network of figure 5.

(a) The manipulator moves from a starting configuration (dotted lines) to the prescribed position of the end effector (cross). (b) The temporal changes of the three joint angles α, β, and δ during relaxation. (c, d) Movement of the manipulator when the desired endpoint coordinates (cross) lie outside its workspace. Only the manipulator configuration of every fifth cycle is shown in (c). (d) and (b): Abscissa is the number of iteration cycles (i.t.).

Conclusion

Thus, both examples show that the investigation of systems with complex motor output addresses problems that may not occur when dealing with systems having only a small number of degrees of freedom. In the first case, the degrees of freedom are not exploited to solve variable tasks. The high number of degrees of freedom result from a repetition of more or less identical segments—a millipede would be a more extreme case—that have to cooperate to serve a common goal, namely the propulsion of the body. This task does not appear to require a "manipulate-able" body model, i.e., a model that can be used to "play around" in order to find possible solutions by exploiting all the possibilities of the complex motor system. Instead, the body itself is used.

The second example considers the control of a complex kinematic body that might be expanded by including external objects like tools and therefore might serve not only as an internal body model, but might also be extended to form an internal world model. This leads to the assumption that the ability to control complex kinematic systems may have formed the prerequisite to deal with more general problems, i.e., to become an intelligent system. Examples of systems with the need to control complex kinematics are the grasping and manipulation movements with an arm and a hand shown by different mammals, in particular primates, the control of the trunk in elephants, manipulation of objects with legs and beak in parrots or the above mentioned invertebrate example of Octopus. All appear to be good problem solvers. As a conclusion, therefore, I assume that the understanding of how to control a complex kinematic system is an essential prerequisite to understand the functioning of cognitive systems.

This proposal may also be relevant for the development of artificial cognitive systems. If one is only dealing with the control of a cylindrical, two-wheeled robot, such holistic (recurrent) networks may not be necessary because the task to control such a "trivial" body is simple enough to be solved by using feed-forward systems. This kind of research may, however, preclude the finding of solutions for the very task for which brains have been developed to deal with. Also artificial cognitive systems may have to be built on the basis of holistic systems for motor control (Cruse 1999).

Cognitive Systems

7

Perceptual Invariance and Categorization in an Embodied Model of the Visual System

Nikolaus Almássy and Olaf Sporns

Perceptual invariance is an important prerequisite for the discrimination and categorization of stimuli in a natural environment. Biological nervous systems contain neurons, i.e., within the mammalian inferior temporal cortex, that respond invariantly to specific visual stimuli. Little is known about the role of phenotype, behavior, and environment in the development and experience-dependent plasticity of inferior temporal neuronal responses. To investigate this question, we designed a neuronal model based on visual cortex that is embedded in a real world device capable of autonomous behavior. Initially, visual responses are nonselective and noninvariant. In the course of autonomous behavior, synaptic changes in visual and sensorimotor networks accumulate resulting in neuronal units that are pattern selective and translation invariant. In analyzing the model, we find that the continuity of self-generated movements is essential for the development of these complex response properties; no translation invariance develops if behavior is disrupted and substituted with passive presentations of static stimuli. Voltage-dependent intrinsic connections in the inferior temporal cortex aid in the development of large and sharply defined receptive fields and support rapid and accurate behavioral discrimination. In summary, our studies suggest that at least some perceptual invariances may be the result of the interplay between plasticity intrinsic to the nervous system and extrinsic factors ("embodiment") due to phenotype, behavior and environment.

Organisms are able to behaviorally discriminate highly diverse and often novel visual stimuli and to acquire new perceptual categories throughout their lifetime (Edelman 1987). Traditionally, theoretical frameworks of pattern classification have approached the problem by attempting to devise strategies for partitioning often high-dimensional input spaces into distinct regions corresponding to categories. These approaches do not typically take into account several key characteristics of how biological systems achieve their superior performance in categorizing natural environments. Biological perceptual categorization is not the result of disembodied information processing or of (even neurally implemented) algorithmic procedures. Rather, viewed from a biological perspective, categorization necessarily involves exploration and active movement resulting in sensory exposure and sampling. The construction of basic feature dimensions depends upon statistical patterns in sensory inputs. The generation of these patterns may depend critically on an organism's body structure (including physical properties of its sensory and motor organs, i.e., its "phenotype"), its movement repertoire and on the previous history of its interactions in the real world.

One key prerequisite for successful categorization is the extraction of invariants from the highly variable activity pattern present on the sensory sheet (Epstein 1977, Walsh and Kulikowski 1998). In the visual domain, many organisms (in particular higher vertebrates) are able to categorize stimuli no matter where they are located within the visual field (translation invariance), and, in addition, discount differences in rotational angle, perspective, and illuminant (see schematic in figure 1). In mammalian brains, a possible neural basis for these visual invariances can be found in the receptive field properties of neurons located in the inferior temporal cortex (for reviews see Gross 1992, Logothetis, Pauls, and Poggio 1995, Tanaka 1996). These neurons respond selectively to various kinds of complex visual stimuli (Gross, Rocha-Miranda, and Bender 1972, Desimone et al. 1984, Tanaka et al. 1991). They have large receptive fields giving rise to responses that are invariant with respect to stimulus translation (Gross and Mishkin 1977, Tovee, Rolls, and Azzopardi 1994, Ito et al. 1995). Other invariant properties of visual neurons include rotational invariance, size invariance, viewpoint invariance, and invariance with respect to illuminance.

Here, we address two questions concerning the highly characteristic patterns of neuronal responses observed in mammalian inferior temporal cortex. The first question concerns the developmental origin of the complex response properties of such neurons. There is relatively little empirical data on the development and experience-dependence of these properties. Evidence suggests that tuning properties of visual cortical neurons are subject to significant postnatal modification and refinement (Rodman 1994), at least in part as a result of exposure to actual stimuli (Kobatake, Wang, and Tanaka 1998). Our modeling studies investigate what developmental mechanisms might be involved in shaping these responses. The second question concerns potential roles for a class of connections linking neurons within the inferior temporal cortex (also called tangential, horizontal, or long-range intrinsic connections). Such connections have been described in primary visual cortex (Gilbert and Wiesel 1983, Callaway and Katz 1990, Gilbert 1993) as well as in inferior temporal cortex (Fujita and Fujita 1996, Tanigawa et al. 1998). They link distinct groups of pyramidal neurons over distances of up to several millimeters. We investigated what effects such

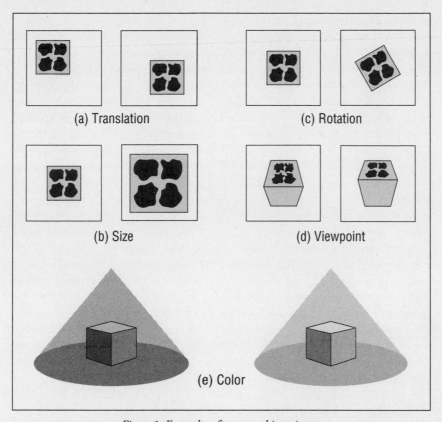

Figure 1. Examples of perceptual invariances.

In each panel two separate views of an object (with a "bloblike" texture) are shown. (a) Translation invariance. (b) Size invariance. (c) Rotation invariance. (d) Viewpoint invariance. (e) Color invariance.

connections might have on local response properties of inferior temporal neurons as well as on categorization behavior.

In a series of previous modeling studies Reeke et al. 1990, Reeke, Sporns, and Edelman 1990, Edelman et al. 1992, Reeke and Sporns 1993, Verschure et al. 1995), we have designed simulations of neuronal models that could be interfaced with a behaving phenotype and interact with an environment to produce autonomous behavior. We have called our approach "synthetic neural modeling" to indicate our central aim: to interrelate realistically modeled neural processes across multiple scales of organization (from synapses to the function of entire neural systems) in the context of a behaving system. Other approaches, based on embodied models of brain and behavior have been proposed (such as Chiel and Beer 1997, Clark 1997, Mataric 1998, Pfeifer and Scheier 1999); several of these are reviewed in this book.

Our most recent set of studies (Almássy, Edelman, and Sporns 1998, Almássy and Sporns 1998, Sporns, Almássy and Edelman 2000) was aimed at the role of behavior and changes in environmental input during visual development. We designed Darwin V, a neuronal model based on visual cortex embedded in a real world device, and behaving in an environment containing objects that differed in their visual patterns. In brief, Darwin V operated as follows: Visual input acquired by a video camera was transmitted to a primary visual area (VAp) and from there to a secondary visual area (VAs) resembling inferior temporal cortex. Connections of VAp to VAs were widely divergent and modifiable according to a synaptic rule allowing for potentiation and depression. Connections of VAs to motor centers were modifiable depending upon value elicited by "taste" (conductivity). Before visual experience, VAs responses were weak, nonselective and noninvariant, and behaviorally Darwin V did not discriminate between stimuli. In the course of visual experience, groups of VAs units emerged that were more sharply tuned, and responded selectively for distinct stimulus patterns and invariantly with respect to their location. After conditioning, Darwin V was able to discriminate objects, approaching nonconductive ones, while avoiding conductive ones. The emergence of translation invariance was impaired if the temporal continuity of stimulus sequences due to self-generated movements was disrupted. The map of units within VAs reflected the history of stimulus encounters and was sensitive to changes in sensory input due to behavior. In the course of development, a patchy network of long-range intrinsic connections developed within area VAs, resulting in larger and more sharply defined receptive fields of neurons within VAs as well as improved categorization behavior.

Overall, our results are consistent with the view that the development of pattern selective and translation invariant neuronal responses depends critically on self-generated movement, the stimulus content of the environment and the dynamics of ongoing behavior.

Implementation

In this chapter, the implementation of Darwin V, in particular the construction of its robotic phenotype and the simulated nervous system, are only described in outline. Details of the implementation (including parameter values) are contained in previous publications (Almássy, Edelman, and Sporns 1998, Almássy and Sporns 1998, Sporns, Almássy, and Edelman 1999).

A mobile device called NOMAD was equipped with a miniature CCD camera, six infrared sensors that trigger collision-avoidance reflexes, and a rigid electromagnetic "snout" that provides a binary "taste" signal to the nervous system. The experiments were conducted in an enclosed area with black cloth-covered walls and a black floor. Six to nine metal cubes (ten centimeters wide, subtend-

Figure 2. NOMAD in its environment.

ing a visual angle of about 7.5 degrees) were evenly distributed in the environment, and the robot's control architecture allowed the exploration and sampling of two types of test stimuli. "Appetitive" tasting stimuli were marked with five white "stripes" (width five millimeters, evenly spaced) and "aversive" stimuli showed "blobs" (four white patches, Ø 2.5 centimeters).

During autonomous behavior NOMAD performs obstacle avoidance, visual ex-

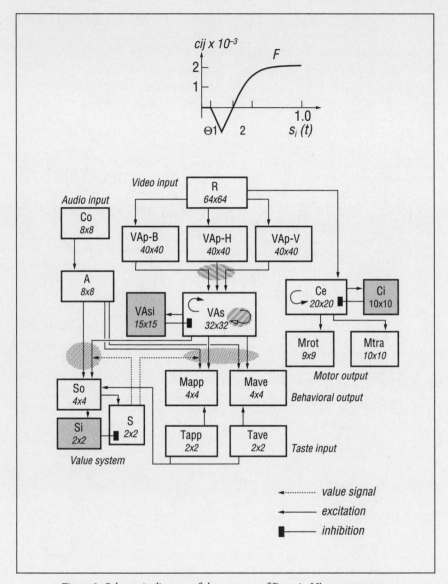

Figure 3. Schematic diagram of the anatomy of Darwin V's nervous system.

Boxes indicate different anatomical areas (numbers within boxes indicate their dimensions in neuronal units), shaded boxes indicate inhibitory units, arrows indicate major pathways, typically comprising hundreds or thousands of individual connections. The open arrowhead (in area VAs) indicates voltage-dependent long-range intrinsic connections. All other connections are voltage-independent. Cross-hatched areas indicate plastic connections. Value projections are represented by a stippled arrow and area of termination indicates projections that are subject to value-dependent modification. Insert on top is a sketch of postsynaptic function F (see equation 4).

ploration, tracking, gripping and conductivity (taste) sensing, as well as appetitive and aversive behaviors. Appetitive behavior consists of prolonged gripping, movement and sensing of taste, while aversive behavior consists of releasing the object and turning away. The last two modes of behavior are activated either by the sensing of taste (the unconditioned stimulus, US, triggering an unconditioned response, UR), or by inputs from another sensory modality, such as vision (the conditioned stimulus, CS, followed by a conditioned response, CR). Appetitive or aversive behavior is triggered as soon as the difference in instantaneous activity between motor areas Mapp and Mave (see below) exceeds a behavioral threshold β. If visual inputs act to trigger aversive behavior, the aversive turning response (CR) is executed instantaneously, resulting in immediate removal of the aversive object from the visual field; no taste sensing (UR) occurs.

Nervous System

Darwin V's nervous system consists of a number of areas representing different brain regions containing neuronal units of different types. Such units are taken to represent local populations of neurons, often corresponding to neuronal groups (Edelman 1987). In the instantiation used in the present experiments, the simulated nervous system contains a total of approximately 15,000 neuronal units and 600,000 synaptic connections. There are five major components: a visual system, a taste system, sets of motor neurons capable of triggering behavior, a visual tracking system, and a value system. A schematic diagram of the major components of Darwin V's nervous system is shown in figure 3.

The pixel image captured by NOMAD's camera is relayed to a receiving area R and transmitted via topographic connections to a primary visual area VAp. The spatial arrangement (resembling feature matrices) of these connections results in various stimulus selectivities within interleaved subpartitions of VAp. There are three subpartitions, one each selective for visual "blobs," "horizontal" and "vertical" stripes. Topographic, mutually inhibitory connections result in sharpening and disambiguation of responses. Dynamically, responses within VAp are brisk and closely follow stimulus onset and lateral displacements. All subpartitions of VAp project to a secondary visual area VAs, containing both excitatory and inhibitory units. Local excitatory-excitatory, excitatory-inhibitory, and inhibitory-excitatory interactions produce firing patterns that are characterized by focal regions of excitation (diameter about three to five neuronal units) surrounded by inhibition; responses tend to be more long-lasting than those in VAp.

The taste system consists of two kinds of sensory units responsive to either the presence or absence of conductivity across the surface of stimulus objects (as measured by sensors in NOMAD's snout). These units emit all-or-none responses that are transmitted to appropriate motor centers by innately specified ("prewired") connections. In addition, both taste units send a uniform, nonplastic input to the value system.

The motor system consists of two groups of units capable of triggering two distinct behaviors, appetitive (Mapp) and aversive (Mave). These two groups receive pre-specified and fixed connections from the taste system (Tapp to Mapp and Tave to Mave) and have mutually inhibitory connections. In addition they receive initially weak nonspecific connections from the visual system (VAs to Mapp and Mave) that are subject to value-dependent modification.

The visual tracking system controls navigational movements, in particular approach of objects identified by brightness contrast with respect to the background. The visual receiving area R emits a projection to an area C ("colliculus"), containing excitatory (Ce) and inhibitory (Ci) units. The pattern of connectivity within area C helps to sharpen Ce responses to visual targets and partially disambiguates such responses when multiple targets are present. Ce activity triggers translational and rotational motion of NOMAD (via activation of Mtra and Mrot, respectively) ultimately producing visual approach behavior. Connection strengths in projections from Ce to Mtra and Mrot were assigned initial values resembling distributions obtained in earlier work by value-dependent synaptic modification during sensorimotor training (Edelman et al. 1992).

Cell Activation and Synaptic Rules

As in previous models (such as Reeke, Sporns, and Edelman 1990), activity values $s_i(t)$ of neuronal units at cycle t represent the average firing rate of a local population of neurons. Synaptic strengths c_{ij} may be subject to activity-dependent modification (see below).

Synaptic inputs can be voltage-independent or voltage-dependent. The total input to unit i from voltage-independent (VI) connections is given by

$$A_i^{VI}(t) = \sum_{\ell=1}^{M} \sum_{j=1}^{N_\ell} c_{ij} s_j(t) \tag{1}$$

where M is the number of different anatomically defined connection types and N_ℓ is the number of connections per type ℓ projecting to unit i. Negative values for c_{ij} correspond to inhibitory connections. The total contribution from voltage-dependent (VD) connections is given by

$$A_i^{VD}(t) = \sum_{\ell=1}^{M} \tanh\left(A_i^{VI}(t) + \omega s_i(t) \right) \sum_{j=1}^{N_\ell} c_{ij} s_j(t) \tag{2}$$

where ω determines the persistence of unit activity from one cycle to the next. Voltage-dependent connections have no effect unless there is sufficient postsynaptic activity due to other, voltage-independent inputs.

The activity level of unit i is given by

$$s_i(t+1) = \phi_{\sigma_i}\left(\tanh\left(g_i \left[A_i^{VI}(t) + A_i^{VD}(t) + \omega s_i(t) \right] \right) \right) \tag{3}$$

where ϕ_{σ_i} is a unit-specific firing-threshold function and g_i is a scale factor. In the model, several types of connections (both voltage-dependent and voltage-in-dependent, see figure 3) are subject to activity-dependent modification according to a synaptic rule:

$$\Delta c_{ij}(t) = \varepsilon\big(c_{ij}(0) - c_{ij}(t)\big) + \eta s_j(t)F\big(s_i(t)\big) \tag{4}$$

where $s_i(t)$ and $s_j(t)$ are activities of post- and presynaptic units, respectively, η is a fixed learning rate, ε is a decay constant ($\varepsilon \ll 1$), and $c_{ij}(0)$ is the initial ($t = 0$) weight of connection c_{ij}. Synaptic changes depend upon both pre- and postsynaptic activity and can result in either strengthening or weakening of connections as determined by the function F (see figure 3, inset), which sets limits and rates for synaptic potentiation and depression depending upon the postsynaptic activity (compare Bienenstock, Cooper and Munro 1982). For some connections (e.g., VAs to Mapp and Mave), this modification depends on value (for more detail see Sporns, Almássy, and Edelman 2000). The long-range intrinsic connections within area VAs studied in this chapter are modifiable, with changes in c_{ij} solely depending on pre- and postsynaptic activity.

Results

In this chapter we present some exemplary results obtained from experiments reported previously (Almássy, Edelman, and Sporns 1998, Almássy and Sporns 1998, Sporns, Almássy, and Edelman 1999). These results address the problem of how perceptual invariants arise during development and how their emergence relates to aspects of a behaving system's embodiment. First, we briefly describe the overall behavior of Darwin V and its development over time. Then, we describe the development of visual properties of neuronal units within the "higher" visual area VAs, in particular the development of translation invariance and object selectivity.

Overall Behavior of Darwin V

Figures 4 and 5 provide a summary of relevant neural and behavioral states recorded during several stimulus encounters. Neural states of visual, taste, motor and value networks are indicated as average activity levels over time (figure 4). Before development, Darwin V indiscriminately approaches all visual objects until they are located within the visual fovea. Then, all objects are gripped to allow sensing of their conductivity ("taste"). Taste sensing triggers either appetitive or aversive behavior. Visual neuronal responses in area VAs are still nonspecific and do not allow the translation invariant recognition of objects. Therefore, all behavior is initially driven by "taste" sensing only. After some time, synaptic changes in connections linking visual areas VAp and VAs have ac-

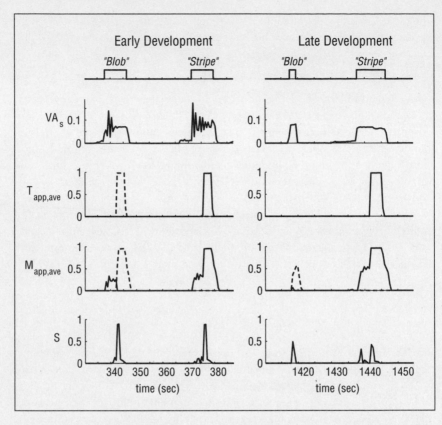

Figure 4. Average neural states of several sensory and motor networks of Darwin V recorded before (left) and after (right) visual development and conditioning.

Traces for two individual encounters with a "blob" and a "stripe" are shown, with (top to bottom) traces for average visual activity in VAs, taste sensing (Tave, broken line; Tapp, solid line), behavioral motor activity (Mave, broken line; Mapp solid line), and the value system *S*. For description see text.

cumulated and neuronal responses within VAs have developed that allow the visual recognition of objects. This results in visual responses becoming linked directly to behavior (figure 5). After this developmental stage is completed, Darwin V will still approach objects that "taste good," but will avoid objects that "taste bad," i.e., if encountered, trigger avoidance behavior.

Development of Translation Invariant and Object Selective Neuronal Responses

During visual exploration and approach, neuronal units in the primary (VAp) and secondary (VAs) visual areas show responses with different temporal char-

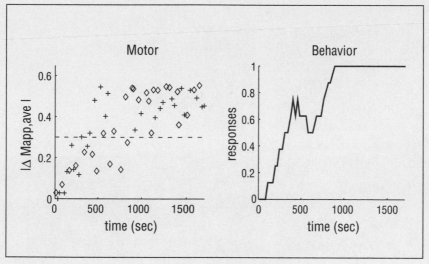

Figure 5. Learning curves.

On the left, symbols indicate the difference in average activities of Mave and Mapp for "stripes" (+) and "blobs" (◇), with a stippled line indicating the behavioral threshold ($\beta = 0.3$) used in the present experiments. On the right, the percent incidence of conditioned responses (aversive and appetitive) are indicated. Note that after about 1,000 seconds (30 minutes) of experience only conditioned responses occur, i.e., responses that are triggered by vision alone.

acteristics. Neuronal units in VAp have small receptive fields and respond to local features of the image, i.e. short segments of vertical lines. Due to stimulus displacement during approach, line segments quickly move in and out of the unit's receptive fields and unit responses are brief in duration. In our experiments, no modification of VAp responses occurred with development. At higher levels of the cortical model (VAs), neuronal units receive highly convergent inputs from a large region within VAp. Due to local dynamics of excitatory/inhibitory interactions, lateral displacement of stimuli within the visual field is accompanied by sustained activation or suppression of subsets of units within VAs. For many units, such responses either increase or decrease in both amplitude and temporal duration during development, producing an overall sharpening of unit responses.

Next, we tested the neuronal response patterns we obtained from area VAs for translation invariance (figure 6). For this purpose, we presented visual objects at different locations within the field of view and compared the activity patterns within area VAs. Recording the activity values for all nine hundred units within area VAs for a given pair of object locations yielded two activation vectors **a** and **b**. Their mutual overlap (degree of pair-wise correlation) is estimated as

$$\cos(\phi) = \frac{\mathbf{ab}}{|\mathbf{a}| \cdot |\mathbf{b}|}$$

(5)

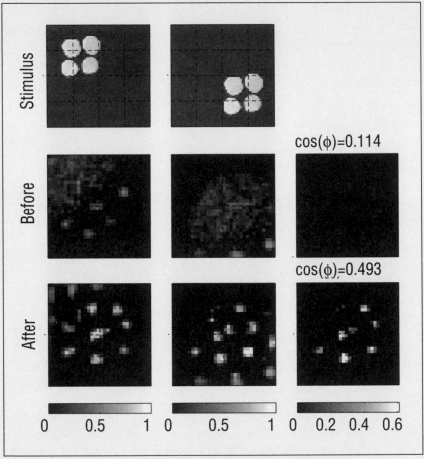

Figure 6. Patterns of neural activity in VAs before and after development.

Presentation of an object in two different positions (top) and resulting activity patterns in *VAs* before (middle) and after (bottom) development. Element-by-element product of unit activities is indicated at right.

Before development, VAs activation was characterized by variable foci of activity due to local excitation and inhibition. Exemplary activity patterns for the same object presented at two different locations are shown in figure 6. Their overlap before development ($\cos(\phi)$ = 0.114) indicated a very small number of units that respond invariantly with respect to translation of the object. After development (4,083 cycles, 82 objects) VAs activity patterns were more sharply tuned and overlapped significantly for the same object presented at different locations indicating translation invariance ($\cos(\phi)$ = 0.493). On average, during development the overlap increased significantly for all object distances (Almássy, Edelman, and Sporns 1998).

So far, we have shown that translation invariant and pattern selective neuronal responses emerged in the course of development as Darwin V interacted with numerous objects in its environment. A key question arises: does the emergence of these properties depend on movement and how is it affected if the continuity of Darwin V's movements is disrupted? To address this question, we compared Darwin V's neuronal responses before and after "normal" development to those of a separately trained Darwin V that had been immobilized and presented with sequences of stationary images of visual patterns flashed at random positions within its narrow-angle field of view ("discontinuous" development). Patterns used consisted of a training set of "blobs" and "stripes" (in horizontal and vertical orientations) that were presented with equal frequency. To keep the overall amount of sensory stimulation comparable to "normal" development, individual patterns were presented for about seven seconds (twenty cycles) separated by about twenty-five seconds (seventy blank cycles that simulated the times for visual search and exploration).

We recorded activity levels and calculated $\cos(\phi)$ (equation 5) for pairs of object presentations at a distance of sixteen and thirty-two pixels (corresponding to a viewing angle of 6.4 and 12.8 degrees, respectively) distributed evenly over all parts of the field of view. The overall level of activity within VAs ($s_i(t) > 0.0$) was unchanged between "normal" and "discontinuous" modes of stimulation, although a significantly larger number of units showed strong ($s_i(t) > 0.5$) and sustained responses in the former versus the latter condition. While "normal" development significantly increased the overlap measure $\cos(\phi)$, which is an indicator of the degree of translation invariance, "discontinuous" development did not result in a similar increase and $\cos(\phi)$ remained at baseline levels.

Receptive field maps of individual VAs units were examined and compared before and after "normal" and "discontinuous" development. VAs responses were recorded while presenting an object in a regularly spaced array of 32×32 locations within the narrow-angle field of view. An individual receptive field map was obtained by plotting the steady-state activity level of a single neuronal unit for all spatial locations. Figure 7 shows representative examples of such maps for a unit located near the center of VAs, which received highly convergent anatomical input from a large, central portion of VAp. Before development, receptive field maps were patchy and showed weak pattern selectivity over much of their spatial extent (figure 7, "before"). After "normal" development, neuronal units with high selectivity for a particular visual pattern (in this case "horizontals") had receptive fields that were coherent in their selectivity, consisting in most cases of a single large region; at the same time, parts of the receptive field showing responses to other patterns decreased (figure 7, "normal"). After "discontinuous" development, receptive field maps changed only slightly and retained many of their initial characteristics (figure 7, "discontinuous"). In particular, these receptive field maps did not extend across large regions of the visual field and did not show coherent regions of high pattern selectivity. No improve-

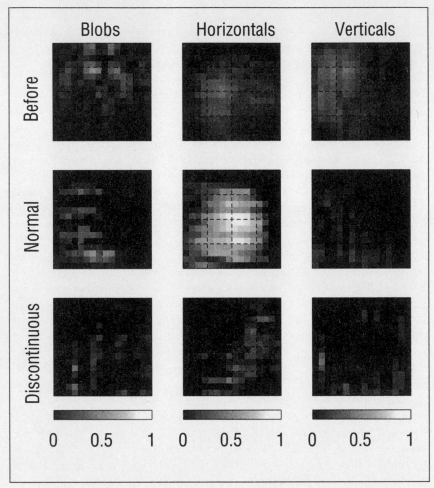

Figure 7. Effect of continuous movements on development of receptive field maps.

Receptive field maps were obtained by recording VAs responses while presenting an object in a regularly spaced array of 32 × 32 locations within the narrow-angle field of view. Pixel values represent neural activity for a single presentation of an object centered at that location and are spatially averaged over 2 × 2 subregions. Receptive field maps are plotted before (top), after "normal" (middle) and after "discontinuous" (bottom) visual development. For each condition, a single receptive field map is shown with three components (responses to "blobs," "horizontals" and "verticals") displayed side by side.

ment was found even after very long runs (data not shown). From all of these results, we reach the conclusion that disrupting the continuity of self-generated movements strongly impaired the development of translation invariance for VAs neuronal units.

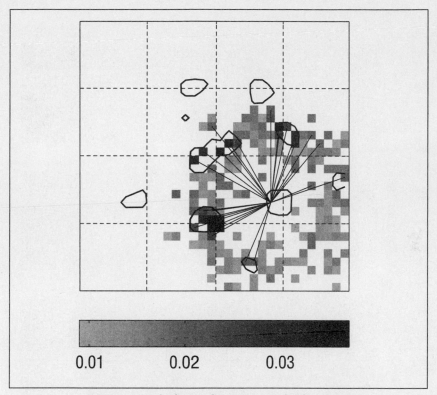

*Figure 8. Axonal arbors and synaptic strengths of long-range
intrinsic connections within VAs to an excitatory neuronal unit
selective for "blobs" (located on the lower right of the array), after visual development.*

The contour lines mark groups of neurons (similar to those shown in figure 6 that respond selectively to "blobs." Note that connections are strongest between neurons with similar response properties (selectivity for "blobs").

Potential Functional Role of Intrinsic Connections

Recently, long-range intrinsic connections have been described in inferior temporal cortex, but their functional role remains unknown. One possible functional role concerns their involvement in translation invariance and in helping to generate robust categorization behavior. In the model, long-range intrinsic connections were implemented as voltage-dependent connections. Before visual experience, long-range intrinsic connections within area VAs had relatively weak connection strengths and were distributed randomly between neuronal units in VAs. After development (figure 8), strengthened long-range intrinsic connections selectively linked groups of neuronal units that had similar response properties; other long-range intrinsic connections were weakened ("pruned away").

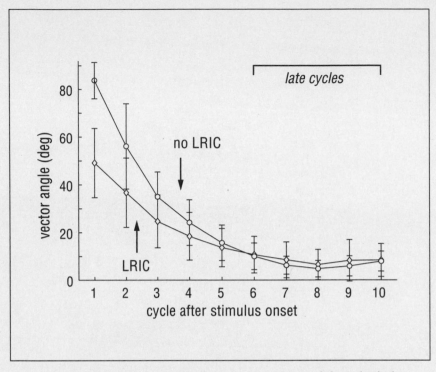

Figure 9. Population vector angles between VAs activity sampled at individual cycles after stimulus onset and an average "late" pattern (cycles 6-10).

Without long-range intrinsic connections (LRIC), the angle is significantly larger during the first three cycles after stimulus onset (ttest2: p-values = 2.6 x 10-7, 0.0079, 0.027, respectively). In addition, arrows indicate when, on average, behavior is triggered.

This pattern allowed distant groups of neuronal units to interact through a patchy network of voltage-dependent connections.

Long-range intrinsic connections affected the dynamics of firing patterns within VAs. During early development, these firing patterns tended to fluctuate and showed little stability and selectivity with respect to particular visual stimuli. This was due to the still immature patterns of afferent and intrinsic synaptic strengths. A prerequisite for reliable categorization of visual stimuli is a relatively stable firing pattern that ensures the consistent development of sensorimotor connections linking VAs to the motor units. To quantify how quickly the population response stabilized after stimulus onset we evaluated the overlap in VAs response patterns (activity vectors) between individual time points during stimulus encounter. In particular, we compared the "late" (stabilized) pattern (sampled after the time when behavior is initiated) and "early" firing patterns sampled directly after stimulus onset (figure 9). We found that when long-range intrinsic connections were present, the overlap (vector angle ϕ) between early

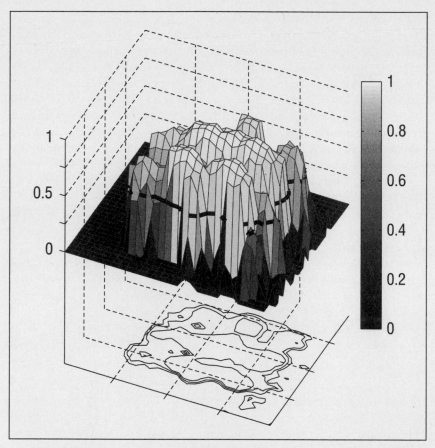

Figure 10. Receptive field of a neuronal unit (shown in figure 8) selective for "blobs."
The contour line in the surface plot indicates half the maximal response. The sharpness of the receptive field was defined as the average gradient around that line.

and late population vectors decreased more quickly than in a model where long-range intrinsic connections had been "lesioned" (by setting their c_{ij}'s to zero). This indicated that the population response organized more quickly into a pattern that allowed the initiation of a motor response. Overall levels of activity were similar between the two models.

Long-range intrinsic connections had significant effects on the size and shape of receptive fields within VAs (figure 10). Before development, the receptive field maps of units in VAs were patchy and weak, indicating inconsistent selectivity over much of their spatial extent. After normal visual development during behavior, neuronal units exhibiting object selectivity and translation invariance had receptive field maps that were coherent in their selectivity, consisting in most cases of a single large region. The receptive field maps of 118 neuronal units sampled from a model with long-range intrinsic connections were compared to the receptive fields of 90 neuronal units sampled from a model that did not have long-range intrinsic connections but received the same visual experience. We found that the receptive field sizes in the model with long-range intrinsic connections increased by about thirty percent compared to the model without long-range intrinsic connections and the average neuronal response within the receptive field increased by thirteen percent. Furthermore, the average gradient along the half maximal contour line of the receptive field (the "sharpness") increased by thirty-eight percent. All differences are statistically significant (data not shown).

Models that included long-range intrinsic connections in area VAs showed a significant improvement in categorizing performance. On average, behavior was triggered significantly earlier when long-range intrinsic connections were present (after 2.5 cycles, versus 3.5 for a model without long-range intrinsic connections, twelve trials, behavioral threshold $\beta = 0.3$; one-way Anova, $df = 1$, $F = 6$, $p = 0.023$, see figure 9). Also, categorization was more reliable, with the rate of errors in behavioral discrimination increasing from one to five (out of twelve trials, in a representative simulation segment) as long-range intrinsic connections are omitted from the model.

Discussion

The development of object selectivity and translation invariance in visual neuronal responses is a prerequisite for the behavioral discrimination of objects. In this chapter, we describe exemplary results obtained from a biologically based neuronal model of visual cortex that is embedded in a real world device and is capable of autonomous behavior. Most previous models of form recognition or categorization have dealt with these processes as purely sensory or perceptual phenomena, independent of motor activity and ongoing behavior. Our modeling study suggests that in autonomous systems the development of cortical selective and invariant neuronal responses may depend critically on self-generated movement and behavior. Overall, our study is consistent with the notion that the behavioral activity of organisms in their econiche is an important factor in the development and subsequent elaboration of their neural circuitry. Self-generated movement and behavior play important roles in the ability of an organism to sense and discriminate objects and events in its environment.

The Development of Object Selectivity and Translation Invariance

Biological object recognition is typically achieved in a manner that is invariant with respect to natural transformations, such as translation, size or rotation.

Neurophysiological evidence (Gross, Rocha-Miranda, and Bender 1972, Logothetis, Pauls, and Poggio 1995, Tanaka 1996) suggests that the object selective and translation invariant responses of neurons in the inferotemporal cortex play a key role in this process. While recognition of some visual patterns may be innate, developmental studies in primates (Spinozzi 1996) and humans (Bertenthal 1996) strongly suggest that exposure to visual stimuli is required for normal (selective and invariant) neuronal responses to emerge. In Darwin V, we modeled the development of such responses in the course of successive exposure to various objects present in its environment.

In the primate visual system, areas within "lower" hierarchical levels contain neurons that are selective only for elementary (simple) features of visual objects, such as line segments. Invariant and object-selective visual responses arise only at "higher" hierarchical levels and depend for their construction on the progressive elaboration of visual input from "lower" to "higher" areas via convergent/divergent feed-forward connectivity (for a review see Rolls 1992). In our model, for reasons of computational expediency, we have simplified the multi-level hierarchical arrangement of the primate visual system to include only two areas (VAp and VAs), with properties characteristic for primary/secondary (V1/V2) and inferior temporal cortices (IT), respectively. These two areas are linked by widely convergent/divergent connections, arising from neurons with different stimulus selectivity in VAp and terminating on a single set of neurons in VAs. Intrinsic connections within VAs link distinct populations of excitatory and inhibitory units. Activity patterns within VAs are sustained (lasting for several time steps, corresponding to several hundred milliseconds of real time) and are characterized by local foci of activation surrounded by lateral inhibition. Before visual experience, these foci are highly dynamic and unstable, appearing at different locations within the VAs map depending upon small fluctuations in the input. During synaptic modification, repeated sustained coactivation of neighboring units tends to produce similar patterns of synaptic change in their afferent and efferent connectivity. Inhibition tends to spread apart and limit the size of emerging functional neuronal groups selective for specific objects. Intrinsic excitatory-inhibitory interactions within VAs enhance competition between neuronal populations in different parts of the array, sharpening their responses and leading to the emergence of distinct neuronal groups.

Several computational models of inferior temporal have been developed previously (Gochin 1994, Wallis and Rolls 1997). Different proposals have been made to account for the translation invariant properties of inferior temporal neurons. An important set of models (Földiàk 1991, Oram and Földiàk 1996, Wallis and Rolls 1997, Wallis and Bülthoff 1999) has utilized a Hebbian-type learning mechanism (the so-called trace rule) to develop translation invariant neuronal responses. The trace rule incorporates temporal delays into the learning mechanism, providing an effective way to link successive images of objects. In our model, such linkage is achieved directly through neuronal dynamics, i.e.

the sustained activation of neurons in area VAs. This dynamical process, in conjunction with lateral displacement of objects at a time scale commensurate with synaptic changes, serves to allow units within VAs to become responsive to signals arriving over an extended region of the visual field.

Intrinsic Organization of Inferior Temporal Cortex

A functional columnar organization of inferior temporal cortex has been shown in a series of electrophysiological and optical imaging studies (Fujita et al. 1992, Wang, Tanaka, and Tanifuji 1996); this pattern of organization is strikingly similar to the pattern of neuronal groups emerging during visual development in our modeled area VAs (figure 6). These neuronal groups contain units that share object selectivity and generate translation invariant responses. Such local functional coupling is consistent with the observed higher incidence of functional interactions for neurons located within about one hundred micrometers (Gochin et al. 1991). While neuronal groups are generated through dynamic interactions over short distances, they become mutually linked over longer distances through voltage-dependent intrinsic connections. Synaptic changes in these connections result in connection patterns that resemble the patchy network of intra-areal connections present within the inferior temporal cortex (Fujita and Fujita 1996, Tanigawa et al. 1998). After development, strong connections tend to link groups of neurons that have similar response properties. We found that the presence of these connections had significant effects on the size and shape of receptive fields within VAs; they tended to increase both overall areal extent and sharpness of receptive fields and thus contributed to an increase in translation invariance. Also, firing patterns within area VAs emerged more quickly after the onset of a visual stimulus and converged more rapidly towards patterns that allowed the initiation of a motor response. This dynamic effect produced an effect on behavior. We found that, on average, appropriate motor responses were triggered earlier within a behavioral trial. These effects on receptive fields and behavior of intrinsic connections within our modeled area VAs are suggestive of potential functional roles of such connections in inferior temporal cortex.

Conclusion

The essential role of behavioral and environmental interactions in the development of translation invariance is demonstrated by the drastic effects on neuronal responses if such interactions are impaired. No translation invariant responses develop if the continuity of stimulus displacement is selectively destroyed, even if equivalent levels of sensory input and synaptic changes are allowed. We conclude that in systems showing autonomous behavior, complex neuronal responses are in part determined by self-generated behavioral interactions in the environment. Such interactions can help in sampling and generating statistical regularities in the environment that can be captured by developing neuronal circuitry. Similar mechanisms may also be responsible for generating other perceptual invariances, such as those for object size, rotation, view-independence, or color (see figure 1). In general, our study is consistent with the hypothesis that the ongoing behavioral and motor activity of organisms constitute essential prerequisites for the extraction of invariants by specialized neurons.

Acknowledgments

This work was carried out in the W.M. Keck Foundation Machine Psychology Laboratory at The Neurosciences Institute and supported by a grant from the W.M. Keck Foundation to Neurosciences Research Foundation.

8

Investigating Models of Social Development Using a Humanoid Robot

Brian Scassellati

Research on humanoid robotics has been motivated by a variety of different goals. Some research groups have focused on the construction of machines with humanlike form and motion to meet anticipated commercial needs as a flexible factory worker, a domestic assistant, or to operate in areas that are dangerous to humans (Hirai et al. 1998, Kawamura et al. 1996). Other research has focused on the construction of humanoid robots to examine issues of human-robot interaction and cooperation (Takanishi, Hirano, and Sato 1998; Morita, Shibuya, and Sugano 1998), or to examine issues of sensory-motor integration and architectural techniques from artificial intelligence (Kanehiro et al. 1998). The majority of these research efforts have focused on the challenging engineering issues of building intelligent and adaptive systems.

My colleagues and I have proposed that humanoid robotics research can also investigate scientific questions about the nature of human intelligence (Brooks et al. 1998). We believe that humanoid robots can serve as a unique tool to investigators in the cognitive sciences. Robotic implementations of cognitive, behavioral, and developmental models provide a test-bed for evaluating the predictive power and validity of those models. An implemented robotic model allows for more accurate testing and validation of these models through controlled, repeatable experiments. Slight experimental variations can be used to isolate and evaluate single factors (whether environmental or internal) independent of many of the confounds that affect normal behavioral observations. Experiments can also be repeated with nearly identical conditions to allow for easy validation. Further, internal model structures can be manipulated to observe the quantitative and qualitative effects on behavior. A robotic model can also be subjected to controversial testing that is potentially hazardous, costly, or unethical to conduct on humans; the "boundary conditions'" of the models can be explored by testing alternative learning and environmental conditions. Finally, a robotic model can be used to suggest and evaluate potential intervention strategies before applying them to human subjects.

In this chapter, I discuss the potential biological and engineering questions that can be examined by implementing models of human social development on a humanoid robot. Our group has implemented biological models at many different abstraction levels, including interaction models of infant-caregiver interactions (Breazeal and Scassellati 1998), behavioral models of the development of infant reaching (Marjanovic, Scassellati, and Williamson 1996) and neural models of spinal motor neurons (Williamson 1996, Williamson 1998). In this chapter, we present an on-going implementation of one behavioral model of social development that focuses on the recognition and production of joint attention behaviors (Scassellati 1996, Scassellati 1998).

Models of Joint Attention

One of the critical precursors to social learning in human development is the ability to selectively attend to an object of mutual interest. Humans have a large repertoire of social cues, such as gaze direction, pointing gestures, and postural cues, that all indicate to an observer which object is currently under consideration. These abilities, collectively named mechanisms of joint (or shared) attention, are vital to the normal development of social skills in children. Joint attention to objects and events in the world serves as the initial mechanism for infants to share experiences with others and to negotiate shared meanings. Joint attention is also a mechanism for allowing infants to leverage the skills and knowledge of an adult caregiver in order to learn about their environment, in part by allowing the infant to manipulate the behavior of the caregiver and in part by providing a basis for more complex forms of social communication such as language and gestures.

Joint attention has been investigated by researchers in a variety of fields. Experts in child development are interested in these skills as part of the normal developmental course that infants acquire extremely rapidly, and in a stereotyped sequence (Scaife and Bruner 1975, Moore and Dunham 1995). Additional work on the etiology and behavioral manifestations of pervasive developmental disorders such as autism and Asperger's syndrome have focused on disruptions to joint attention mechanisms and demonstrated how vital these skills are in human social interactions (Cohen and Volkmar 1997, Baron-Cohen 1995). Philosophers have been interested in joint attention both as an explanation for issues of contextual grounding and as a precursor to a theory of other minds (Whiten 1991, Dennett 1991). Evolutionary psychologists and primatologists have focused on the evolution of these simple social skills throughout the animal kingdom as a means of evaluating both the presence of theory of mind and as a measure of social functioning (Povinelli and Preuss 1995, Hauser 1996, Premack 1988).

The investigation of joint attention asks questions about the development and origins of the complex nonverbal communication skills that humans so easily master: What is the progression of skills that humans must acquire to engage in shared attention? When something goes wrong in this development, as it seems to do in autism, what problems can occur, and what hope do we have for correcting these problems? What parts of this complex interplay can be seen in other primates, and what can we learn about the basis of communication from these comparisons?

Decomposing Social Skills

The most relevant studies to our purposes have occured as developmental and evolutionary investigations of "theory of mind" (see Whiten 1991 for a collection of these studies). The most important finding, repeated in many different forms, is that the mechanisms of joint attention are not a single monolithic system. Evidence from childhood development shows that not all mechanisms for joint attention are present from birth, and there is a stereotypic progression of skills that occurs in all infants at roughly the same rate (Hobson 1993). For example, infants are always sensitive to eye direction before they can interpret and generate pointing gestures.

There are also developmental disorders, such as autism, that limit and fracture the components of this system (Frith 1990). Autism is a pervasive developmental disorder of unknown etiology that is diagnosed by a set of behavioral criteria centered around abnormal social and communicative skills (*Diagnostic and Statistical Manual of Mental Disorders*, 1994; The *ICD-10 Classification of Mental and Behavioral Disorders*, 1993). Individuals with autism tend to have normal sensory and motor skills, but have difficulty with certain socially relevant tasks. For example, autistic individuals fail to make appropriate eye contact, and while they can recognize where a person is looking, they often fail to grasp the implications of this information. While the deficits of autism certainly cover many other cognitive abilities, some researchers believe that the missing mechanisms of joint attention may be critical to the other deficiencies (Baron-Cohen 1995). In comparison to other mental retardation and developmental disorders (like Williams and Downs Syndromes), the social deficiencies of autism are quite specific (Karmiloff-Smith et al. 1995).

Evidence from research into the social skills of other animals has also indicated that joint attention can be decomposed into a set of subskills. The same ontological progression of joint attention skills that is evident in human infants can also be seen as an evolutionary progression in which the increasingly complex set of skills can be mapped to animals that are increasingly closer to humans on a phylogenetic scale (Povinelli and Preuss 1995). For example, skills that infants acquire early in life, such as sensitivity to eye direction, have been demonstrated in relatively simple vertebrates, such as snakes (Burghardt and Greene 1990), while skills that are acquired later tend to appear only in the primates (Whiten 1991).

A Theoretical Decomposition

One of the most influential models of joint attention comes from Baron-Cohen (1995). Baron-Cohen's model gives a coherent account of the observed developmental stages of joint attention behaviors in both normal and blind children, the observed deficiencies in joint attention of children with autism, and a partial explanation of the observed abilities of primates on joint attention tasks.

Baron-Cohen describes four Fodorian modules: the eye-direction detector (EDD), the intentionality detector (ID), the shared attention module (SAM), and the theory-of-mind module (TOMM) (see figure 1). In brief, the eye-direction detector locates eyelike shapes and extrapolates the object that they are focused upon while the intentionality detector attributes desires and goals to objects that appear to move under their own volition. The outputs of these two modules (EDD and ID) are used by the shared attention module to generate representations and behaviors that link attentional states in the observer to attentional states in the observed. Finally, the theory-of-mind module acts on the output of SAM to predict the thoughts and actions of the observed individual. In normal development, the interaction of EDD, ID, and SAM produce a variety of normal behaviors. Furthermore, the model proposes that autistic behavior can be explained by including the EDD and ID modules without any of the competencies of the shared attention module.

Decomposition Based on Observable Behaviors

In order to implement and test a complex social model, representative behaviors that can be independently tested and observed must be identified for each part of the model. A behavioral decomposition allows us to evaluate the performance of the system incrementally and to match the observed behavior of our robot with observed behavior in humans. The skill decomposition that we are pursuing is a set of representative behaviors from EDD, ID, and SAM for two social modalities (eye contact and pointing). This decomposition includes four observable and testable behaviors: maintaining eye contact, gaze following, imperative pointing, and declarative pointing. Figure 2 shows simple cartoon illustrations of these four skills in which the smaller figure on the left in each cartoon represents the novice and the larger figure on the right represents the caregiver. These skills were selected as representative behaviors because the ontogeny and phylogeny of the skills have been intensively studied, because they are possible with

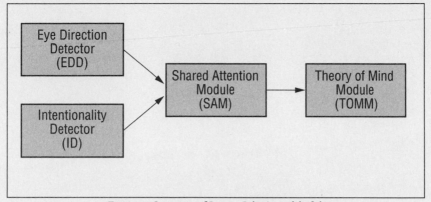

*Figure 1. Overview of Baron-Cohen's model of the
development of joint attention and theory of mind.*

current robot technology, and because they are significant improvements to the
behavioral repertoire of our humanoid robot (Scassellati 1998).

The simplest behavioral manifestation of Baron-Cohen's eye direction detector (EDD) is the recognition and maintenance of eye contact. Many animals have
been shown to be extremely sensitive to eyes that are directed at them, including
reptiles like the hognosed snake (Burghardt and Greene 1990), avians like the
chicken (Scaife 1976) and the plover (Ristau 1991), and all primates (Cheney
and Seyfarth 1990). Identifying whether or not something is looking at you
provides an obvious evolutionary advantage in escaping predators. In many
mammals, especially primates, the recognition that another is looking at you also carries social significance. In monkeys, eye contact is significant for maintaining a social dominance hierarchy (Cheney and Seyfarth 1990). In humans, the
reliance on eye contact as a social cue is even more striking. Infants have a
strong preference for looking at human faces and eyes, and maintain (and thus
recognize) eye contact within the first three months. Maintenance of eye contact
will be the first testable behavioral goal for the eye direction detector.

The simplest shared attention behavior is gaze following, the rapid alterna-
tion between looking at the eyes of the individual and looking at the distal object of their attention. As part of the shared attention module (SAM), gaze following utilizes information about eye direction and mutual gaze from the eye
direction detector (EDD) and extrapolates to external objects of focus. While
many animals are sensitive to eyes that are gazing directly at them, only primates
show the capability to extrapolate from the direction of gaze to a distal object,
and only the great apes will extrapolate to an object that is outside their immediate field of view (Povinelli and Preuss 1995). This evolutionary progression is
also mirrored in the ontogeny of social skills. At least by the age of three
months, human infants display maintenance (and thus recognition) of eye contact. However, it is not until nine months that children begin to exhibit gaze

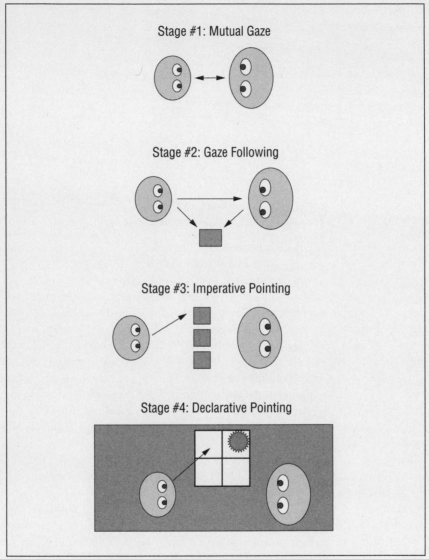

Figure 2. A four-part task-based decomposition of joint attention skills.

The capabilities for maintaining mutual gaze lead to the ability of gaze following. Imperative pointing skills, combined with gaze following, results in declarative pointing. For further information, see the text.

following, and not until eighteen months that children will follow gaze outside their field of view (Baron-Cohen 1995). Gaze following is an extremely useful imitative gesture, which serves to focus the child's attention on the same object that the caregiver is attending to. Even this simple mechanism of joint attention is believed to be critical for social scaffolding (Thelen and Smith 1994), development of theory of mind (Baron-Cohen 1995), and providing shared meaning for learning language (Wood, Bruner, and Ross 1976).

While gaze following and eye contact constitute one mechanism for joint attention, I believe that it will also be instructive to examine a second mechanism for establishing joint attention. I selected pointing as the second behavior. The development of pointing to direct attention is based upon much more complex sensory-motor control than eye gaze; pointing forces us to utilize the robot's arms and to recognize gesture cues. However, a pointing gesture can be used for purposes other than to direct attention. The same arm motion can also be utilized to reach for an object.

Developmental psychologists distinguish between imperative pointing, which is a gesture to obtain an object that is out of reach, and declarative pointing, which is a joint attention mechanism. Imperative pointing is first seen in human children at about nine months of age (Baron-Cohen 1995), and occurs in many monkeys (Cheney and Seyfarth 1990). However, there is nothing particular to the infant's behavior that is different from a simple reach—the infant is initially as likely to perform imperative pointing when the caregiver is attending to the infant as when the caregiver is looking in the other direction or when the caregiver is not present. The caregiver's interpretation of the infant's gesture provides the shared meaning. Over time, the infant learns when the gesture is appropriate. One can imagine the child learning this behavior through simple reinforcement. The reaching motion of the infant is interpreted by the adult as a request for a specific object, which the adult then acquires and provides to the child. The acquisition of the desired object serves as positive reinforcement for the contextual setting that preceded the reward (the reaching action in the presence of the attentive caregiver). Generation of this behavior is then a simple extension of a primitive reaching behavior.

Declarative pointing differs from imperative pointing in both form and function. Declarative pointing is characterized by an extended arm and index finger designed to draw attention to a distal object. Unlike imperative pointing, it is not necessarily a request for an object; children often use declarative pointing to draw attention to objects that are clearly outside their reach, such as the sun or an airplane passing overhead. Declarative pointing also only occurs under specific social conditions; children do not point unless there is someone to observe their action. From the perspective of Baron-Cohen's model, we can formulate declarative pointing as the application of SAM and ID to the motor abilities of imperative pointing combined with imitative learning. When the intentionality detector identifies motion that matches a pointing gesture, the shared attention module extrapolates to identify the distal target. The recognition of pointing gestures builds upon the competencies of gaze following; the infrastructure for extrapolation from a body cue is already present from gaze following, it need only be applied to a new domain. The generation of declarative pointing gestures builds upon the motor capabilities of imperative pointing; by imitating the successful pointing gestures of other individuals, the child can learn to make use of similar gestures.

The involvement of imitation as a learning mechanism is consistent with ontological and a phylogenetic evidence. From an ontological perspective, declarative pointing begins to emerge at approximately twelve months in human infants, which is also the same time that other complex imitative behaviors such as pretend play begin to emerge. From the phylogenetic perspective, declarative pointing has not been identified in any nonhuman primate (Premack 1988). This also corresponds to the phylogeny of imitation; no nonhuman primate has ever been documented to display complex imitative behavior under general conditions (Hauser 1996).

Evaluating the Robotic Implementation

A robotic implementation of a behavioral model provides a standardized evaluation mechanism. Behavioral observation and classification techniques that are used on children and adults can be applied to the behavior of our robot with only minimal modifications. Because of their use in the diagnosis and assessment of autism and related disorders, evaluation tools for joint attention mechanisms, such as the Vineland Adaptive Behavior Scales, the Autism Diagnostic Interview, and the Autism Diagnostic Observation Schedule, have been extensively studied (Sparrow et al. 1997, Powers 1997). With the evaluations obtained from these tools, the success of our implementation efforts can be tested using the same criteria that are applied to human behaviors. The behavior of the complete robotic implementation can be compared with developmental data from normal children. Furthermore, operating with only the EDD and ID modules should produce behavior that can be compared with developmental data from autistic children. With these evaluation techniques, we can determine the extent to which our model matches the observed biological data. However, what conclusions can we draw from the outcomes of these studies?

One possible outcome is that the robotic implementation will match the expected behavior evaluations, that is, the complete system will demonstrate normal uses of joint attention. In this case, our efforts have provided evidence that the model is internally consistent in producing the desired behaviors, but says nothing about the underlying biological processes. We can verify that the model provides a possible explanation for the normal (and abnormal) development of joint attention, but we cannot verify that this model accurately reflects what happens in biology.

If the robotic implementation does not meet the same behavioral criteria, the reasons for the failure are significant. The implementation may be unsuccessful because of an internal logical flaw in the model. In this case, we can identify shortcomings of the proposed model and potentially suggest alternate solutions.

A more difficult failure may result if our environmental conditions differ too significantly from normal human social interactions. While the work of Reeves and Nass (1996) leads us to believe that this result will not occur, this possibility allows us to draw conclusions only about our implementation and not the model or the underlying biological factors.

Building Social Skills

A robotic approach to studies of joint attention and social skill development has three main advantages. First, human observers readily anthropomorphize their social interactions with a humanlike robot. Second, the construction of a physically embodied system may be computationally simpler than the construction of a simulation of sufficient detail. Third, the skills that must be implemented to test these models are useful for a variety of other practical robotics tasks.

Interactions with a robotic agent are easily anthropomorphized by children and adults. An embodied system with human form allows for natural social interactions to occur without any additional training or prompting. Observers need not be trained in special procedures necessary to interact with the robot; the same behaviors that they use for interacting with other people allow them to interact naturally with the robot. In our experience, and in the empirical studies by Reeves and Nass (1996), people readily treat a robot as if it were another person. Human form also provides important task constraints on the behavior of the robot. For example, to observe an object carefully, our robot must orient its head and eyes toward a target. These task constraints allow observers to easily interpret the behavior of the robot.

A second reason for choosing a robotic implementation is that physical embodiment may actually simplify the computation necessary for this task. The direct physical coupling between action and perception reduces the need for an intermediary representation. For an embodied system, internal representations can be ultimately grounded in sensory-motor interactions with the world (Lakoff 1987); there is no need to model aspects of the environment that can simply be experienced (Brooks 1986, Brooks 1991). The effects of gravity, friction, and natural human interaction are obtained for free, without any computation. Embodied systems can also perform some complex tasks in relatively simple ways by exploiting the properties of the complete system. For example, when putting a jug of milk in the refrigerator, you can exploit the pendulum action of your arm to move the milk (Greene 1982). The swing of the jug does not need to be explicitly planned or controlled, since it is the natural behavior of the system. Instead of having to plan the whole motion, the system only has to modulate, guide, and correct the natural dynamics.

The social skills that must be implemented to test these models are also im-

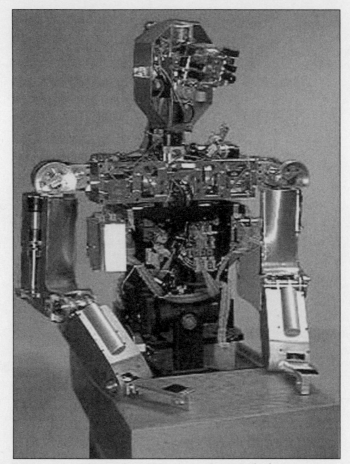

Figure 3. Cog, an upper-torso humanoid robot.

Cog has twenty-one degrees of freedom and a variety of sensory systems including visual, auditory, tactile, kinesthetic, and vestibular systems.

portant from an engineering perspective. A robotic system that can recognize and engage in joint attention behaviors will allow for human-machine interactions that have previously not been possible. The robot would be capable of learning from an observer using normal social signals in the same way that human infants learn; no specialized training of the observer would be necessary. The robot would also be capable of expressing its internal state (emotions, desires, goals, etc.) through social interactions without relying upon an artificial vocabulary. Further, a robot that can recognize the goals and desires of others will allow for systems that can more accurately react to the emotional, attentional, and cognitive states of the observer, can learn to anticipate the reactions of the observer, and can modify its own behavior accordingly.

Robotic Hardware

Our humanoid robot, called Cog, was designed to investigate a variety of scientific and engineering issues; constraints imposed by social interaction studies were balanced with constraints from other parallel investigations, as well as constraints from cost and availability of components (Brooks and Stein 1994, Brooks et al. 1998). To allow for natural social interactions, and to provide similar task constraints, our robot was built with humanlike sensory systems and motor abilities (see figure 3).

To approximate human motion, Cog has a total of twenty-one mechanical degrees of freedom. Cog's torso has six degrees of freedom: the waist bends side-to-side and front-to-back, the "spine" can twist, and the neck tilts side-to-side, nods front-to-back, and twists left-to-right. To approximate human eye motion, each eye can rotate about an independent vertical axis (pan) and a coupled horizontal axis (tilt). Each arm has six compliant degrees of freedom, each of which is powered by a series elastic actuator (Pratt and Williamson 1995), which provides a sensible "natural" behavior: if it is disturbed, or hits an obstacle, the arm simply deflects out of the way.

To obtain information about the environment, Cog has a variety of sensory systems including visual, vestibular, auditory, tactile, and kinesthetic senses. The visual system mimics some of the capabilities of the human visual system, including binocularity and space-variant sensing (Scassellati 1998a). To allow for both a wide field of view and high resolution vision, there are two cameras per eye, one that captures a wide-angle view of the periphery [$88.6° \times 115.8°$ field of view] and one that captures a narrow-angle view of the central (foveal) area [$18.4° \times 24.4°$ field of view] with the same resolution. Vestibular function is approximated with three rate gyroscopes and two inclinometers. The robot has two microphones for ears, and simple pinnae. We have also begun implementing a tactile system using arrays of resistive force sensors for the torso and hands. Kinesthetic information, including joint position from shaft encoders and potentiometers, temperature measurements from the motors and motor driver chips, and torque measurements from strain gauges on the arms, is also available on our robot.

Cog has a distributed, heterogeneous computational network. Similar to the decomposition in humans, specialized subsystems operate on specific aspects of the robot's behavior. Each joint has a dedicated on-board motor controller that performs low-level functions and simple reflexes, similar to the spinal cord. A network of industrial Pentium processors, a network of custom-built Motorola 68332 processor boards, and a digital signal processor network for auditory and visual processing combine to provide higher-level functionality.

Implementing Joint Attention

Even the simplest of joint attention behaviors require the coordination of a large number of perceptual, sensory-motor, attentional, and cognitive processes, including basic eye motor skills, face and eye detection, determination of eye direction, gesture recognition, attentional systems that allow for social behavior selection at appropriate moments, emotive responses, arm motor control, image stabilization, and many others. We have begun to construct many of these component pieces, and many results from this work have been published previously (Brooks et al. 1998, Scassellati 1998d, Scassellati 1998, Marjanovic, Scassellati, and Williamson 1996, Breazeal and Scassellati 1998, Breazeal 1998). In this section, we will review some of the capabilities of our robot that have direct bearing on implementing joint attention.

Implementing Maintenance of Eye Contact

Implementing the first stage in our developmental framework, recognizing and responding to eye contact, requires mostly perceptual abilities. We require at least that the robot be capable of finding faces, determining the location of the eye within the face, and determining if the eye is looking at the robot. The only necessary motor abilities are to maintain a fixation point.

Many computational methods of face detection on static images have been investigated by the machine vision community, for example Sung and Poggio (1994) and Rowley, Baluja, and Kanade (1995). However, these methods are computationally intensive, and current implementations do not operate in real time. However, a simpler strategy for finding faces can operate in real time and produce good results under dynamic conditions (Scassellati 1998). The strategy that we use is based on the ratio-template method of object detection reported by Sinha (1994). In summary, finding a face is accomplished with the following five steps:

1. Use a motion-based prefilter to identify potential face locations in the peripheral image.
2. Use a ratio-template based face detector to identify target faces.
3. Saccade to the target using a learned sensory-motor mapping.
4. Convert the location in the peripheral image to a foveal location using a learned mapping.
5. Extract the image of the eye from the foveal image.

A short summary of these steps appears below, and additional details can be found in Scassellati (1998).

To identify face locations, the peripheral image is converted to grayscale and passed through a prefilter stage (see figure 4). The prefilter allows us to search only locations that are likely to contain a face, greatly improving the speed of the detection step. The prefilter selects a location as a potential target if it has had

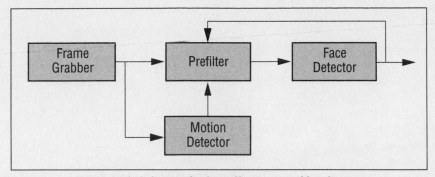

Figure 4. Block diagram for the prefiltering stage of face detection.

The prefilter selects target locations based upon motion information and past history. The prefilter allows face detection to occur at 20 Hz with little accuracy loss.

motion in the last 4 frames, was a detected face in the last 5 frames, or has not been evaluated in 3 seconds. A combination of the prefilter and some early-rejection optimizations allows us to detect faces at 20 Hz with little accuracy loss.

Face detection is done with a template-based method called "ratio templates" designed to recognize frontal views of faces under varying lighting conditions (Sinha 1996). A ratio template is composed of a number of regions and a number of relations, as shown in figure 5. Overlaying the template with a grayscale image location, each region is convolved with the grayscale image to give the average grayscale value for that region. Relations are comparisons between region values, such as "the left forehead is brighter than the left temple." In figure 5, each arrow indicates a relation, with the head of the arrow denoting the lesser value. The match metric is the number of satisfied relations; the more matches, the higher the probability of a face.

Once a face has been detected, two sensory-motor mappings must be used to extract the eye image (see figure 6). First, the face location is converted into a motor command to center the face in the peripheral image. To maintain portability and to ensure accuracy in the sensory-motor behaviors, we require that all of our sensory-motor behaviors be learned by on-line adaptive algorithms (Brooks et al. 1998). The mapping between image locations and the motor commands necessary to foveate that target is called a saccade map. This map is implemented as a 17×17 interpolated lookup table, which is trained by the following algorithm:

1. Initialize with a linear map obtained from self-calibration.
2. Randomly select a visual target.
3. Saccade using the current map.
4. Find the target in the post-saccade image using correlation.
5. Update the saccade map based on L_2 error.
6. Go to step 2.

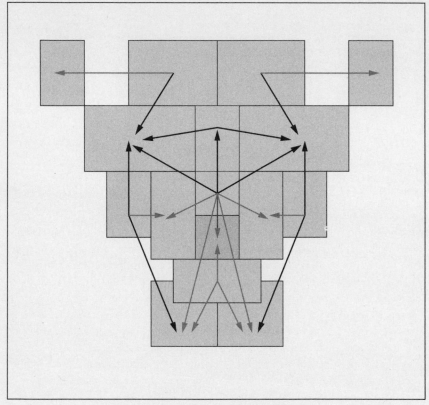

Figure 5. A ratio template for face detection.
The template is composed of 16 regions (the gray boxes) and 23 relations (shown by arrows).

The system converges to an average of less than one pixel of error per saccade after 2000 trials (1.5 hours). More information on this technique can be found in Marjanovic, Scassellati, and Williamson (1996).

Because humans are rarely motionless, after the active vision system has saccaded to the face, we first verify the location of the face in the peripheral image. The face and eye locations from the template in the peripheral camera are then mapped into foveal camera coordinates using a second learned mapping. The mapping from foveal to peripheral pixel locations can be seen as an attempt to find both the difference in scales between the images and the difference in pixel offset. In other words, we need to estimate four parameters: the row and column scale factor that we must apply to the foveal image to match the scale of the peripheral image, and the row and column offset that must be applied to the foveal image within the peripheral image. This mapping can be learned in two steps. First, the scale factors are estimated using active vision techniques: while

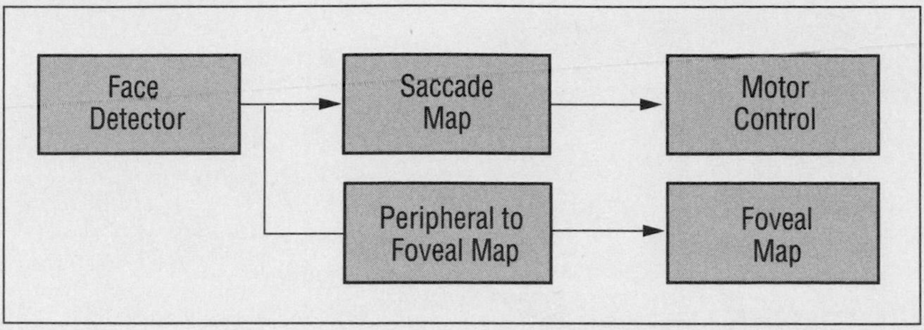

Figure 6. Block diagram for finding eyes and faces.

Once a target face has been located, the system must saccade to that location, verify that the face is still present, and then map the position of the eye from the face template onto a position in the foveal image.

moving the motor at a constant speed, we measure the optic flow of both cameras. The ratio of the flow rates is the ratio of the image sizes. Second, we use correlation to find the offsets. The foveal image is scaled down by the discovered scale factors, and then correlated with the peripheral image to find the best match location.

Once this mapping has been learned, whenever a face is foveated we can extract the image of the eye from the foveal image. This extracted image is then ready for further processing. The left image of figure 7a shows the result of the face detection routines on a typical grayscale image before the saccade. The right image of figure 7a shows the extracted subimage of the eye that was obtained after saccading to the target face. Additional examples of successful detections on a variety of faces can be seen in figure 7b. This method achieves good results in a dynamic real-world environment; in a total of one hundred and forty trials distributed between seven subjects, the system extracted a foveal image that contained an eye on one hundred thirty-one trials (ninety-four percent accuracy) (Scassellati 1998b).

In order to accurately recognize whether or not the caregiver is looking at the robot, we must take into account both the position of the eye within the head and the position of the head with respect to the body. Work on extracting the location of the pupil within the eye and the position of the head on the body has begun, but is still in progress.

Implementing Gaze Following

Once our system is capable of detecting eye contact, we require three additional subskills to achieve gaze following: extracting the angle of gaze, extrapolating the angle of gaze to a distal object, and motor routines for alternating between the distal object and the caregiver. Extracting angle of gaze is a generalization of detecting someone gazing at you, and requires the skills noted in the preceding

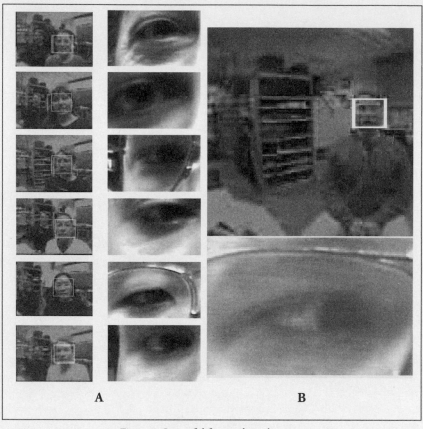

Figure 7. Successful face and eye detections.

A. The 128 × 128 grayscale image was captured by the active vision system, and then processed by the prefiltering and ratio template detection routines. One face was found within the peripheral image, shown at left. The right subimage was then extracted from the foveal image using a learned peripheral-to-foveal mapping.

B. The system locates faces in the peripheral camera, saccades to that position, and then extracts the eye image from the foveal camera. The position of the eye is inexact, in part because the human subjects are not motionless.

section. Extrapolation of the angle of gaze can be more difficult. By a geometric analysis of this task, we would need to determine not only the angle of gaze, but also the degree of vergence of the observer's eyes to find the distal object. However, the ontogeny of gaze following in human children demonstrates a simpler strategy.

Butterworth (1991) has shown that at approximately six months, infants will begin to follow a caregiver's gaze to the correct side of the body, that is, the child can distinguish between the caregiver looking to the left and the caregiver look-

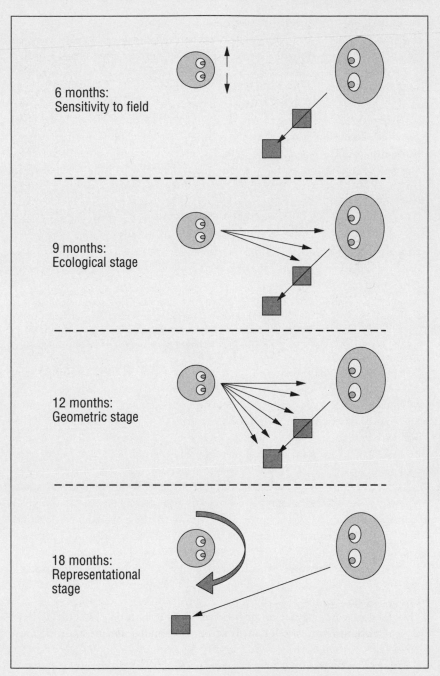

Figure 8. Proposed developmental progression of gaze following adapted from Butterworth (1991).

ing to the right (see figure 8). Over the next three months, their accuracy increases so that they can roughly determine the angle of gaze. At nine months, the child will track from the caregiver's eyes along the angle of gaze until a salient object is encountered. Even if the actual object of attention is further along the angle of gaze, the child is somehow "stuck" on the first object encountered along that path. Butterworth labels this the "ecological" mechanism of joint visual attention, since it is the nature of the environment itself that completes the action. It is not until twelve months that the child will reliably attend to the distal object regardless of its order in the scan path. This "geometric" stage indicates that the infant successfully can determine not only the angle of gaze but also the vergence. However, even at this stage, infants will only exhibit gaze following if the distal object is within their field of view. They will not turn to look behind them, even if the angle of gaze from the caregiver would warrant such an action. Around eighteen months, the infant begins to enter a "representational" stage in which it will follow gaze angles outside its own field of view, that is, it somehow represents the angle of gaze and the presence of objects outside its own view.

At six months, infants show sensitivity only to the side that the caregiver is gazing. At nine months, infants show a particular strategy of scanning along the line of gaze for salient objects. By one year, the child can recognize the vergence of the caregiver's eyes to localize the distal target, but will not orient if that object is outside the field of view until eighteen months of age.

Implementing this progression for a robotic system provides a simple means of bootstrapping behaviors. The capabilities used in detecting and maintaining eye contact can be extended to provide a rough angle of gaze. By tracking along this angle of gaze, and watching for objects that have salient color, intensity, or motion, our robot can mimic the ecological strategy. From an ecological mechanism, we can refine the algorithms for determining gaze and add mechanisms for determining vergence. A rough geometric strategy can then be implemented, and later refined through feedback from the caregiver. A representational strategy requires the ability to maintain information on salient objects that are outside of the field of view including information on their appearance, location, size, and salient properties. The implementation of this strategy requires us to make assumptions about the important properties of objects that must be included in a representational structure, a topic beyond the scope of this chapter.

Implementing Imperative Pointing

Implementing imperative pointing is accomplished by implementing the more generic task of reaching to a visual target. Children pass through a developmental progression of reaching skills (Diamond 1990). The first stage in this progression appears around the fifth month and is characterized by a very stereotyped reach that always initiates from a position close to the child's eyes and

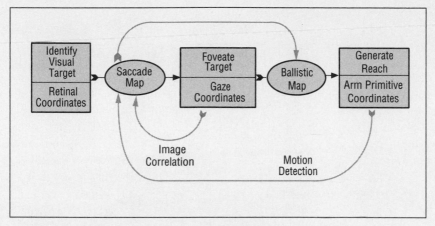

*Figure 9. Reaching to a visual target is the product of two subskills: foveating
a target and generating a ballistic reach from that eye position.*

Image correlation can be used to train a saccade map that transforms retinal coordinates into gaze
coordinates (eye positions). This saccade map can then be used in conjunction with motion detection to train a ballistic map that transforms gaze coordinates into a ballistic reach.

moves ballistically along an angle of gaze directly toward the target object.
Should the infant miss with the first attempt, the arm is withdrawn to the starting position and the attempt is repeated.

To achieve this stage of reaching on our robotic system, we have utilized the
foveation behavior to train the arm to reach (Marjanovic, Scassellati,
Williamson 1996). To reach to a visual target, the robot must learn the mapping
from retinal image coordinates $\mathbf{x} = (x, y)$ to the head-centered gaze coordinates
of the eye motors $\mathbf{e} = (pan, tilt)$ and then to the coordinates of the arm motors α
$= (\alpha_0 ... \alpha_5)$ (see figure 9). The saccade map $\mathbf{S}: \mathbf{x} \rightarrow \mathbf{e}$ relates positions in the
camera image with the motor commands necessary to foveate the eye at that lo-
cation. Our task then becomes to learn the ballistic movement mapping head-
centered coordinates $\mathbf{e}$ to arm-centered coordinates α. To simplify the dimen-
sionality problems involved in controlling a six degree-of-freedom arm, arm
positions are specified as a linear combination of basis posture primitives.

The ballistic mapping $\mathbf{B}: \mathbf{e} \rightarrow \alpha$ is constructed by an on-line learning algorithm that compares motor command signals with visual motion feedback clues
to localize the arm in visual space. Once the saccade map has been trained, we
can utilize that mapping to generate error signals for attempted reaches (see figure 10). By tracking the moving arm, we can obtain its final position in image
coordinates. The vector from the tip of the arm in the image to the center of the
image is the visual error signal, which can be converted into an error in gaze coordinates using the saccade mapping. The gaze coordinates can then be used to
train a forward and inverse model of the ballistic map using a distal supervised

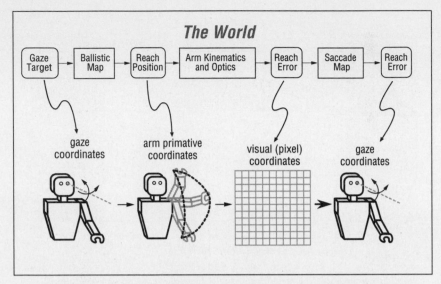

Figure 10. Generation of error signals from a single reaching trial.
Once a visual target is foveated, the gaze coordinates are transformed into a ballistic reach by the ballistic map. By observing the position of the moving hand, we can obtain a reaching error signal in image coordinates, which can be converted back into gaze coordinates using the saccade map.

learning technique (Jordan and Rumelhart 1992). A single learning trial proceeds as follows:

1. Locate a visual target.
2. Saccade to that target using the learned saccade map.
3. Convert the eye position to a ballistic reach using the ballistic map.
4. As the arm moves, use motion detection to locate the end of the arm.
5. Use the saccade map to convert the error signal from image coordinates into gaze positions, which can be used to train the ballistic map.
6. Withdraw the arm, and repeat.

This learning algorithm operates continually, in real time, and in an unstructured "real-world" environment without using explicit world coordinates or complex kinematics. This technique successfully trains a reaching behavior within approximately three hours of self-supervised training.

Implementing Declarative Pointing

The task of recognizing a declarative pointing gesture can be seen as the application of the geometric and representational mechanisms for gaze following to a new initial stimulus. Instead of extrapolating from the vector formed by the an-

Figure 11. Images captured from a videotape of the robot imitating head nods.

The upper two images show the robot imitating head nods from a human caregiver. The output of the face detector is used to drive fixed yes/no nodding responses in the robot. The face detector also picks out the face from stuffed animals, and will also mimic their actions.[1]

gle of gaze to achieve a distal object, we extrapolate the vector formed by the position of the arm with respect to the body. This requires a rudimentary gesture recognition system, but otherwise utilizes the same mechanisms.

We have proposed that producing declarative pointing gestures relies upon the imitation of declarative pointing in an appropriate social context. We have not yet begun to focus on the problems involved in recognizing these contexts, but we have begun to build systems capable of simple mimicry. By adding a tracking mechanism to the output of the face detector and then classifying these outputs, we have been able to have the system mimic yes/no head nods of the caregiver, that is, when the caregiver nods yes, the robot responds by nodding yes (see figure 11). The face detection module produces a stream of face locations at 20Hz. An attentional marker is attached to the most salient face stimulus, and the location of that marker is tracked from frame to frame. If the position of the marker changes drastically, or if no face is determined to be salient, then the tracking routine resets and waits for a new face to be acquired. Otherwise, the position of the attentional marker over time represents the motion of the face stimulus. The motion of the attentional marker for a fixed-duration window is classified into one of three static classes: a *yes* class, a *no* class, and a *no-motion* class. Two metrics are used to classify the motion, the cumulative sum of the displacements between frames (the relative displacement over the time window) and the cumulative sum of the absolute values of the displacements (the total distance traveled by the marker). If the horizontal total trip distance exceeds a threshold (indicating some motion), and if the horizontal cumulative displacement is below a threshold (indicating that the motion was back and forth around a mean), and if the horizontal total distance exceeds the vertical total distance, then we classify the motion as part of the *no* class. Otherwise, if the vertical cumulative total trip distance exceeds a threshold (indicating some motion), and if the vertical cumulative displacement is below a threshold (indicating that the motion was up and down around a mean), then we classify the motion as part of the *yes* class. All other motion types default to the *no-motion* class. These simple classes then drive fixed-action patterns for moving the head and eyes in a yes or no nodding motion. While this is a very simple form of imitation, it is highly selective. Merely producing horizontal or vertical movement is not sufficient for the head to mimic the action—the movement must come from a facelike object.

Future Work

The implementation of Baron-Cohen's model is still work in progress. All of the basic sensory-motor skills have been demonstrated. The robot can move its eyes in many humanlike ways, including saccades, vergence, tracking, and maintaining fixation through vestibulo-ocular and opto-kinetic reflexes. Orientation with the neck to maximize eye range has been implemented, as well as coordinated arm pointing. Perceptual components of EDD and SAM have also been constructed; the robot can detect and foveate faces to obtain high-resolution images of eyes.

These initial results are incomplete, but have provided encouraging evidence that the technical problems faced by an implementation of this nature are within our grasp. Cog's perceptual systems have been successful at finding faces and eyes in real-time, and in real-world environments. Simple social behaviors, such as eye-neck orientation and head-nod imitation, have been easy to interpret by human observers who have found their interactions with the robot to be both believable and entertaining.

Our future work will focus on the construction and implementation of the remainder of the EDD, ID, and SAM modules from Baron-Cohen's model. From an engineering perspective, this approach has already succeeded in providing adaptive solutions to classical problems in behavior integration, space-variant perception, and the integration of multiple sensory and motor modalities. From a scientific perspective, we are optimistic that when completed, this implementation will provide new insights and evaluation methods for models of social development.

Note

1. The original video clips are available at www.ai.mit.edu/projects/cog/.

Epilog

Barbara Webb and Thomas R. Consi

T he chapters collected in this book cover a highly diverse range of research endeavors—from insect neurobiology to human cognitive development and from mechanical design considerations to high-level learning algorithms. Nevertheless the participants in the AAAI symposium from which this book is derived felt a strong sense of common ground. This lay, not in the subject matter per se, but in the approach and methodology adopted to address these apparently diverse topics. "Biorobotics" was seen as the true intersection of biology and robotics: where one system addressed and answered questions in both fields. At the meeting we held extensive and productive discussions of key issues for this methodology. For example, how closely should the biology be represented in the robot model? What advantages accrue in building physical rather than simulation models and what technological problems get in the way? What evaluation methods are most appropriate? What systems look promising for application of the approach in the near future? What are the longer-term possibilities for scaling up? In this epilog we will attempt to summarize and synthesize some of the outcomes of these discussions. It should be stressed that all the authors in this book (and the other AAAI symposium participants) have contributed points to the discussion we present.

Copying Biology

While a great deal has been said over the last twenty years or so about the possible technological benefits of copying biology, what is common to the research reported here is that a serious attempt has been made to do so. Rather than simply being "inspired" by some vaguely understood notions of how animal systems work, these studies identify specific, well studied animal systems and attempt to build truly representative models of them. Much of this research involves direct collaboration between biologists and robotic engineers. A thorough knowledge of the relevant biological data is taken to be necessary, so that the risk of misinterpretation is minimized. Having said this, it is important to add that biorobotics does not simply consist in taking an example from biology and directly translating it in hardware and software. While the animal serves as a "default" point of reference in design decisions, it is rare for any biological system to be sufficiently well studied that all the answers needed to build the system are directly available. Indeed, for a number of the systems discussed here there are substantial gaps in the data. For example, almost nothing may be known about the neural underpinnings of a behavior, or measurements of sensory or motor capabilities may not available, or a number of hypothetical control mechanisms may be consistent with the data.

A problem always to be solved is how to go from the results of neuroethological research to specifications for robotic implementation. First it needs to be clear what are the current hypotheses in the field: both explicit and implicit. Are there already mathematical or computer models of the system, and if so what is the robot model intended to add? There are then a variety of different ways in which the implementation can be constrained: by behavioral evidence, by physiological evidence or neural plausibility of the mechanisms, by the information processing problem posed, by the environment, and by the physical limitations of sensory and motor capacities. Obviously it is useful if extensive information is available, but a complete story from the biology is not necessary before robot building can make a contribution. Indeed, building a robot can be extremely productive in determining critical areas needing further biological research.

The other major consideration is how to determine which aspects of the known biology should be included in the robot model. What details are crucial and what are irrelevant? One conclusion of the AAAI symposium was that no a priori judgment (e.g. that a low-level model of neural processes is always better; or that exact replication of a sensing device is needed before any conclusions about processing can be made) could be universally applied. It needs to be determined for each different example with reference to current understanding and current questions that the system can hope to answer. This may be easier to do when the system is intended as a means to test a very specific hypothesis, but more difficult when the system is a more open-ended project intended to achieve a biological level of competence in some task or tasks. This determination also applies to the correctness of the choice to build a physical model in the first place, which is linked to assumptions about the importance of the physical plant and the environment in understanding behavior, and the need to close the loop between sensing and action. Making a "realistic" model is not necessarily in the sense of highly accurate detail, but rather in the sense of addressing the essential aspects of the problem. Two kinds of (unavoidable) abstraction can be identified: in isolating the problem to be tackled, e.g. taking the animal behavior out of the context of survival and propagation of the species; and in making the mapping between the animal and the available technology to implement the model.

Certain biological systems might be particularly fruitful to explore with current technology. Criteria for identifying such systems include the following. The animal must be a good "model" system for a class of behavior. The phenomenon must have been well investigated in biology and be "ripe" for more rigorous modeling. There must be relatively clear evaluation criteria (measurement and experimental protocols) for the success of the model. Finally, the behavior must have some inherent fascination for the researcher to be willing to take the time to obtain nontrivial training in another field (biology or engineering). Our meeting came up with a number of suggestions for future work, i.e. biological systems that seem ready for a biorobotics approach (some of these have in fact already begun to be studied). Specific biological systems and phenomena include: escape behaviors, nematodes, electrolocation in fish, bird song, jumping-spider trajectory planning, magnetic sensing in birds and other animals, and construction behaviors such as bird nests and spider webs. More abstract phenomena for which biological examples can be found include: object invariance, extracting energy from the environment (e.g. an oil-spill eating robot), complex multimodal systems (e.g. body stabilization via optical and vestibular inputs), long distance navigation, the use of biological signal processing and control strategies to compensate for noisy sensors and sloppy actuators, error correction, self-repair, and reproduction.

Physical Implementations

The previous section encouraged robotics researchers to embrace details of biology; this section encourages biological researchers to embrace the nitty-gritty of building real robotic systems rather than limiting themselves to computational, mathematical or box-and-arrow models. Not that "biorobotics" is always or only the correct approach for model building—other methods are sometimes more appropriate. Rather, biorobotics is particularly useful in situations when it is suspected that the complexity of the stimulus is important and simulations cannot adequately represent that complexity. It is also useful where it is desired to critically address perceptual problems in context of actions, or motor problems in context of the plant. Counter to what seems expected by some biologists, robots can be very useful even where we have a rather limited notion of how the animal performs the behavior of interest. In these situations biorobotics is a rapid, yet stringent, way of evaluating many alternative hypotheses. It is especially useful for eliminating ideas that are physically unreasonable, e.g. the animal cannot use a particular algorithm without certain data that is, in fact, unobtainable given its sensing limitations or the environmental constraints.

Why go to the trouble of building real robotic systems to test biological or cognitive hypotheses? What emerges again and again in the literature is that the physical implementations raised critical, central issues that had not been previously anticipated or addressed. To make a robotic system work you really have to solve the full problem, which may be more difficult than realized (e.g. underwater odor plume tracking, chapter 2). On the other hand, it may be discovered that certain problems can be solved more simply than expected by novel, often noncomputational, solutions that exploit the physical constraints (e.g. the cricket ear, chapter 1).

However, one should bear in mind that physical implementations are strongly constrained by current technology and that these constraints, though sometimes similar to those faced by animals, are by no means guaranteed to be so. Limitations in technology are a major issue in biorobotics. Compared to their biological counterparts, sensors are typically more bulky and more limited in dynamic range. Linear actuators of the size and form factor of real muscles are simply not available. Robots have almost no ability to extract energy from their surroundings, as animals do, and thus have operational times that are constrained by the amount of energy they can carry. Finally there is the ever-present reliability problem, which grows rapidly with the complexity (i.e. number of components, size of the software) of the robot. Limits in microprocessors are mostly in their interfaces to sensors and actuators and not in their computational abilities. Our wish-list of new technology for biorobotics includes: muscle-like actuators (motor, housing, transmission, power and sensing in one cheap package), tough, compliant, and conformable materials for skin and joint coverings, sensor arrays that can be easily embedded in a biorobot's skin, improved chemical sensors, better power sources (from biology-derived ideas for low-power consumption and energy conserving strategies), and parallel processor architectures tailored for easy implementation of neural-like computational strategies.

Experimental Approach

The preceding considerations—both engineering and biological justifications for the biorobotics approach— feed into the third major issue: evaluation. In strict robotics terms this is an important consideration not always sufficiently attended to, that is, the necessity to evaluate how well the robot can perform a task. This becomes increasingly important when claims are made regarding the advantages of adopting biologically based approaches. For example, biological sensing strategies are often claimed to be more robust but how can this be demonstrated? This is equally important with regard to the biological understanding that can be derived from a robot experiment. Given that technology constrains a model's accuracy, it is important to consider how this affects the experimental data and the conclusions drawn from that data. It can be hard to pinpoint the cause of a failure to replicate a desired behavior: is it a weakness in the theory itself, or in the physical match between the animal and the robot, or simply a failure of the robot builders to be clever enough in their implementation? On the other hand, success might be due to nonbiological features of the model.

The high biological fidelity of biorobots confers the advantage that the experimental methods developed by biologists can be directly applied to biorobotic experiments. Indeed, a good practical yardstick of biological adequacy is whether or not the biorobot can be put in the same experimental apparatus as used for the animal. The use of the same experimental methods permits a rigorous test of biological relevance in that it enables verifiable predictions to be made on the behavior of the animal under study. Another advantage of the biorobotic approach is the ability to perform experiments that explore the performance of the model in situations beyond its original design space. This feature is most important to evaluating the utility of the biological idea in nonbiological applications.

To summarize—the biorobotic method should be carried out in the same stages as other forms of modeling. First is the identification of the target phenomenon and the specific question that is to be resolved. Next is the development of a mapping between the biological and robotic systems using appropriate representations that include physical as well as symbolic analogs. Having built the model, it is tested in the appropriate ways, often through the use of the same experimental apparatus as that used for parallel biological studies. The results of the experiments are then analyzed and biological predictions are made for further biological and robotic explorations. The key to this methodology is the continuous back and forth between the biological and robotic systems during both the developmental and the experimental stages of the investigation. Note that the robot is not an endpoint in the study: a well-evaluated hypothesis is the goal. It is a mistake to consider the robot as finished product in the sense of, for example, an automobile. Rather, a good biorobot is a dynamic breadboard for testing biological ideas, devices and software are added and subtracted as dictated by the needs of the experiments.

The Challenge of Multidisciplinary Research

Several practical issues were raised by the participants with regard to the problems inherent in working in a novel interdisciplinary field. First is the communication difficulties often experienced between collaborating biologists and engineers. Both fields have their own particular language, point of view, and priorities, and a willingness to understand and appreciate these divergences is important. Second, effort should be devoted to clearly establishing the nature of the collaboration (research priorities, publication authorship, etc.) to ensure that no member of the team feels left out or exploited. Third is the challenge of training students. To work with this methodology, biology students will need to get some engineering training; and engineering students will need a reasonable grounding in biology; neither typically occurs in current standard degree programs. Encouragingly, there do seem to be more "cross-over" programs being introduced.

Funding of biorobotics is currently easier to achieve from engineering resources, which can sometimes undermine the biological relevance with the focus being placed on immediate technological results. A more long-term view—that really understanding how biological systems work, rather than just superficially taking inspiration from them, will have multiple payoffs—needs to be brought to the attention of funding bodies. Finally, we considered avenues of publication for biorobotics research. There is especially a need to go beyond the specialist forums, such as the AAAI symposium, and present biorobotics research to the larger biological and engineering communities. Thus we considered it inappropriate to attempt to establish a journal or conference series, which would only isolate this area from the main streams from which it draws its strength and justification. On the other hand it would be useful to have a forum for communication by which the relevant research that currently appears in highly diverse places can be brought to attention of workers in the field. Internet-based resources seem the most appropriate mechanism for this kind of interdisciplinary networking. A website and mailing list resulting from the AAAI symposium can be found at: http://www.ai.mit.edu/~scaz/biorobotics/

Scaling the Achievements

So far biorobotics has been most successful in the study of single sensorimotor systems or "isolated" motor control, particularly in invertebrates. Can biorobotics scale up to explore more complex systems? The chapters in this book suggest that this is possible. First, there are several obvious ways in which existing systems might be combined (e.g. taxis and walking) and such collaborative efforts were one outcome of the meeting. Second, implicit even in some of the invertebrate systems discussed was the issue of limits of simple "reactivity" and need for more complex notions of behavioral control. Third, is the explicit idea that sensory and motor complexity in robots are needed as driving forces to make us face the real problems solved by animal systems (chapter 6). Finally, the last two chapters in this book have provided examples of the successful application of biorobotics to research where the aim is to investigate mammalian and human systems. Our general feeling was one of confidence that, in synergy with developments in biology and robot technology, the methodology of biorobotics will have a significant role in future research in exploring and understanding a wide range of animal behaviors.

Bibliography

Alexander, R. M. 1988. *Elastic Mechanisms in Animal Movement.* Cambridge, U.K.: Cambridge University Press.

Almàssy, N., and Sporns, O. 1998. Role of Behavior in the Development of Complex Neuronal Properties. In *From Animals to Animats 5: Proceedings of the Fifth International Conference on Simulation of Adaptive Behavior* eds. R. Pfeifer, B. Blumberg, J. A. Meyer, and S. W. Wilson, 311–320. Cambridge, Mass.: The MIT Press.

Almàssy, N.; Edelman, G. M.; and Sporns, O. 1998. Behavioral Constraints in the Development of Neuronal Properties: A Cortical Model Embedded in a Real-World Device. *Cerebral Cortex* 8(4): 346–361.

Anderson, M. A. 1977. A Model for Landmark Learning in the Honey-Bee. *Journal of Comparative Physiology.* A 114: 335–355.

American Psychological Association. 1994. *Diagnostic and Statistical Manual of Mental Disorders.* Washington D.C.: American Psychiatric Association (APA).

Arbib, M. 1972. *The Metaphorical Brain.* New York: Wiley.

Arbib, M., and Liaw, J. 1995. Sensorimotor Transformations in the Worlds of Frogs and Robots. *Artificial Intelligence* 72(1–2): 53–79.

Arkin, R. 1987. Motor Schema–Based Mobile Robot Navigation. In Proceedings of the IEEE International Conference on Robotics and Automation. Washington, D.C.: IEEE Computer Society.

Ashby, W. R. 1952. *Design for a Brain.* London: Chapman and Hall.

Ayers, J.; Zavracky, P.; Mcgruer, N.; Massa, D.; Vorus, V.; Mukherjee, R.; and Currie, S. 1998. A Modular Behavioral-Based Architecture for Biomimetic Autonomous Underwater Robots. Paper presented at the Autonomous Vehicles in Mine Countermeasures Symposium. December. Naval Postgraduate School, Monterey, Calif.

Bachmann, R. J.; Nelson, G. M.; Flannigan, W. C.; Quinn, R. D.; Watson, J. T.; and Ritzmann, R. E. 1997. Construction of a Cockroach-Like Hexapod Robot. Paper presented at the Eleventh VPI&SU Symposium on Structural Dynamics and Control, Blacksburg, Virginia, May 12–14.

Baird, R. C.; Johari, H.; and Jumper, G. 1996. Numerical Simulation of Environmental Modulation of Chemical Signal Structure and Odor Dispersal in the Open Ocean. *Chemical Senses*. 21(2): 121–134.

Barbin, G. 1998. The Role of Olfaction in Homing and Estuarine Migratory Behavior of Yellow-Phase American Eels. *Canadian Journal of Fisheries and Aquatic Sciences* 55(3): 564–575.

Baron-Cohen, S. 1995. *Mindblindness*. Cambridge, Mass.: The MIT Press.

Bartlett, S. L.; Hampapur, A.; Huber, M. J.; Kortenkamp, D.; and Moezzi, S. 1995. Vision for Mobile Robots. In *Advances in Image Processing and Machine Vision,* ed. J. Sanz, 1–117. New York: Springer-Verlag.

Basil, J. 1994. Lobster Orientation in Turbulent Odor Plumes: Simultaneous Measurement of Tracking Behavior and Temporal Odor Patterns. *Biological Bulletin* 187(2): 272–273.

Beckers, R.; Holland, O. E.; and Deneubourg, J. L. 1996. From Local Actions to Global Tasks: Stigmergy and Collective Robotics. In *Artificial Life IV, Proceedings of the Fourth International Workshop on the Synthesis and Simulation of Living Systems,* 181–189, ed. R. Brooks and P. Maes. Cambridge, Mass.: The MIT Press.

Beer, R. D. 1996. Toward the Evolution of Dynamical Neural Networks for Minimally Cognitive Behavior. In *From Animals to Animats 4: Proceedings of the Fourth International Conference on Simulation of Adaptive Behavior* eds. P. Maes, M. J. Mataric, J.-A. Meyer, J. Pollack, and S. W. Wilson, 421–429. Cambridge Mass.: The MIT Press.

Beer, R. D.; Ritzmann, R. E.; and McKenna, T., eds. 1993. *Biological Neural Networks in Invertebrate Neuroethology and Robotics*. San Diego, Calif.: Academic Press.

Beer, R. D.; Quinn, R. D.; Chiel, H. J.; and Ritzmann, R. E. 1997. Biologically Inspired Approaches to Robotics. *Communications of the ACM* 40(3): 30–38.

Beglane, P. F.; Grasso, F. W.; Basil, J. A.; and Atema, J. 1997. Far Field Chemo-Orientation in the American Lobster, Homarus Americanus: Effects of Unilateral Ablation and Lesioning of the Lateral Antennule. *Biological Bulletin* 193(2): 214–215.

Bekey, G. A. 1996. Biologically Inspired Control of Autonomous Robots. *Robotics and Autonomous Systems* 18(1–2): 21–31.

Belanger, J. H., and Willis, M. A. 1996. Adaptive Control of Odor-Guided Locomotion: Behavioral Flexibility as an Antidote to Environmental Unpredictability. *Adaptive Behavior* 4(3–4): 217–253.

Berg, H. C., and Purcell, E. M. 1977. The Physics of Chemoreception. *Biophysical Journal* 20(2): 193–219.

Berkemeier, M., and Desai, K. 1996. Design of a Robot Leg with Elastic Energy Storage, Comparison to Biology, and Preliminary Experimental Results. In Proceedings of the IEEE International Conference on Robotics and Automation, Volume 1, 213–218. Washington, D.C.: IEEE Computer Society.

Bertenthal, B. I. 1996. Origins and Early Development of Perception, Action, and Representation. In *Annual Reviews in Neuroscience* 47: 431–459. Palo Alto, Calif.: Annual Reviews.

Bienenstock, E. L.; Cooper, L. N.; and Munro, P. 1982. Theory for the Development of Neuron Selectivity: Orientation Selectivity and Binocular Interaction in Visual Cortex. *Journal of Neuroscience* 2(1): 23–48.

Biewener, A., and Full, R. J. 1992. Force Platform and Kinematic Snalysis. *Biomechanics: Structures and Systems, A Practical Approach*, 45–73. Oxford, U.K.: Oxford University Press.

Binnard, M. B. 1995. Design of a Small Pneumatic Walking Robot. Master's thesis, Dept. of Mechanical Engineering, Massachusetts Institute of Technology, Cambridge, Mass. (ftp://ftp.ai.mit.edu/pub/users/binn/SMthesis.zip).

Blanchard, M.; Verschure, P. F. M. J.; and Rind, F. C. 1999. Using a Mobile Robot to Study Locust Collision-Avoidance Responses. *International Journal of Neural Systems* 9(5): 405–410.

Bohm, H., and Schildberger, K. 1992. Brain Neurons Involved in the Control of Walking in the Cricket Gryllus Bimaculatus. *Journal of Experimental Biology* 166(1): 113–130.

Braitenberg, V. 1984. *Vehicles: Experiments in Synthetic Psychology*. Cambridge, Mass.: The MIT Press.

Breazeal, C. 1998. A Motivational System for Regulating Human-Robot Interaction. In Proceedings of the Fifteenth National Conference on Artificial Intelligence (AAAI-98), 54–61. Menlo Park, Calif.: American Association for Artificial Intelligence.

Breazeal, C., and Scassellati, B. 2000. Infant-Like Social Interactions between a Robot and a Human Caretaker. *Adaptive Behavior* 8(1): 49–74.

Breeder, C. M. 1926. The Locomotion of Fishes. *Zoologica* 4(5):159–297.

Brooks, R. A. 1986a. A Robust Layered Control System for a Mobile Robot. *IEEE Journal of Robotics and Automation* RA-2:14–23.

Brooks, R. A. 1986b. Achieving Artificial Intelligence through Building Robots. AI Memo, 1439, Artificial Intelligence Laboratory, Massachusetts Institute of Technology, Cambridge, Mass.

Brooks, R. A. 1991a. Intelligence without Reason. In Proceedings of the Thirteenth International Joint Conference on Artificial Intelligence, 569–595. San Francisco: Morgan Kaufmann.

Brooks, R. A. 1991b. Intelligence without Representation. *Artificial Intelligence Journal* 47(1–3): 139–160.

Brooks, R. A., and Stein, L. A. 1993. Building Brains for Bodies. AI Memo, 1439, Artificial Intelligence Laboratory, Massachusetts Institute of Technology, Cambridge, Mass.

Brooks, R. A., and Stein, L. A. 1994. Building Brains for Bodies. *Autonomous Robots* 1(1): 7–25.

Brooks, R. A.; Breazeal, C.; Irie, R.; Kemp, C. C.; Marjanovic, M.; Scassellati, B.; and Williamson, M. M. 1998. Alternative Essences of Intelligence. In Proceedings of the Fifteenth National Conference on Artificial Intelligence (AAAI-98), 961–968. Menlo Park, Calif.: American Association for Artificial Intelligence.

Brüwer, M., and Cruse, H. 1990. A Network Model for the Control of the Movement of a Redundant Manipulator. *Biological Cybernetics* 62(6): 549–555.

Buchner, E. 1984. Behavioral Analysis of Spatial Vision in Insects. *NATO ASI Series* A(74), 561–621. New York: Plenum.

Burgess, N.; Donnett, J. G.; Jeffery, K. J.; and O'Keefe, J. 1997. Robotic and Neuronal Simulation of the Hippocampus and Rat Navigation. *Philosophical Transactions of the Royal Society B*352: 1535–1543.

Burghardt, G. M., and Greene, H. W. 1990. Predator Simulation and Duration of Death Feigning in Neonate Hognose Snakes. *Animal Behavior* 36(6): 1842–1843.

Butterworth, G. 1991. The Ontogeny and Phylogeny of Joint Visual Attention. In *Natural Theories of Mind*, 223–232, ed. A. Whiten. Oxford, U.K.: Blackwell.

Callaway, E. M., and Katz, L. C. 1990. Emergence and Refinement of Clustered Horizontal Connections in Cat Striate Cortex. *Journal of Neuroscience* 10(4): 1134–1153.

Calvin, W. H. 1996. *How Brains Think*. New York: Basic Books.

Cartwright, B. A., and Collett, T. S. 1983. Landmark Learning in Bees. *Journal of Comparative Physiology* A151: 521–543.

Cartwright, B. A., and Collett, T. S. 1987. Landmark Maps for Honeybees. *Biological Cybernetics* 57(1–2): 85–93.

Cassinis, R.; Grana, D.; and Rizzi, A. 1996. Using Color Information in an Omnidirectional Perception System for Autonomous Robot Localization. In Proceedings of EUROBOT'96, 172–176. Washington, D.C.: IEEE Computer Society.

Chang, C., and Gaudiano, P., eds. 2000. Biomimetic Robotics. *Robotics and Autonomous Systems* 30(1–2): 1-2.

Chang, C., and Gaudiano, P. 1998. Application of Biological Learning Theories to Mobile Robot Avoidance and Approach Behaviors. *Journal of Complex Systems* 1(1): 79–114.

Chapman, T., and Webb, B. 1999. A Neuromorphic Hair Sensor Model of Wind-Mediated Escape in the Cricket. *International Journal of Neural Systems* 9(5): 397–403.

Chapuis, A., and Droz, E. 1958. *Automata*. Neuchatel, Switzerland: Editions du Griffon.

Cheng, K.; Collett, T. S.; Pickhard, A.; and Wehner, R. 1987. The Use of Visual Landmarks by Honeybees: Bees Weight Landmarks according to Their Distance from the Goal. *Journal of Comparative Physiology* A161: 469–475.

Cheney, D. L., and Seyfarth, R. M. 1990. *How Monkeys See the World*. Chicago: University of Chicago Press.

Chiel, H. J., and Beer, R. D. 1997. The Brain Has a Body: Adaptive Behavior Emerges from Interactions of Nervous System, Body, and Environment. *Trends in Neurosciences* 20(12): 553–557.

Clark, A. 1997. *Being There. Putting Brain, Body, and World Together Again*. Cambridge, Mass.: The MIT Press.

Clark, J. J. 1998. Spatial Attention and Saccadic Camera Motion. In Proceedings of the IEEE International Conference on Robotics and Automation, 3247–252. Washington, D.C.: IEEE Computer Society.

Cohen, D. J., and Volkmar, F. R., eds. 1997. *Handbook of Autism and Pervasive Developmental Disorders*. 2d ed. New York: Wiley.

Collett, T. S. 1980. Angular Tracking and the Optomotor Response: An Analysis of Visual Reflex Interaction in a Hoverfly. *Journal of Comparative Physiology* 140(2): 145–158.

Collewijn, H. 1972. An Analog Model of the Rabbit's Optokinetic System. *Brain Research* 36:71–88.

Consi, T. R.; Grasso, F; Mountain, D.; and Atema, J. 1995. Explorations of Turbulent Odor Plumes with an Autonomous Underwater Robot. *Biological Bulletin* 189(2): 231–232.

Consi, T. R.; Atema, J.; Goudey, C. A.; Cho, J; and Chryssostomidis, C. 1994. AUV Guidance with Chemical Signals. In Proceedings of the IEEE Symposium on Autonomous Underwater Vehicle Technology, 450–455. Washington, D.C.: IEEE Computer Society.

Corke, P. I. 1996. Dynamic Issues in Robot Visual-Servo Systems. In *Robotics Research*, eds. G. Giralt and G. Hirzinger, 488–498. Berlin: Springer-Verlag.

Cox, C.; Hunt, J. A.; Lyons, W. G.; and Davis, G. E. 1997. Nocturnal Foraging of the Caribbean Spiny Lobster (Panurlis Argus) on Offshore Reefs of Florida, USA. *Marine Freshwater Resources* 48: 671–679.

Cruse, H. 1990. What Mechanisms Coordinate Leg Movement in Walking Arthropods? *Trends in Neurosciences* 13(1): 15–21.

Cruse, H. 1999. Feeling Our Body—The Basis of Cognition? *Evolution and Cognition* 5(2): 162–173.

Cruse, H.; Bartling, C. H.; Brunn, D. E.; Dean, J.; Dreifert, M.; Kindermann, T.; and Schmitz, J. 1995. Walking: A Complex Behavior Controlled by Simple Systems. *Adaptive Behavior* 3(4): 385–418.

Cruse, H.; Kindermann, T.; Schumm, M.; Dean, J.; and Schmitz, J. 1998. Walknet—A Biologically Inspired Network to Control Six-Legged Walking. *Neural Networks* 11(7–8): 1435–1447.

Cruse, H.; Steinkühler, U.; Burkamp, C. 1998. MMC—A Recurrent Neural Network Which Can Be Used as Manipulable Body Model. In *From Animals to Animats 5: Proceedings of the Fifth International Conference on Simulation of Adaptive Behavior*, eds. R. Pfeifer, B. Blumberg, J. A. Meyer, and S. W. Wilson, 381–389. Cambridge, Mass.: The MIT Press.

Dale, J. 1997. Chemosensory Search Behavior in the Starfish Asterias Forbesii. *Biological Bulletin* 193(2): 210–212.

Dario, P.; Sandini, G.; and Aebischer, P. 1993. Robots and Biological Systems: Toward a New Bionics? *NATO ASI Series F, Volume 102*. Berlin: Springer-Verlag.

Delcomyn, F. 1971. The Locomotion of the Cockroach Periplaneta Americana. *Journal of Experimental. Biology* 54(2): 443–452.

Delcomyn, F. 1985. Walking and Running. In *Comprehensive Insect Physiology, Biochemistry, and Pharmacology: Nervous System: Structure and Motor Function*, 439–466. Oxford, U.K.: Pergamon.

Delcomyn, F., and Nelson, M. E. 2000. Architectures for a Biomimetic Hexapod Robot. *Robotics and Autonomous Systems* 30(1–2): 5–15.

Dennett, D. C. 1991. *Consciousness Explained*. New York: Little, Brown.

Dennett, D. C. 1998. *Brainchildren: Essays on Designing Minds*. Cambridge, Mass.: The MIT Press.

Desimone, R.; Albright, T. D.; Gross, C. G.; and Bruce, C. 1984. Stimulus-Selective Properties of Inferior Temporal Neurons in the Macaque. *Journal of Neuroscience* 4(8): 2051–2062.

De Solla Price, D. J. 1964. Automata in History: Automata and the Origins of Mechanism and Mechanistic Philosophy. *Technology and Culture* 5(1): 9–23.

Devine, D. V., and Atema, J. 1982. Function of Chemoreceptor Organs in Spatial Orientation of the Lobster, Homarus Americanus: Differences and Overlap. *Biological Bulletin* 163(2): 144–153.

de Vauconson, J. [1738] 1979. Le Mecanisme du Fluteur Automate. Reprint, translation by J. T. Desaguliers. Uitgeverij Frits Kauf.

Diamond, A. 1990. Developmental Time Course in Human Infants and Infant Monkeys, and the Neural Bases of Inhibitory Control in Reaching. In *The Development and*

Neural Bases of Higher Cognitive Functions, Volume 608, 637–676. New York: New York Academy of Sciences.

Dickinson, M. H.; Lehmann, F. O.; and Sane, S. P. 1999. Wing Rotation and the Aerodynamic Basis of Insect Flight. *Science* 284(5422): 1954–1960.

Dittmer, K.; Grasso, F. W.; and Atema, J. 1995. Effects of Varying Plume Turbulence on Temporal Concentration Signals Available to Orienting Lobsters. *Biological Bulletin* 189(2): 232–233.

Dittmer, K.; Grasso, F W..; and Atema, J. 1996. Obstacles to Flow Produce Distinctive Patterns of Odor Dispersal on a Scale That Could Be Detected by Marine Animals. *Biological Bulletin* 191(2): 313–314.

Dodson, J. J., and Dohse, L. A. 1984. A Model of Olfactory-Mediated Conditioning of Directional Bias in Fish Migrating in Reversing Tidal Currents Based on the Homing Migration of American Shad (Alosa Sapidissima). In *Mechanisms of Migration in Fishes*, eds. J. D. McCleave; G. P. Arnold; J. J. Dodson; and W. H. Neill, 263–281. New York: Plenum Press.

Doherty, J. A. 1985. Trade-Off Phenomena in Calling Song Recognition and Phonotaxis in the Cricket. *Journal of Comparative Physiology A*156: 787–801.

Dunsenberry, D. 1992. Guiding. In *Sensory Ecology*, 413–436. New York: Freeman.

Edelman, G. M. 1987. *Neural Darwinism*. New York: Basic Books.

Edelman, G. M.; Reeke, G. N.; Gall, W. E.; Tononi, G.; Williams, D.; and Sporns, O. 1992. Synthetic Neural Modeling Applied to a Real-World Artifact. *Proceedings of the National Academy of Sciences* 89(15): 7267–7271.

Edwards, D. H.; Heitler, W. J.; and Krasne, F. B. 1999. Fifty Years of a Command Neuron: The Neurobiology of Escape Behavior in Crayfish. *Trends in Neurosciences* 22(4): 153–161.

Elsner, N. 1994. The Search for the Neural Centers of Cricket and Grasshopper Song. In *Neural Basis of Behavioral Adaptations*, eds. K. Schildberger and N. Elsner, 167–193. Stuttgart, Germany: G. Fischer

Epstein, W. 1977. *Stability and Constancy in Visual Perception*. London: Wiley.

Erkman, I.; Erkman, A. M.; Takkaya, A. E.; and Pasinlioglu, T. 1999. Haptic Perception of Shape and Hollowness of Deformable Objects Using the Anthrobot-III Robot Hand. *Journal of Robotic Systems* 16(1): 9–24.

Espenschied, K. S.; Quinn, R. D.; Beer, R.; and Chiel, H. J. 1996. Biologically Based Distributed Control and Local Reflexes Improve Rough Terrain Locomotion in a Hexapod Robot. *Robotics and Autonomous Systems* 18(1–2): 59–64.

Espenschied, K. S.; Quinn, R. D.; Chiel, H. J.; and Beer, R. D., 1995. Biologically Inspired Hexapod Robot Project: Robot II. In Video Proceedings of the IEEE International Conference on Robotics and Automation (ICRA'95). Washington, D.C.: IEEE Computer Society.

Fearing, R. S.; Chiang, K. H.; Dickinson, M.; Pick, D. L.; Sitti, M.; and Yan, J. 2000. Wing Transmission for a Micromechanical Flying Insect. In Proceedings of the IEEE International Conference on Robotics and Automation, 1509–1516. Washington, D.C.: IEEE Computer Society.

Ferrell, C. 1995. Comparison of Three Insect-Inspired Locomotion Controllers. *Robotics and Autonomous Systems* 16(2–4): 135–159.

Finelli, C. M.; Pentcheff, N. D.; Zimmer-Faust, R. K.; and Wethey, D. S. 1999. Odor Transport in Turbulent Flows: Constraints on Animal Navigation. *Limnology and Oceanography* 44(4): 1056–1071.

Flynn, A. M., and Brooks, R. A. 1989. Battling Reality. AI Memo, 1148, Artificial Intelligence Laboratory, Massachusetts Institute of Technology, Cambridge, Mass.

Földiàk, P. 1991. Learning Invariance from Transformation Sequences. *Neural Computation* 3(2): 194–200.

Fraenkel, G. S., and Gunn, D. L. 1961. *The Orientation of Animals: Kineses, Taxes, and Compass Reactions.* New York: Dover.

Franceschini, N., and Chagneux, R. 1997. Repetitive Scanning in the Fly Compound Eye. In Proceedings of the Göttingen Neurobiology Conference, eds. H. Wassle and N. Elsner. Stuttgart: Thierne.

Franceschini, N.; Blanes, C; and Oufar, L. 1986. Appareil de mesure passif et sans contact de la vitesse d'un objet quelconque. (Passive, Noncontact Measuring Device for Assessing the Speed of an Object, Technical Patent) *Dossier Technique ANVAR/DVAR N° 51 549*, Paris.

Franceschini, N.; Pichon, J. M.; and Blanes, C. 1992. From Insect Vision to Robot Vision. *Philosophical Transactions of the Royal Society B*337: 283–294.

Franceschini, N.; Riehle, A.; and Le Nestour, A. 1989. Directionally Selective Motion Detection by Insect Neurons. In *Facets of Vision,* eds. D. G. Stavenga and R. C. Hardie, 360–390. Berlin: Springer-Verlag.

Franklin, G. F.; Powell, J. D.; and Emami-Naeini, A. 1994. *Feedback Control of Dynamic Systems,* Reading, Mass.: Addison Wesley.

Franz, M. O., and Mallot, H. A. 2000. Biomimetic Robot Navigation. *Robotics and Autonomous Systems* 30(1–2): 133–153.

Franz, M. O.; Schölkopf, B.; Mallot, H. A.; and Bülthoff, H. H. 1998a. Learning View Graphs for Robot Navigation. *Autonomous Robots* 5(1): 111–125.

Franz, M. O.; Schölkopf, B.; Mallot, H. A.; and Bülthoff, H. H. 1998b. Where Did I Take That Snapshot? Scene-Based Homing by Image Matching. *Biological Cybernetics* 79(3): 191–202.

Frazier, S. F.; Larsen, G. S.; Neff, D.; Quimby, L.; Carney, M. DiCaprio, R. A.; and Zill, S. N. 1999. Elasticity and Movements of the Cockroach Tarsus in Walking. *Journal of Comparative Physiology.* 185(2): 157–172.

Frik, M.; Guddat, M.; Karatas, M.; and Losch, C. D. 1999. A Novel Approach to Autonomous Control of Walking Machines. In *Proceedings of the Second International Conference on Climbing and Walking Robots CLAWAR 99, 13–15 September, Portsmouth, UK,* eds. G. S. Virk, M. Randall, and D. Howard, 333–342. Edmunds, U.K.: Professional Engineering.

Frith, U. 1990. *Autism: Explaining the Enigma.* Oxford, U.K.: Blackwell.

Fujita, I., and Fujita, T. 1996. Intrinsic Connections in the Macaque Inferior Temporal Cortex. *Journal of Comparative Neurology* 368(4): 467–486.

Fujita, I.; Tanaka, K.; Ito, M.; and Cheng, K. 1992. Columns for Visual Features of Objects in Monkey Inferotemporal Cortex. *Nature* 360(26): 343–346.

Full, R. J. 1993. Integration of Individual Leg Dynamics with Whole Body Movement in Arthropod Locomotion. In *Biological Neural Networks in Invertebrate Neuroethology and Robotics*, 3–20, eds. R. D. Beer, R. E. Ritzman, and T. McKenna, 3–20. San Diego, Calif.: Academic Press.

Full, R. J.; Blickhan, R; and Ting, L. H. 1991. Leg Design in Hexapedal Runners. *Journal of Experimental Biology.* 158(1): 369–390.

Fuster, J. M. 1995. *Memory in the Cerebral Cortex: An Empirical Approach to Neural Networks in the Human and Nonhuman Primate.* Cambridge, Mass.: The MIT Press.

Gaussier, P.; Banquet, J. P.; Joulain, C.; Revel, A.; and Zrehen, S. 1997. Validation of a Hippocampal Model on a Mobile Robot. Paper Presented at the International Conference on Vision, Recognition, Action: Neural Models of Mind and Machine. 29–31 May, Boston, Mass.

Gaussier, P.; Joulain, C.; Zrehen, S.; Banquet, J. P.; and Revel, A. 1997. Visual Navigation in an Open Environment without Map. In Proceedings of the IEEE/RSJ International Conference on Intelligent Robots and Systems (IROS'97), 545–550. Washington, D.C.: IEEE Computer Society.

Gelenbe, E.; Schmajuk, N.; Staddon, J.; and Reif, J. 1997. Autonomous Search by Robots and Animals: A Survey. *Robotics and Autonomous Systems* 22(1): 23–34.

Georgopoulos, A. P.; Lurito, J. T.; Petrides, M.; Schwartz, A. B.; and Massey, J. T. 1989. Mental Rotation of the Neuronal Population Vector. *Science* 243(4888) (13 January): 234–236.

Gilbert, C. D. 1993. Circuity, Architecture, and Functional Dynamics of Visual Cortex. *Cerebral Cortex* 3(5): 373–386.

Gilbert, C. D., and Wiesel, T. N. 1983. Clustered Intrinsic Connections in Cat Visual Cortex. *Journal of Neuroscience* 3(5): 1116–1133.

Gochin, P. M. 1994. Properties of Simulated Neurons from a Model of Primate Inferior Temporal Cortex. *Cerebral Cortex* 4(5): 532–543.

Gochin, P. M.; Miller, E. K.; Goss, C. G.; and Gerstein, G. L. 1991. Functional Interactions among Neurons in Inferior Temporal Cortex of the Awake Macaque. *Experimental Brain Research* 84(3): 505–516.

Gomez, G., and Atema, J. 1996a. Temporal Resolution in Olfaction: Stimulus Integration Time of Lobster Chemoreceptor Cells. *Journal of Experimental Biology* 199(8): 1771–1779.

Gomez, G., and Atema, J. 1996b. Temporal Resolution in Olfaction. II: Time Course of Recovery from Adaptation in Lobster Chemoreceptor Cells. *Journal of Neurophysiology* 76(2): 1340–1343.

Gomez, G.; Voigt, R.; and Atema, J. 1992. High-Resolution Measurement and Control of Chemical Stimuli in the Lateral Antennule of the Lobster Homarus Americanus. *Biological Bulletin* 183(2): 353–354.

Gomez, G.; Voigt, R.; and Atema, J. 1994a. Frequency Filter Properties of Lobster Chemoreceptors Cells Determined with High-Resolution Stimulus Measurement. *Journal of Comparative Physiology A*174: 803–811.

Gomez, G.; Voigt, R.; and Atema, J. 1994b. Tuning Properties of Chemoreceptor Cells of the American Lobster: Temporal Filters. In *Olfaction and Taste XI,* 788–789, ed N. Suzuki, L. Kurihara, and H. Ogawa. Berlin: Springer-Verlag.

Gorassini, M. A.; Prochazka, A.; Hiebert, G. W.; and Gauthier, M. J. A. 1994. Corrective Responses to Loss of Ground Support during Walking: I. Intact Cats. *Journal of Neurophysiolgy* 71(2): 603–610.

Grasso, F. W., and Di Lorenzo, P. M. 1997. GUSSTO: A Neuronal Network Model of Gustatory Processing in the Rat NTS and PBN. In *Computational Neuroscience*, ed. J. M. Bower, 321–326. New York: Plenum.

Grasso, F. W.; Basil, J. A.; and Atema, J. 1998. Toward the Convergence: Robot and Lobster Perspectives of Tracking Odors to Their Source in the Turbulent Marine Environment. In Proceedings of the 1998 IEEE, 259–264. Washington, D.C.: IEEE Computer Society.

Grasso, F W..; Consi, T.; Mountain, D.; and Atema, J. 1996. Locating Odor Sources in Turbulence with a Lobster-Inspired Robot. In *From Animals to Animats 4: Proceedings of the Fourth International Conference on Simulation of Adaptive Behavior,* 104–112. Cambridge, Mass.: The MIT Press.

Grasso, F W..; Consi, T.; Mountain, D.; and Atema, J. 2000. Biomimetic Robot Lobster Performs Chemo-Orientation in Turbulence Using a Pair of Spatially Separated Sensors: Progress and Challenges. *Robotics and Autonomous Systems* 30(1–2): 115–131.

Grasso, F. W.; Dale, J. H.; Consi, T. R.; Mountain, D. C.; and Atema, J. 1996. Behavior of Purely Chemotactic Robot Lobster Reveals Different Odor-Dispersal Patterns in the Jet Region and the Patch Field of a Turbulent Plume. *Biological Bulletin* 191(2): 312–313.

Grasso, F. W.; Dale, J. H.; Consi, T. R.; Mountain, D. C.; and Atema, J. 1997. Effectiveness of Continuous Bilateral Sampling for Robot Chemotaxis in a Turbulent Odor Plume: Implications for Lobster Chemo-Orientation. *Biological Bulletin* 193(2): 215–216.

Grasso, F. W.; Gaito, S. T.; and Atema, J. 1999. Behavior, Peripheral Chemo-Reception and Information in Turbulent Odor Plume Tracking: Results from Simulation Studies. *Society for Neuroscience Abstacts* 29: 550.3.

Grasso, F. W.; Voigt, R.; and Atema, J. 1998. Lobster Chemoreceptor Dynamics in Turbulent Odor Plumes: Transmission of Environmental Cues from the Periphery to the CNS. *Society for Neuroscience Abstracts* 28: 711.2.

Greene, P. H. 1982. Why Is It Easy to Control Your Arms? *Journal of Motor Behavior* 14 (4): 260–286.

Gross, C. G. 1992. Representation of Visual Stimuli in Inferior Temporal Cortex. *Philosophical Transactions of the Royal Society London B* 335: 3–10.

Gross, C. G., and Mishkin, M. 1977. The Neural Basis of Stimulus Equivalence across Retinal Translation. In *Lateralization in the Nervous System*, eds. S. Harnad, R. Doty, L. Goldstein, J. Jaynes, and G. Krauthammer, 109–122. San Diego, Calif.: Academic Press.

Gross, C. G.; Rocha-Miranda, C. E.; and Bender, D. B. 1972. Visual Properties of Neurons in Inferotemporal Cortex of the Macaque. *Journal of Neurophysiology* 35(1): 96–111.

Hallam, B.; Halperin, J. R.; and Hallam, J. C. 1994. An Ethological Model for Implementation in Mobile Robots. *Adaptive Behavior* 3(1): 51–79.

Hanna, J. P.; Grasso, F. W.; and Atema, J. 1999. Temporal Correlation between Sensor Pairs in Different Plume Positions: A Study of Concentration Information Available to the American Lobster, Homarus Americanus, during Chemotaxis. *Biological Bulletin* 197(2): 26–27.

Hannaford, B.; Winters, J.; Chou, C.-P.; and Marbot, P. H. 1995. The Anthroform Biorobotic Arm: A System for the Study of Spinal Circuits. *Annals of Biomedical Engineering* 23(4): 39–408.

Hardie R. C. 1985. Functional Organization of Fly Retina. In *Progress in Sensory Physiology* 5, ed. D. Ottoson, 1–79. Berlin: Springer-Verlag.

Harmon, L. D. 1961. Neural Analogs. In Proceedings of the Institute of Radio Engineers, 1316. New York: Institute of Radio Engineers.

Harrison, R. R., and Koch, C. 1999. A Robust Analog VLSI Motion Sensor Based on the Visual System of the Fly. *Autonomous Robotics* 7(3): 211–224.

Hauck, A.; Sorg, M.; Faerber, G.; and Schenk, T. 1998. Biologically Motivated Model for the Control of Visually Guided Reach-to-Grasp Movements. In Proceedings of the IEEE International Symposium on Intelligent Control, 295–300. Washington, D.C.: IEEE Computer Society.

Hauser, M. D. 1996. *Evolution of Communication.* Cambridge, Mass.: The MIT Press.

Hedrick, A. V., and Dill, L. M. 1993. Mate Choice by Female Crickets Is Influenced by Predation Risk. *Animal Behavior* 46(1): 193–196.

Hirai, K.; Hirose, M.; Haikawa, Y.; and Takenaka, T. 1998. The Development of the Honda Humanoid Robot. In Proceedings of the IEEE International Conference on Robotics and Automation, 1321–1326. Washington, D.C.: IEEE Computer Society.

Hirose, S. 1993. *Biologically Inspired Robots: Snake-Like Locomotors and Manipulators.* Oxford: Oxford University Press.

Hobson, R. P. 1993. *Autism and the Development of Mind.* Hillsdale, N.J.: Lawrence Erlbaum.

Hoff, J., and Bekey, G. 1997. Cerebellar Approach to Adaptive Locomotion for Legged Robots. In Proceedings of IEEE International Symposium on Computational Intelligence in Robotics and Automation, Cira, 94–100. Washington, D.C.: IEEE Computer Society.

Holland, O. E., and Melhuish, C. 1999. Stigmergy, Self-Organization and Sorting in Collective Robotics. *Artificial Life* 5(2): 173–202.

Holland, O. E.; Beckers, R.; and Deneubourg, J. L. 1994. From Local Actions to Global Tasks: Stigmergy and Collective Robotics. In *Artifical Live IV, Proceedings of the Fourth International Workshop on the Synthesis and Stimulation of Living Systems,* 181–189. Cambridge, Mass.: The MIT Press.

Hong, J.; Tan, X.; Pinette, B.; Weiss, R.; and Riseman, E. M. 1992. Image-Based Homing. *IEEE Control Systems Magazine,* 12(1): 38–45.

Honma, A. 1996. Construction Robot for Three-Dimensional Shapes Based on the Nesting Behavior of Paper Wasps. *Seimitsu Kogaku Kaishi (Journal of the Japan Society for Precision Engineering)* 62: 805–809.

Horak, F. B., and MacPherson, J. M. 1995. Postural Orientation and Equilibrium. In *Handbook of Physiology, Section 12: Exercise: Regulation and Integration of Multiple Systems.* Eds. Loring B. Rowell and John T. Shepherd, 255–292. New York: Oxford University Press.

Horiuchi, T. 1997. An Auditory Localization and Co-Ordinate Transform Chip. In *Advances in Neural Information Processing Systems 8.* Cambridge, Mass.: The MIT Press.

Horiuchi, T. K., and Koch, C. 1999. Analog VLSI-Based Modeling of the Primate Oculomotor System. *Neural Computation* 11(1): 243–264.

Horridge, G. A., and Sandeman, D. C. 1964. Nervous Control of Optokinetic Responses in the Crab *Carcinus.* In Proceedings of the Royal Society of London B 161: 216–246, London: The Royal Society.

Horseman, G., and Huber, F. 1994. Sound Localization in Crickets: II. Modeling the Role of a Simple Neural Network in the Prothoracic Ganglion. *Journal of Comparative Physiology A*175: 399–413.

Hoshino, H.; Mura, F.; Morii, H.; Suematsu, K.; and Shimoyama, I. 1998. A Small-Sized Panoramic Scanning Visual Sensor Inspired by the Fly's Compound Eye. In Proceedings of the IEEE International Conference on Robotics and Automation, 1641–1646. Washington, D.C.: IEEE Computer Society.

Huang, J.; Ohnishi, N.; and Sugie, N. 1995. A Biomimetic System for Localization and Separation of Multiple Sound Sources. *IEEE Transactions on Instrumentation and Measurement* 44(3): 733–738.

Huber, F., and Thorson, J. 1985. Cricket Auditory Communication. *Scientific American* 253(6): 47–54.

Huber, F.; Moore, T. E.; and Loher, W., eds. 1989. *Cricket Behavior and Neurobiology*. Ithaca, N.Y.: Cornell University Press.

Huber, S. A., and Bülthoff, H. H. 1998. Simulation and Robot Implementation of Visual Orientation Behavior of Flies. In *From Animals to Animats 5: Proceedings of the Fifth International Conference on Simulation of Adaptive Behavior,* 77–85. Cambridge, Mass.: The MIT Press.

Ilg, W.; Berns, K.; Jedele, H.; Albiez, J.; Dillmann, R.; Fischer, M.; Witte, H.; Biltzinger, J.; Lehmann, R.; and Schilling, N. 1998. BISAM: From Small Mammals to a Four-Legged Walking Machine. In *From Animals to Animats 5: Proceedings of the Fifth International Conference on Simulation of Adaptive Behavior.* Cambridge, Mass.: The MIT Press.

Indiveri, G. 1998. Analog VLSI Model of Locust DCMD Neuron Response for Computation of Object Approach. In *Neuromorphic Systems: Engineering Silicon from Neurobiology,* eds. L. Smith and A. Hamilton. London: World Scientific.

Ishida, H.; Kobayashi, A.; Nakamoto, T.; and Moriisumi, T. 1999. Three-Dimensional Odor Compass. *IEEE Transactions on Robotics and Automation* 15(2): 251–257.

Ishii, I..; Yoshihiro, Y.; and Ishikawa, M. 1996. Target-Tracking Algorithm for 1-ms Visual Feedback System Using Massively Parallel Processing. In Proceedings of IEEE Robotics and Automation, 2309–2314. Washington, D.C.: IEEE Computer Society.

Ito, M. 1993. Movement and Thought: Identical Control Mechanisms by the Cerebellum. *Trends in Neuroscience* 16(11): 448-450.

Ito, M.; Tamura, H.; Fujita, I.; and Tanaka, K. 1995. Size and Position Invariance of Neuronal Responses in Monkey Inferotemporal Cortex. *Journal of Neurophysiology* 73(1): 218–226.

Jordan, M. I., and Rumelhart, D. E. 1992. Forward Models: Supervised Learning with a Distal Teacher. *Cognitive Science* 16(3): 307–354.

Kanehiro, F.; Mizuuchi, I.; Koyasako, K.; Kakiuchi, Y.; Inaba, M.; and Inoue, H. 1998. Development of a Remote-Brained Humanoid for Research on Whole Body Action. In Proceedings of the 1998 IEEE International Conference on Robotics and Automation (ICRA-98), 1302–1307. Washington, D.C.: IEEE Computer Society.

Kanzaki, R. 1996. Behavioral and Neural Basis of Instinctive Behavior in Insects: Odor-Source Searching Strategies without Memory and Learning. *Robotics and Autonomous Systems* 18(1–2): 33–43.

Karmiloff-Smith, A.; Klima, E.; Bellugi, U.; Grant, J.; and Baron-Cohen, S. 1995. Is There a Social Module? Language, Face Processing, and Theory of Mind in Individuals with Williams Syndrome. *Journal of Cognitive Neuroscience* 7(2): 196–208.

Kato, M., and Inaba, T. 1998. Guidance and Control of Fish Robot with Apparatus of Pectoral Fin Motion. In Proceedings of the IEEE International Conference on Robotics and Automation 1, 446–451. Washington, D.C.: IEEE Computer Society.

Kawamura, K.; Wilkes, D. M.; Pack, T.; Bishay, M.; and Barile, J. 1996. Humanoids: Future Robots for Home and Factory. In Proceedings of the First International Symposium on Humanoid Robots, 53–62. Tokyo, Japan: Waseda University.

Keijzer, F. A. 1998. Some Arm Chair Worries about Wheeled Behavior. In *From Animals to Animats 5: Proceedings of the Fifth International Conference on Simulation of Adaptive Behavior,* eds. R. Pfeifer, B. Blumberg, J.-A. Meyer, and S. W. Wilson, 13–21. Cambridge, Mass.: The MIT Press.

Kennedy, J. S. 1986. Some Current Issues in Orientation to Odor Sources. In *Mechanisms in Insect Olfaction,* 11–25, eds. T. L. Payne; M. C. Birch; and C. E. J. Kennedy. Oxford, U.K.: Clarendon.

Kennedy, J. S. 1992. *The New Anthropomorphism.* Cambridge, U.K.: Cambridge University Press.

Kindermann, T.; Cruse, H.; and Dean, J. 1998. Biologically Motivated Controller for a Six-Legged Walking System. In Proceedings of IECON (Industrial Electronics Conference), 2168–2173. Washington, D.C.: IEEE Industrial Electronics Society.

Kobatake, E.; Wang, G.; and Tanaka, K. 1998. Effects of Shape-Discrimination Training on the Selectivity of Inferotemporal Cells in Adult Monkeys. *Journal of Neurophysiology* 80(1): 324–330.

Kortenkamp, D. 1993. Cognitive Maps for Mobile Robots: A Representation for Mapping and Navigation. Ph.D. dissertation, Computer Science and Engineering Department, University of Michigan, Ann Arbor, Mich.

K-Team. 1994. *Khepera User Manual.* Lausanne: EPFL.

Kube, C. R., and Bonabeau, E. 2000. Cooperative Transport by Ants and Robots. *Robotics and Autonomous Systems* 30(1–2): 85–101.

Kuc, R. 1997. Biomimetic Sonar Recognizes Objects Using Binaural Information. *Journal of the Acoustical Society of America* 102(2): 689–696.

Kuipers, B. J., and Byun, Y.-T. 1988. A Robust, Qualitative Approach to a Spatial Learning Mobile Robot. In SPIE Sensor Fusion: Spatial Reasoning and Scene Interpretation, 1003. Bellingham, Wash.: SPIE—The International Society for Optical Engineering.

Kuwana, Y.; Shimoyama, I.; and Miura, H. 1995. Steering Control of a Mobile Robot Using Insect Antennae. In Proceedings of the IEEE International Conference on Intelligent Robots and Systems, 530–535. Washington, D.C.: IEEE Computer Society.

Lakoff, G. 1987. *Women, Fire, and Dangerous Things: What Categories Reveal about the Mind.* Chicago: University of Chicago Press.

Lambrinos, D.; Maris, M.; Kobayashi, H.; Labhart, T.; Pfeifer, R.; and Wehner, R. 1997. An Autonomous Agent Navigating with a Polarized Light Compass. *Adaptive Behavior* 6(1): 175–206.

Lambrinos, D.; Möller, R.; Labhart, T.; Pfeifer, R.; and Wehner, R. 2000. A Mobile Robot Employing Insect Strategies for Navigation. *Robotics and Autonomous Systems* 30(1–2): 39–64.

Lambrinos, D.; Möller, R.; Pfeifer, R.; and Wehner, R. 1998. Landmark Navigation without Snapshots: The Average Landmark Vector Model. In Proceedings of the Twenth-

Sixth Göttingen Neurobiology Conference Report, eds. E. Elsner and R. Wehner, 30a. Stuttgart, Germany: Georg Thieme Verlag.

Langton, C. G., ed. 1989. *Artificial Life*. Reading, Mass.: Addison-Wesley.

Laurent, G., and Richard, D. 1986. The Organization and Role during Locomotion of the Proximal Musculature of the Cricket Foreleg: I. Anatomy and Innervation. *Journal of Experimental Biology* 123(1): 255–283.

Leoni, F.; Guerrini, M.; Laschi, C.; Taddeucci, D.; Dario, P.; and Staritao, A. 1998. Implementing Robotic Grasping Tasks Using a Biological Approach. In Proceedings of the IEEE International Conference on Robotics and Automation, 2274–2280. Washington, D.C.: IEEE Computer Society.

Lewis, M. A., and Nelson, M. E. 1998. Look before You Leap: Peering Behavior for Depth Perception. In *From Animals to Animats 5: Proceedings of the Fifth International Conference on Simulation of Adaptive Behavior,* 98–103. Cambridge, Mass.: The MIT Press.

Loeb, J. 1918. *Forced Movements, Tropisms, and Animal Conduct*. Philadelphia: Lippincott. Reprinted in 1973 by Dover Publications, New York, N.Y.

Logothetis, N. K.; Pauls, J.; and Poggio, T. 1995. Shape Representation in the Inferior Temporal Cortex of Monkeys. *Current Biology* 5(5): 552–563.

Lund, H.; Webb, B.; and Hallam, J. 1997. A Robot Attracted by the Cricket Species Gryllus Bimaculatus. In *Proceedings of the Fourth European Conference on Artificial Life,* 246–255, eds. P. Husbands and I. Harvey. Cambridge Mass.: The MIT Press.

Lund, H.; Webb, B.; and Hallam, J. 1998. Physical and Temporal Scaling Considerations in a Robot Model of Cricket-Calling Song Preference. *Artificial Life* 4(1): 95–107.

Maes, P. 1991. A Bottom-Up Mechanism for Behavior Selection in an Artificial Creature. In *From Animals to Animats,* eds. J.-A. Meyer and S. W. Wilson, 238–246. Cambridge, Mass.: The MIT Press.

Marjanovic, M. J.; Scassellati, B.; and Williamson, M. M. 1996. Self-Taught Visually Guided Pointing for a Humanoid Robot. In *From Animals to Animats 3: Proceedings of the Third International Conference on Simulation of Adaptive Behavior,* 35–44. Cambridge, Mass.: The MIT Press.

Mataric, M. J. 1998. Behavior-Based Robotics as a Tool for Synthesis of Artificial Behavior and Analysis of Natural Behavior. *Trends in Cognitive Sciences* 2(3): 82–86.

McFarland, D., and Bösser, T. 1993. *Intelligent Behavior in Animals and Robots*. Cambridge, Mass.: The MIT Press.

Mel, B. W. 1997. SEEMORE: Combining Color, Shape, and Texture Histogramming in a Neurally Inspired Approach to Visual Object Recognition. *Neural Computation* 9(4) (15 May): 777–804.

Melhuish, C.; Holland, O.; and Hoddell, S. 1998. Collective Sorting and Segregation in Robots with Minimal Sensing. In *From Animals to Animats 5: Proceedings of the Fifth International Conference on Simulation of Adaptive Behavior.* Cambridge, Mass.: The MIT Press.

Meyer, J. A., and Guillot, A. 1990. Simulation of Adaptive Behavior in Animats: Review and Prospect. In *Proceedings of the First International Conference on the Simulation of Adaptive Behavior,* 2–14. Cambridge, Mass.: The MIT Press.

Michelsen, A.; Popov, A. V.; and Lewis, B. 1994. Physics of Directional Hearing in the Cricket Gryllus Bimaculatus. *Journal of Comparative Physiology A* 175: 153–164.

Miller, G. 2001. Snake Robots. In *Neurotechnology for Biomimetic Robots,* ed. J. Ayers, J. Davis, and J. Rudolph. Cambridge, Mass.: The MIT Press.

Mjos, K.; Grasso, F.; and Atema, J. 1999. Antennule Use by the American Lobster, Homarus Americanus, during Chemo-Orientation in Three Turbulent Odor Plumes. *Biological Bulletin* 197(2): 25–26.

Mojarrad, M., and Shahinpoor, M. 1997. Biomimetic Robotic Propulsion Using Polymeric Artificial Muscles. In Proceedings of the IEEE International Conference on Robotics and Automation, 2152–2157. Washington, D.C.: IEEE Computer Society.

Möller, R. 1999. Visual Homing in Analog Hardware. *International Journal of Neural Systems* 9(5): 383–389.

Möller, R. 2000. Insect Visual Homing Strategies in a Robot with Analog Processing. *Biological Cybernetics.* 83(3): 231–243.

Möller, R.; Maris, M.; and Lambrinos, D. 1999. A Neural Model of Landmark Navigation in Insects. *Neurocomputing* 26–27: 801–808.

Möller, R.; Lambrinos, D.; Pfeifer, R.; Labhart, T.; and Wehner, R. 1998. Modeling Ant Navigation with an Autonomous Agent. In *From Animals to Animats 5, Proceedings of the Fifth International Conference on Simulation of Adaptive Behavior,* eds. R. Pfeifer, B. Blumberg, J.-A. Meyer, and S. W. Wilson, 185–194. Cambridge, Mass.: The MIT Press.

Moore, C., and Dunham, P. J., eds. 1995. *Joint Attention: Its Origins and Role in Development.* Hillsdale, N.J.: Lawrence Erlbaum.

Moore, P. A., and Atema, J. 1991. Spatial Information in the Three-Dimensional Fine Structure of an Aquatic Plume. *Biological Bulletin* 181(3): 408–418.

Moore, P. A., and Lepper, D. M. E. 1997. Role of Chemical Signals in the Orientation Behavior of the Sea Star Asterias Forbsii. *Biological Bulletin* 192(3): 410–417.

Moore, P. A.; Scholz, N.; and Atema, J. 1991. Chemical Orientation of Lobsters, Homarus Americanus, in Turbulent Odor Plumes. *Journal of Chemical Ecology* 17(8): 1293–1307.

Morita, T.; Shibuya, K.; and Sugano, S. 1998. Design and Control of Mobile Manipulation System for Human Symbiotic Humanoid. In Proceedings of the 1998 IEEE International Conference on Robotics and Automation (ICRA-98), 1315–1320. Washington, D.C.: IEEE Computer Society.

Morse, T. M.; Ferree, T. C.; and Lockery, S. R. 1998. Robust Spatial Navigation in a Robot Inspired by Chemotaxis in Caenorrhabditis Elegans. *Adaptive Behavior* 6(3–4): 393–410.

Mura, F., and Franceschini, N. 1996. Biologically Inspired Retinal Scanning Enhances Motion Perception of a Mobile Robot. Paper presented at the First Europe-Asia Congress on Mechatronics, 1–3 October, Bensacon, France.

Mura, F., and Franceschini, N. 1994. Visual Control of Altitude and Speed in a Flying Agent. In *Proceedings: From Animals to Animats 3: Proceedings of the Third International Conference on Simulation of Adaptive Behavior,* eds. E. Clif, P. Husbands, J. A. Meyer, and S. W. Wilson, 91–99. Cambridge, Mass.: The MIT Press.

Mura, F., and Shimoyama, I. 1998. Visual Guidance of a Small Mobile Robot Using Active, Biologically Inspired, Eye Movements. In Proceedings of the IEEE Conference on Robotics and Automation, 1859–1864. Washington, D.C.: IEEE Computer Society.

Murlis, J.; Elkinton, J. S.; and Carde, R. T. 1992. Odor Plumes and How Insects Use Them. In *Annual Review of Entomology* 37: 505–532. Palo Alto: Calif.: Annual Reviews.

Mussa-Ivaldi, F. A.; Morasso, P.; and Zaccaria, R. 1988. A Distributed Model for Representing and Regularizing Motor Redundancy. *Biological Cybernetics* 60(1): 1–16.

Nelson, G. M. 1995. Modeling and Control of a Cockroach-Like Hexapod Robot. Master's thesis, Mechanical and Aerospace Engineering Department, Case Western Reserve University.

Nelson, G. M., and Quinn, R. D. 1995. A Lagrangian Formulation in Terms of Quasicoordinates for Dynamic Simulations of Multibody Systems such as Insects and Robots. Paper presented at the ASME International Mechanical Engineering Congress and Exposition (IMECE 1995), November 15–17, San Francisco, California.

Nelson, G. M., and Quinn, R. D. 1996. A Quasicoordinate Formulation for Dynamic Simulations of Complex Multibody Systems with Constraints. In *Dynamics and Control of Structures in Space III,* eds. C. L. Kirk and D. J. Inman, 523–538. Southampton, U.K.: Computational Mechanics.

Nelson, G. M., and Quinn, R. D. 1998. Posture Control of a Cockroach-Like Robot. In Proceedings of the IEEE International Conference on Robotics and Automation, 157–162. Washington, D.C.: IEEE Computer Society.

Nelson, G. M.; Bachmann, R. J.; Quinn, R. D.; Watson, J. T.; and Ritzmann, R. E. 1998. Posture Control of a Cockroach-Like Robot. In Video Proceedings of the IEEE International Conference on Robotics and Automation (ICRA '98). Washington, D.C.: IEEE Computer Society.

Nelson, G. M.; Quinn, R. D.; Bachmann, R. J.; Flannigan, W. C.; Ritzmann, R. E.; and Watson, J. T. 1997. Design and Simulation of a Cockroach-Like Hexapod Robot. Paper presented at the 1997 IEEE International Conference on Robotics and Automation, April 22–24. Washington, D.C.: IEEE Computer Society.

Nelson, R. C. 1989. Visual Homing Using Associative Memory. In *Proceedings of the Image Understanding Workshop,* 245–262. San Francisco, Calif.: Morgan Kaufmann.

Oldfield, B. P. 1980. Accuracy of Orientation in Female Crickets, Teleogryllus Oceanicus (Gryllidae): Dependence on Song Spectrum. *Journal of Comparative Physiology A* 141(1): 93–99.

Oliver, S. J.; Grasso, F.; and Atema, J. 1996. Filament Tracking and Casting in American Elvers (Anguilla Rostrata). *Biological Bulletin* 191(2): 314–315.

Oram, M. W., and Földiàk, P. 1996. Learning Generalization and Localization: Competition for Stimulus Type and Receptive Field. *Neurocomputing* 11(2–4): 297–321.

Patel, G. N.; Holleman, J. H.; and DeWeerth, S. P. 1998. Analog VLSI Model of Intersegmental Coordination with Nearest-Neighbour Coupling. In *Advances in Neural Information Processing Systems 10,* eds. M. I. Jordan, M. J. Kearns, and S. A. Solla, 719–726. Cambridge, Mass.: The MIT Press.

Pearson, K. 1976. The Control of Walking. *Scientific American* 235(6): 72–86.

Pearson, K. G., and Iles J. F. 1970. Discharge Patterns of Coxal Levator and Depressor Motoneurones of the Cockroach, Periplaneta americana. *Journal of Experimental Biology* 52(1): 139–165.

Pearson, K. G., and Iles, J. F. 1971. Innervation of Coxal Depressor Muscle in the Cockroach, Periplaneta Americana. *Journal of Experimental Biology* 54(1): 215–232.

Peremans, H.; Walker, A.; and Hallam, J. C. T. 1998. 3D Object Localization with a Binaural Sonar Head—Inspirations from Biology. In Proceedings of the IEEE International Conference on Robotics and Automation 2795–2800. Washington, D.C.: IEEE Computer Society.

Pfeifer, R. 1996. Building "Fungus Eaters": Design Principles of Autonomous Agents. In *From Animals to Animats 4: Proceedings of the Fourth International Conference on Simulation of Adaptive Behavior*, eds. P. Maes, M. J. Mataric, J.-A. Meyer, J. Pollack, and S. W. Wilson, 3–12. Cambridge Mass.: The MIT Press.

Pfeiffer, F.; Etze, J.; and Weidemann, H. 1995. Six-Legged Technical Walking Considering Biological Principles. *Robotics and Autonomous Systems* 14(2–3): 223–232.

Pfeifer, R., and Scheier, C. 1999. *Understanding Intelligence*. Cambridge, Mass.: The MIT Press.

Pfeifer R., and Verschure, P. F. M. J. 1992. Distributed Adaptive Control: A Paradigm for Designing Autonomous Agents. In *Proceedings of the First European Conference on Artificial Life*, 21–30. Cambridge, Mass.: The MIT Press.

Pichon, J. M.; Blanes, C.; and Franceschini, N. 1989. Visual Guidance of a Mobile Robot Equipped with a Network of Self-Motion Sensors. In Mobile Robots 4, 44–53. Bellingham, Wash.: The International Society for Optical Engineering (SPIE).

Platt, J. R. 1964. Strong Inference. *Science* 146(3642): 347–352.

Pollack, G. S. 1998. Neural Processing of Acoustic Signals. In *Comparative Hearing: Insects*, eds. R. R. Hoy, A. N. Popper, and R. R. Fay, 139–196. New York: Springer-Verlag.

Popov, A. V., and Shuvalov, V. F. 1977. Phonotacic Behavior of Crickets. *Journal of Comparative Physiology* 119(1): 111–126.

Povinelli, D. J., and Preuss, T. M. 1995. Theory of Mind: Evolutionary History of a Cognitive Specialization. *Trends in Neuroscience*. 18(9): 418–424.

Powers, M. D. 1997. Behavioral Assessment of Individuals with Autism. In *Handbook of Autism and Pervasive Developmental Disorders*, 448–459, eds. D. J. Cohen and F. R. Volkmar. 2d ed. New York: Wiley.

Pratt, G. A., and Williamson, M. M. 1995. Series Elastic Actuators. In Proceedings of the IEEE/RSJ International Conference on Intelligent Robots and Systems (IROS-95), Volume 1, 399–406. Washington, D.C.: IEEE Computer Society.

Pratt, J. 1995. Virtual Model Control of a Biped Walking Robot. Master's thesis, Department of Electrical Engineering and Computer Science, Massachusetts Institute of Technology, Cambridge, Mass.

Pratt, J.; Dilworth, P.; and Pratt, G. 1997. Virtual Model Control of a Bipedal Walking Robot. Paper presented at the IEEE International Conference on Robotics and Automation (ICRA 97), April 22–24. Washington, D.C.: IEEE Computer Society.

Pratt, J. E., and Pratt, G. A. 1998. Exploiting Natural Dynamics in the Control of a Planar Biped Walking Robot. Paper presented at the Thirty-Sixth Annual Allerton Conference on Communication, Control, and Computing, 23–25 September, Monticello, Ill.

Premack, D. 1988. Does the Chimpanzee Have a Theory of Mind? Revisited. In *Machiavellian Intelligence: Social Expertise and the Evolution of Intellect in Monkeys, Apes, and Humans*, 160–179, eds. R. Byrne and A. Whiten. Oxford, U.K.: Oxford University Press.

Prescott, T. J., and Ibbotson, C. 1997. A Robot Trace Maker: Modeling the Fossil Evidence of Early Invertebrate Behavior. *Artificial Life* 3(4): 289–306.

Quinn, R. D., and Espenschied, K. S. 1993. Control of a Hexapod Robot Using a Biologically Inspired Neural Network. In *Biological Neural Networks in Invertebrate Neuroethology and Robotics*, eds. R. D. Beer, R. E. Ritzman, and T. McKenna. 365–381. San Diego, Calif.: Academic Press.

Raibert, M. H. 1986. *Legged Robots That Balance*. Cambridge, Mass.: The MIT Press.

Raibert, M. H.; Chepponis, M.; and Brown, H. B., Jr. 1986. Running on Four Legs as Though They Were One. *IEEE Journal of Robotics and Automation* RA-2(2): 70–82.

Recce, M., and Harris, K. D. 1996. Memory for Places: A Navigational Model in Support of Marr's Theory of Hippocampal Function. *Hippocampus* 6(6): 735–748.

Reeke, Jr., G. N., and Sporns, O. 1993. Behaviorally Based Modeling and Computational Approaches to Neuroscience. In *Annual Reviews in Neuroscience*, 16: 597–623. Palo Alto, Calif.: Annual Reviews.

Reeke, Jr., G. N.; Sporns, O.; and Edelman, G. M. 1990. Synthetic Neural Modeling: The Darwin Series of Recognition Automata. In Proceedings of the IEEE, Volume 78, 1498–1530. Washington, D.C.: IEEE Computer Society.

Reeke, Jr., G. N.; Finkel, L. H.; Sporns, O.; and Edelman, G. M. 1990. Synthetic Neural Modeling: A Multilevel Approach to the Analysis of Brain Complexity. In *Signal and Sense: Local and Global Order in Perceptual Maps*, eds. G. M. Edelman, W. E. Gall, and W. M. Cowan, 607–707. New York: Wiley.

Reeves, B., and Nass, C. 1996. *The Media Equation: How People Treat Computers, Televisions, and New Media Like Real People and Places*. Cambridge, U.K.: Cambridge University Press.

Ristau, C. A. 1991. Before Mindreading: Attention, Purposes, and Deception in Birds? In *Natural Theories of Mind*, 209–222, ed. A. Whiten. Oxford, U.K.: Blackwell.

Rodman, H. R. 1994. Development of Inferior Temporal Cortex in the Monkey. *Cerebral Cortex* 4(5): 484–498.

Rolls, E. T. 1992. Neurophysiological Mechanisms Underlying Face Processing within and beyond the Temporal Cortical Visual Areas. *Philosophical Transactions of the Royal Society London B*335: 11–21.

Rosheim, M. E. 1994. *Robot Evolution: The Development of Anthrorobotics*. New York: Wiley.

Rowley, H.; Baluja, S.; and Kanade, T. 1995. Human Face Detection in Visual Scenes. Technical Report, CMU-CS-95-158, Department of Computer Science, Carnegie Mellon University.

Rucci, M.; Edelman, G.; and Wray, J. 1999. Adaptation of Orienting Behavior: From the Barn Owl to a Robotic System. *IEEE Transactions on Robotics and Automation* 15(1): 96–110.

Russell, R. 1998. Odor-Sensing Robot Draws Inspiration from the Insect World. In Proceedings of the Second International Conference on Bioelectromagnetism, 49–50. Washington, D.C: IEEE Computer Society.

Saito, F., and Fukuda, T. 1996. A First Result of the Brachiator III—A New Brachiation Robot Modeled on a Siamang. In *Proceedings of ALife V.* Cambridge, Mass.: The MIT Press.

Saksida, L. M.; Raymond, S. M.; and Touretzky, D. S. 1997. Shaping Robot Behavior Using Principles from Instrumental Conditioning. *Robotics and Autonomous Systems* 22(3–4): 231–249.

Sarpeshkar, R.; Kramer, J.; and Koch, C. 1998. Pulse Domain Neuromorphic Integrated Circuit for Computing Motion. U.S. Patent Number 5,781,648. Washington, D.C.: U.S. Patent Office.

Scaife, M. 1976. The Response to Eye-Like Shapes by Birds: II. The Importance of Staring, Pairedness, and Shape. *Animal Behavior* 24(1): 200–206.

Scaife, M., and Bruner, J. 1975. The Capacity for Joint Visual Attention in the Infant. *Nature* 253(5489): 265–266.

Scassellati, B. 1996. Mechanisms of Shared Attention for a Humanoid Robot. In Embodied Cognition and Action: Papers from the 1996 AAAI Fall Symposium, ed. Maja Mataric. Technical Report FS-96-02, Americal Association for Artificial Intelligence. Menlo Park, Calif.: AAAI Press.

Scassellati, B. 1998a. A Binocular, Foveated Active Vision System. Technical Report, 1628, Artificial Intelligence Lab, Massachusetts Institute of Technology.

Scassellati, B. 1998b. Finding Eyes and Faces with a Foveated Vision System. In Proceedings of the Fifteenth National Conference on Artificial Intelligence (AAAI-98), 961–968. Menlo Park, Calif.: American Association for Artificial Intelligence.

Scassellati, B. 1998c. Imitation and Mechanisms of Shared Attention: A Developmental Structure for Building Social Skills. In Agents in Interaction—Acquiring Competence through Imitation: Papers from a Workshop at the Second International Conference on Autonomous Agents, 473–474. New York: Association for Computing Machinery.

Schall, J., and Hanes, D. 1998. Neural Mechanisms of Selection and Control of Visually Guided Eye Movements. *Neural Networks* 11(7–8): 1241–1251.

Scheier, C., and Pfeifer, R. 1998. Exploiting Embodiment for Category Learning. In *From Animals to Animats 5: Proceedings of the Fifth International Conference on Simulation of Adaptive Behavior*, eds. R. Pfeifer, B. Blumberg, J.-A. Meyer, and S. W. Wilson, 32–37. Cambridge, Mass.: The MIT Press.

Schildberger, K. 1984. Temporal Selectivity of Identified Auditory Interneurons in the Cricket Brain. *Journal of Comparative Physiology A*155: 171–185.

Schildberger, K. 1988. Behavioral and Neuronal Methods of Cricket Phonotaxis. *Experentia* 44: 408–415.

Schildberger, K., and Horner, M. 1988. The Function of Auditory Neurons in Cricket Phonotaxis: I. Influence of Hyperpolarization of Identified Neurons on Sound Localization. *Journal of Comparative Physiology A*163: 621–631.

Schmitz, B.; Scharstein, H.; and Wendler, G. 1982. Phonotaxis in Gryllus Campestris L: I. Mechanism of Acoustic Orientation in Intact Female Crickets. *Journal of Comparative Physiology A*148(4): 431–444.

Schöne, H. 1984. Physiology of Orientation. Chapter two in *Spatial Orientation*, 17–148. Princeton, N.J.: Princeton University Press.

Scutt, T. W. 1994. The Five-Neuron Trick: Using Classical Conditioning to Learn How to Seek Light. In *From Animals to Animats 3: Proceedings of the Fifth International Conference on Simulation of Adaptive Behavior*, eds. D. T. Cliff, P. Huslands, J. A. Meyer, and S. W. Wilson, 87–96. Cambridge, Mass.: The MIT Press.

Scutt, T. W., and Damper, R. I. 1991. Computational Modeling of Learning and Behavior in Small Neuronal Systems. Paper presented at the International Joint Conference on Neural Networks, Singapore.

Scutt, T. W., and Damper, R. 1997. Biologically Motivated Learning in Adaptive Mobile Robots. In Proceedings of the SMC '97 IEEE International Conference on Systems, Man, and Cybernetics, 475–480. Washington, D.C.: IEEE Computer Society.

Scutt, T. W., and Webb, B. 1997. Real Neurons in Real Networks. Paper Presented at the European Symposium on Artificial Neural Networks. 16–17 April, Bruges, Belgium.

Sharkey, N. E, and Ziemke, T., eds. 1998. Biorobotics. *Connection Science* 10(3): 361–391.

Sharpe, T., and Webb, B. 1998. Simulated and Situated Models of Chemical Trail Following in Ants. In *From Animals to Animats 5: Proceedings of the Fifth International Conference on the Simulation of Adaptive Behavior,* 195–204. Cambridge, Mass.: The MIT Press.

Shepard, R. N., and Metzler, J. 1971. Mental Rotation of Three-Dimensional Objects. *Science* 171(3972): 701–703.

Shibata, T., and Schaal, S. 1999. Robot Gaze Stabilization Based on Mimesis of Oculomotor Dynamics and Vestibulocerebellar Learning. *Advanced Robotics* 13(3): 351–352.

Sinha, P. 1994. Object Recognition Via Image Invariants: A Case Study. *Investigative Ophthalmology and Visual Science* 35(3): 1735–1740.

Smithers, T. 2000. On Behavior as Dissipative Structures in Agent-Environment System Interaction Spaces. In *Prerational Intelligence: Adaptive Behavior and Intelligent Systems without Symbols and Logic, Volume 2,* eds. H. Ritter, J. Dean, and H. Cruse, 243–257. New York: Kluwer Academic Press.

Sparrow, S.; Marans, W.; Klin, A.; Carter, A.; Volkmar, F. R.; and Cohen, D. J. 1997. Developmentally Based Assessments. In *Handbook of Autism and Pervasive Developmental Disorders,* 411–447, eds. D. J. Cohen and F. R. Volkmar. Second ed. New York: Wiley.

Spinozzi, G. 1996. Categorization in Monkeys and Chimpanzees. *Behavior and Brain Research* 74(1–2): 17–24.

Spirito, C. P., and Mushrush, D. L. 1979. Interlimb Coordination during Slow Walking in the Cockroach: I. Effects of Substrate Alterations. *Journal of Experimental Biology* 78(1): 233–243.

Sporns, O.; Almássy, N.; and Edelman, G. M. 2000. Plasticity in Value Systems and Its Role in Adaptive Behavior. *Adaptive Behavior* 8(2): 129–148.

Srinivasan, M. V.; Chahl, J. S.; and Zhang, S. W. 1997. Robot Navigation by Visual Dead-Reckoning: Inspiration from Insects. *International Journal on Pattern Recognition and Artificial Intelligence* 11(1): 35–47.

Srinivasan, M. V., and Venkatesh, S., eds. 1997. *From Living Eyes to Seeing Machines.* Oxford, U.K.: Oxford University Press.

Staudacher, E. 1998. Distribution and Morphology of Descending Brain Neurons in the Cricket Gryllus Bimaculatus. *Cell and Tissue Research* 294(1): 187–202.

Steinkühler, U., and Cruse, H. 1998. A Holistic Model for an Internal Representation to Control the Movement of a Manipulator with Redundant Degrees of Freedom. *Biological Cybernetics* 79(6): 457–466.

Stout, J. F., and McGhee, R. 1988. Attractiveness of the Male Acheta Domestica Calling Song to Females: II. The Relative Importance of Syllable Period, Intensity, and Chimp Rate. *Journal of Comparative Physiology A*164: 277–287.

Stumpner, A.; Atkins, G.; and Stout, J. F. 1995. Processing of Unilateral and Bilateral Auditory Input by the ON1 and L1 Interneurons of the Cricket Acheta Domesticus and Comparison to Other Cricket Species. *Journal of Comparative Physiology A*177: 379–388.

Sung, K. K., and Poggio, T. 1994. Example-Based Learning for View-Based Human Face Detection. Technical Report, 1521, Artificial Intelligence Lab, Massachusetts Institute of Technology.

Takanishi, A.; Hirano, S.; and Sato, K. 1998. Development of an Anthropomophic Head-Eye System for a Humanoid Robot. In Proceedings of the IEEE International Conference on Robotics and Automation, 1308–1314. Washington, D.C.: IEEE Computer Society.

Takanobu, H.; Yajima, T.; Nakazawa, M.; Takamishi, A.; Ohtsuki, K.; and Onishi, M. 1998. Quantification of Masticatory Efficiency with a Masticatory Robot. In Proceedings of the IEEE International Conference on Robotics and Automation, 1635–1640. Washington, D.C.: IEEE Computer Society.

Tanaka, K. 1996. Inferotemporal Cortex and Object Vision. In *Annual Review in Neuroscience* 19:109–139. Palo Alto, Calif.: Annual Reviews.

Tanaka, K.; Saito, H.; Fukada, Y.; and Moriya, M. 1991. Coding Visual Images of Objects in the Inferotemporal Cortex of the Macaque Monkey. *Journal of Neurophysiology* 66(1): 170–189.

Tanigawa, H.; Fujita, I.; Kato, M.; and Ojima, H. 1998. Distribution, Morphology, and Gamma-Aminobutyric Acid Immunoreactivity of Horizontally Projecting Neurons in the Macaque Inferior Temporal Cortex. *Journal of Comparative Neurology* 401(1): 129–143.

Thelen, E., and Smith, L. 1994. *A Dynamic Systems Approach to the Development of Cognition and Action*. Cambridge, Mass.: The MIT Press.

Thorson, J.; Weber, T.; and Huber, F. 1982. Auditory Behavior of the Cricket: II. Simplicity of Calling-Song Recognition in Gryllus and Anomolous Taxis at Abnormal Carrier Frequencies. *Journal of Comparative Physiology* A146(3): 361–378.

Tovee, M. J.; Rolls, E. T.; and Azzopardi, P. 1994. Translation Invariance in the Responses to Faces of Single Neurons in the Temporal Visual Cortical Areas of the Alert Macaque. *Journal of Neurophysiology* 72(3): 1049–1060.

Triantafyllou, M. S., and Triantafyllou, G. S. 1995. An Efficient Swimming Machine. *Scientific American* 272(3): 64–70.

Tryba, A. K., and Ritzmann, R. E. 2000. Multi-Joint Coordination during Walking and Foothold Searching in the Blaberus Cockroach. I. Kinematics and Electromyograms. Journal of Neurophysiology. 83(6): 3323-3336.

Van Der Smagt, P. 1998. Cerebellar Control of Robot Arms. *Connection Science* 10(3): 301–320.

Verschure, P. F. M. J.; Wray, J.; Sporns, O.; Tononi, G.; and Edelman, G .M. 1995. Multilevel Analysis of a Behaving Real-World Artifact: An Illustration of Synthetic Neural Modeling. *Robotics and Autonomous Systems* 16(2–4): 247–265.

Viollet, S., and Franceschini, N. 1999. Biologically Inspired Visual Scanning Sensor for Stabilization and Tracking. In Proceedings of the IEEE IROS'99, Intelligent Robots and Systems, 204–209. Washington, D.C.: IEEE Computer Society.

Voegtlin, T., and Verschure, P. F. M. J. 1999. What Can Robots Tell Us about Brains? A Synthetic Approach toward the Study of Learning and Problem Solving. *Reviews in the Neurosciences* 10(3–4): 291–310.

Vogel, S. 1998. *Cats' Paws and Catapults*. New York: Norton.

Wagner, R.; Galiana, H.; and Hunter, I. 1994. Fast Robotic Eye/Head System: Control of Binocular Coordination. In Proceedings of the Annual International Conference of the IEEE Engineering in Medicine and Biology Society, Volume 16, 1045–1046. Washington, D.C.: IEEE Computer Society.

Wallis, G., and Bülthoff, H. 1999. Learning to Recognize Objects. *Trends in Cognitive Sciences* 3(1): 22–31.

Wallis, G., and Rolls, E. T. 1997. A Model of Invariant Object Recognition in the Visual System. *Progress in Neurobiology* 51(2): 167–194.

Walsh, V., and Kulikowski, J., eds. 1998. *Perceptual Constancy: Why Things Look as They Do.* Cambridge, U.K.: Cambridge University Press.

Walter, W. G. 1961. *The Living Brain.* Middlesex, U.K.: Penguin.

Wang, G.; Tanaka, K.; and Tanifuji, M. 1996. Optical Imaging of Functional Organization in the Monkey Inferotemporal Cortex. *Science* 272(5268): 1665–1668.

Watson, J. T., and Ritzmann, R. E. 1997. Leg Kinematics and Muscle Activity during Treadmill Running in the Cockroach, *Blaberus Discoidalis:* I. Slow Running. *Journal of Comparative Physiology A*182(1): 11-22.

Watson, J. T.; Tryba, A. K.; and Ritzmann, R. E. 1996. Analysis of Prothoracic Leg Movement during Walking and Climbing in the Cockroach. *Society for Neuroscience Abstracts* 22: 1077

Watson, J. T.; Tryba, A. K.; Ritzmann, R. E.; and Zill, S. N. 1997. Coordination of Leg Joints during Complex Locomotion in the Cockroach. *Society of Neuroscience Abstracts* 23:767.

Webb, B. 1994. Robotic Experiments in Cricket Phonotaxis. From *Animals to Animats 3: Proceedings of the Fifth International Conference on Simulation of Adaptive Behavior,* 45–54, eds. D. Cliff, P. Husbands, J. A. Meyer, and S. W. Wilson. Cambridge, Mass.: The MIT Press.

Webb, B. 1995. Using Robots to Model Animals: A Cricket Test. *Robotics and Autonomous Systems* 16(2–4): 117–134.

Webb, B. 1996. A Cricket Robot. *Scientific American* 275(6): 62–67.

Webb, B. 2001. Are Biorobots Good Models of Biological Behavior? *Behavior and Brain Sciences.* 24(6).

Webb, B., and Hallam, J. 1996. How to Attract Females: Further Robotic Experiments in Cricket Phonotaxis. In *From Animals to Animats 4: Proceedings of the Fourth International Conference on Simulation of Adaptive Behavior,* 75–83, eds. P. Maes, M. J. Matamic, J.-A. Meyer, J. Pollack, and S. W. Wilson. Cambridge, Mass.: The MIT Press.

Webb, B., and Scutt, T. 2000. A Simple Latency Dependent Spiking Neuron Model of Cricket Phonotaxis. *Biological Cybernetics* 82(3): 247–269.

Weber, K.; Venkatesh, S.; and Srinivasan, M. 1998. An Insect-Based Approach to Robotic Homing. In Proceedings of the Fourteenth International Conference on Pattern Recognition, 297–299. Washington, D.C.: IEEE Computer Society.

Weber, T., and Thorson, J. 1988. Auditory Behavior in the Cricket IV Interaction of Direction of Tracking with Perceived Temporal Pattern in Split-Song Paradigms. *Journal of Comparative Physiology A*163: 13–22.

Wehner, R. 1987. Spatial Organization of Foraging Behavior in Individually Searching Desert Ants, *Cataglyphis* (Sahara Desert) and *Ocymyrmex* (Namib Desert). In *From Individual to Collective Behavior in Social Insects,* 15–42, eds. J. M. Pasteels and J. L. Denebourg. Basel, Switzerland: Birkhäuser

Wehner, R. 1989. Neurobiology of Polarization Vision. *Trends in Neurosciences* 12(9): 353-359.

Wehner, R. 1994. The Polarization-Vision Project: Championing Organismic Biology. In *Neural Basis of Adaptive Behavior,* eds. K. Schildberger and N. Elsner, 103–143. Stuttgart: Fischer.

Wehner, R., and Räber, F. 1979. Visual Spatial Memory in Desert Ants, Cataglyphis Bicolor (Hymenoptera: Formicidae). *Experientia* 35(12): 1569–1571.

Wehner, R.; Michel, B.; and Antonsen, P. 1996. Visual Navigation in Insects: Coupling of Egocentric and Geocentric Information. *Journal of Experimental Biology* 199(1): 129–140.

Wendler, G. 1990. Pattern Recognition and Localization in Cricket Phonotaxis. In *Sensory Systems and Communications in Arthropods.* Basel, Switzerland: BimkhauserVerlag.

Weissburg, M. J., and Zimmer-Faust, R. K. 1994. Odor Plumes and How Blue Crabs Use Them in Finding Prey. *Journal of Experimental Biology* 197(1): 349–375.

Whiten, A., ed. 1991. *Natural Theories of Mind.* Oxford, U.K.: Blackwell.

Williamson, M. M. 1996. Postural Primitives: Interactive Behavior for a Humanoid Robot Arm. In Fourth International Conference on Simulation of Adaptive Behavior, 124–131. Cambridge, Mass.: The MIT Press.

Williamson, M. W. 1998. Rhythmic Robot Arm Control Using Oscillators. In Proceedings of the 1998 IEEE/RSJ International Conference on Intelligent Robots and Systems, 77–83. Washington, D.C.: IEEE Computer Society.

Wohlers, D. W., and Huber, F. 1982. Processing of Sound Signals by Six Types of Neurons in the Prothoracic Ganglion of the Cricket, Gryllus Campestris L. *Journal of Comparative Physiology* A146(2): 161–173.

Wood, D.; Bruner, J. S.; and Ross, G. 1976. The Role of Tutoring in Problem Solving. *Journal of Child Psychology and Psychiatry* 17(2): 89–100.

World Health Organization. 1993. *The ICD-10 Classification of Mental and Behavioral Disorders: Diagnostic Criteria for Research.* Geneva: World Health Organization (WHO).

Worst, R. Robotic Snakes. In Proceedings of the Third German Workshop on Artificial Life. Frankfurt: Veral Haary Deutsch

Yamaguchi, J., and Takanishi, A. 1997. Design of Biped Walking Robots Having Antagonistic Driven Joints Using Non-Linear Spring Mechanism. In Proceedings of the IEEE/RSJ International Conference on Intelligent Robots and Systems, 251–259. Washington, D.C.: IEEE Computer Society.

Young, J. F. 1969. *Cybernetics.* London: Iliffe.

Zill, S. N. 1990. Mechanoreceptors: Exteroceptors and Proprioceptors. *Cockroaches as Models for Neurobiology: Applications in Biomedical Research.* Boca Raton, Fla.: CRC.

Zill, S. N., and Seyfarth, E.-A. 1996. Exoskeletal Sensors for Walking. *Scientific American* 275(1): 86–90.

Zimmer-Faust, R. K.; Finelli, C. M.; Pentcheff, N. D.; and Wethey, D. S. 1995. Odor Plumes and Animal Navigation in Turbulent Water Flow: A Field Study. *Biological Bulletin* 188(2): 111–116.

Zollikofer, C. P. E.; Wehner, R.; and Fukushi, T. 1995. Optical Scaling in Conspecific Cataglyphis Ants. *Journal of Experimental Biology* 198(8): 1637–1646.

Index